the American Short Story
1945 - 1980

A CRITICAL HISTORY

TWAYNE'S CRITICAL HISTORY
OF THE SHORT STORY

William Peden, General Editor
University of Missouri-Columbia

The American Short Story, 1850—1900
   Donald Crowley, University of Missouri-Columbia

The American Short Story, 1900—1945
   Philip Stevick, Temple University

The American Short Story, 1945—1980
   Gordon Weaver, Oklahoma State University

The British Short Story, 1890—1945
   Joseph M. Flora, University of North Carolina-Chapel Hill

The British Short Story, 1945—1980
   Dennis Vannatta, University of Arkansas-Little Rock

The Irish Short Story
   James Kilroy, Vanderbilt University

The Latin American Short Story
   Margaret Sayers Peden, University of Missouri-Columbia

the American Short Story
1945 - 1980

A CRITICAL HISTORY

Gordon Weaver, Editor
Oklahoma State University

Twayne Publishers

The American Short Story
1945—1980:
A Critical History

Published in 1983 by Twayne Publishers
A Division of G. K. Hall & Company
70 Lincoln Street, Boston, Massachusetts 02111

Printed on permanent/durable
acid-free paper and bound in
the United States of America

First Printing

Book design and production
by Barbara Anderson

Typeset in 11 pt. Perpetua
by Compset, Inc. of Beverly, MA

Library of Congress Cataloging in Publication Data

Main entry under title:

The American short story, 1945—1980.

(Twayne's critical history of the short story)
Bibliography: p 111.
Includes index.
1. Short stories, America—History and criticism.
2. American fiction—20th century—History and criticism.
I. Weaver, Gordon.   II. Series.
PS374.S5A37   1983   813'.01'09   82-23423
ISBN 0-8057-9350-X

Contents

Chronology

1945   President Franklin D. Roosevelt dies in Warm Springs, Georgia, April 12.

End of World War II: Germany surrenders to the Allies on May 8; Japan surrenders on August 14.

William March, *Trial Balance: Collected Short Stories* (contains stories from two earlier collections and previously uncollected work published after 1940).

James Thurber, *The Thurber Carnival* (contains stories from four earlier collections and previously uncollected pieces).

1946   Kay Boyle, *Thirty Stories* (contains stories from three earlier collections and previously uncollected stories including thirteen published in or after 1940).

Wilbur Daniel Steele, *The Best Short Stories of Wilbur Daniel Steele* (stories from five collections published between 1918 and 1926).

Edmund Wilson's *Memoirs of Hecate County* suppressed by New York State Court of Special Sessions. Reissued in 1959.

1949   Shirley Jackson, *The Lottery, or the Adventures of James Harris.* The title story, originally published in *The New Yorker,* is said to have elicited the largest reader response in the history of that magazine.

William Faulkner receives the Nobel Prize.

1950   Korean War begins, June 25.

William Faulkner, *Collected Stories* (contains stories from three earlier collections and several previously uncollected stories).

William Carlos Williams, *Make Light of It: Collected Stories* (contains stories from two earlier collections, previously uncollected stories, and thirteen previously unpublished pieces).

1952 *Paris Review* founded, with offices in Paris and New York. *Best Stories from the Paris Review,* with an introduction by William Styron, published in 1959.

1953 End of the Korean War.
John Cheever's first major collection, *The Enormous Radio and Other Stories* (preceded in 1943 by *The Way Some People Live*).
J. D. Salinger, *Nine Stories.*

1954 Ernest Hemingway receives the Nobel Prize.

1957 Isaac Bashevis Singer's first collection, *Gimpel the Fool and Other Stories.*
Bernard Malamud's first collection, *The Magic Barrel,* wins the National Book Award.
Demise of *Collier's Magazine.*

1959 Philip Roth's first book, *Goodbye, Columbus and Five Short Stories,* wins the National Book Award.

1960 *Story* revived under the editorship of Whit and Hallie Burnett (originally founded in Vienna by Whit Burnett and Martha Foley).
Conrad Aiken, *The Collected Short Stories of Conrad Aiken* (contains stories from three earlier collections and several previously uncollected stories).
Death of Richard Wright. His *Eight Men* is published the following year.

1961 Arrival of the first American support troops in Vietnam.
Death of Ernest Hemingway, in Idaho, from a self-inflicted gunshot wound.
Death of James Thurber.

1962 Death of William Faulkner, in Oxford, Mississippi.

1963 President John F. Kennedy assassinated in Dallas.

1964 Death of Flannery O'Connor.

1965 Katherine Anne Porter's *Collected Short Stories* wins the National Book Award.
Fifty Best American Short Stories 1915—1965; edited by Martha Foley from the annual *Best* series begun in 1915 under the editorship of Edward J. O'Brien.

1967 Death of Langston Hughes.

1968 Senator Robert F. Kennedy assassinated in Los Angeles.
The Reverend Dr. Martin Luther King assassinated in Memphis.

1969 *Collected Stories of Jean Stafford,* published posthumously, wins the Pulitzer Prize.
Demise of the *Saturday Evening Post.*

1970 *Fifty Years of the American Short Story,* selected by William Abrahams from the annual O. Henry Awards volumes; edited successively by Blanche Colton Williams, Harry Hansen, Herschel Brickell, and others.
Death of John O'Hara.

1971 *The Complete Stories of Flannery O'Connor.*

1972 Hemingway's *The Nick Adams Stories,* selected from earlier collections and including eight previously unpublished stories and sketches.

1973 United States withdraws from Vietnam.

1974 Watergate scandal and the resignation of President Nixon.

1975 Fiftieth anniversary of *The New Yorker.*

1978 *The Stories of John Cheever.*

1980 Ronald Reagan inaugurated as the fortieth President of the United States.
The Collected Stories of Eudora Welty.

Introduction

As the essays in this book demonstrate, the development of the American short story between 1945 and 1980 exhibits a gradual but ultimately clear movement in two distinct directions with respect to form. On one hand, American writers of serious literary short fiction continued to work within the traditional formal conventions established over the previous century, consolidating and refining the techniques of expression we associate with American masters as far back as Poe and Hawthorne, enriched by the influence of foreign practitioners such as Chekhov and Joyce. On the other hand, very recent contemporaries—perhaps the best example discussed hereafter is Donald Barthelme—indulged in various degrees of formal experimentation and innovation that derive perhaps as much from the impact of post-World War II cultural history as they do from earlier influential literary models. Kafka and Borges, in our century, come to mind, and one can cite fiction as early as Sterne in our novel tradition.

The short story is a very young literary form compared with poetry or even its narrative antecedent, the novel. Poetry's sources for our culture are classical; the novel comes to us from England and Europe. The short story is not only a relatively new genre—perhaps one hundred and seventy-five years in its modern tradition—it is a distinctly American literary phenomenon, despite important non-native influences. It would be presumptuous to declare emphatically that the form's future shape will be traditional or otherwise; the American short story remains dynamic in its esthetic character, flexible and varied, yet still recognizably what it has been, a vital mode of literary expression, continuously evolving toward the limits of its possibilities.

Jeffrey Walker finds that authors writing in the aftermath of World War II, many of whom began their literary careers before or during the war, continued to use the genre as a vehicle for thoughtful depiction and analysis of American social manners, mores, and morality. The stories of John O'Hara, written both then and after a long hiatus during which he wrote his massive novels of manners, can be used as an index to the particular social texture of both prewar and postwar America.

The American writers treated in the following essays use the short story as a lens to view a society within a narrow frame, but close up, magnified to reveal telling detail. This is true of John O'Hara and other *New Yorker* authors then and today; of regionalists such as Peter Taylor, Eudora Welty, and Flannery O'Connor, writing out of the American South in this era; of writers from the American West (Wallace Stegner, William Saroyan); and of those defined not so much by region as by class (Auchincloss), race (Langston Hughes), or even vocation (J. F. Powers).

The story of manners, discussed by Walker, appeared consistently over the years scrutinized here. We note also that a purely regional focus diminished, perhaps due to our increasing cultural homogeneity thanks to geographic mobility and the ubiquity of electronic media after World War II. Finally, many of the authors discussed by E. P. Walkiewicz (John Cheever, R. V. Cassill, William Goyen, Jesse Stuart, I. B. Singer) used the form for the depiction and moral analysis of American society and its constituent groups, whatever other ends their stories may serve.

As a primary, or even a very significant function of the genre, American society per se seems of less interest to most of the writers discussed by James C. Robison. Because the subjects treated by contemporary writers come from their own experience, however, the short story continues to provide a view of the society in which the reader lives.

Like the genre itself, the themes, explicit or implicit, are distinctly American. There are more moral questions than moral conclusions, an attitude that can be traced to the dark Puritan consciousness of Nathaniel Hawthorne. The writers discussed in these essays project two overlapping fields of vision, two separate angles of scope that are almost always in some degree of conflict: society, and the individual's place in and relationship to that society. In American culture, itself so historically new as yet to be declaring its shape and texture (one might pause and remember that Roman legions occupied Britain longer than Western culture has existed in the New World), the cult of individualism has made one's relationship to that culture obscure, even mysterious, as it is closely and profoundly considered by short stories. Thus the themes of individual isolation and alienation repeatedly emerge from the works discussed. In addition to their concern with individuation of psychology and soul, the authors hold up society itself to severe moral scrutiny.

* * *

Hortense Calisher's New Yorkers, the Glass family in J. D. Salinger's stories, James T. Farrell's urban Irish, Wiliam Humphrey's "Texahomans," Langston Hughes's blacks (all surveyed by Jeffrey Walker) are people isolated by class, caste, region, or tortured temperament, from a fulfilling sense of belonging. As they search for identity or quarrel with inadequate social and moral personas imposed on them by their American experience, these characters confront a national culture itself as morally inexplicable or unacceptable as the fictional situations in which they find themselves.

E. P. Walkiewicz examines these themes in short fiction published between 1957 and 1968: John Updike dramatizes the moral complexity that is the modern social institution of marriage on the sensitive planes of spiritual and esthetic sensibility; W. H. Gass's Midwesterners wither on the dry vine of moral sterility in America's heartland; Bernard Malamud's urban Jews, stripped of their Old World religious identities, are torn between a dead or dying tradition and New World chaos; Flannery O'Connor's Deep South grotesques act out a bizarre symbolism for an orthodox Christianity that survives only in the gothic outlines of Bible Belt fundamentalism.

James C. Robison's study of our most recent authors reveals Joyce Carol Oates, Guy Davenport, James Alan McPherson, Leonard Michaels, Daniel Curley, and Barry Targan, among others, challenging traditional esthetic conventions in an effort to find some moral base in society in general or groups within it on which contemporary characters can mount and articulate a vision of individual identity and culture. These authors seek bases for the continuity of human existence itself.

The title story of Shirley Ann Grau's *The Black Prince and Other Stories* (1954) exhibits another confrontation with the Deep South's racial dilemma. It is reminiscent of the work of numerous earlier regional authors, but it anticipates the emerging American social and moral concern that erupted in the turbulence of Little Rock, Selma, and other highwater marks of this cultural preoccupation that, along with the Vietnam conflict, dominated the 1960s. The surface of Grau's story never directly touches on racial segregation, which deeply troubled moral philosophers and social reformers alike for so long, but that phenomenon is implicitly pervasive in her story. It is the evident concern and admiration for what has come to be called black consciousness, the vitality of the life force manifest in black experience that animates the fiction. Much of what has come to be articulated as valuable in black America—its deeply rooted human impulses and responses, quite mythically sensual and sexual in Grau's story—is at the fore in this seemingly melodramatic tale. The story is couched in the traditional tone and outline of myth, and Grau's Black Prince is a traditional demonic hero. "The Black Prince" is at one and the same time a traditionally regional slice of life and an almost prophetic projection of attitudes and beliefs that were to come to popular national consciousness over the next several years.

By the time of Bruce J. Friedman's *Black Angels* (1966) and James Alan McPherson's *Hue and Cry* (1969), the explosive revolution of black awareness, black politics, and black culture as significant elements in the larger society are commonplaces, dramatized as such in American short fiction.

William H. Gass's *In the Heart of the Heart of the Country,* published in 1968, contains several traditional stories that might be called primarily regional evocations of manners, not dramatically different from the story of manners executed with such particularity over the whole period by Louis Auchincloss or John O'Hara. Gass's title story, a long and almost plotless meditation on his life by a narrator in a state of moral and emotional stasis, exhibits formal qualities that seem especially appropriate to the story's mood; the narrator's severe dissociation from self and culture is rendered in his trivial response to the land about him, a rural wasteland, and by his disjointed references to the past that has brought him to this condition of paralyzed isolation.

In "The Black Prince," Grau's segregated Negroes inhabit a world that is fully realized, a geography that imitates a real world of history and sociology. In "In the Heart of the Heart of the Country," Gass brings his reader to a milieu that is still recognizably the American Midwest, but that is now more memory than substance. The subject of the story is the American psyche turning on itself, as morally intense in its painful introspection as it is imprecise in its attempt at moral definition. If Grau's story can be said to anticipate what was to come with respect to the race "problem," Gass's can be seen as depicting the national psychology now out of touch with its traditional points of reference—history, region, fellow citizen—groping toward an as yet indistinct framework on which to reconstruct a new, life-giving moral perception of human experience in "post-modern" America.

Thus as we move in time from Grau's fiction to that of Gass, we observe a marked breakdown in traditional American idealism, whether the focus is race relations or the need for love. This is reflected in deviations from traditional short story form, and is even more pronounced in Gass's later work, which all but abandons correspondence to earlier structure and attempts to enhance its meaning by its altered shape.

In the three collections of stories by Raymond Carver published between 1976 and 1980, traditional form persists, but only minimally. Carver treats the story as epiphany, his brutally spare slices of life so thin as barely to establish viable contexts for their moments of ironic statement or awareness. Another way of viewing Carver's work is that his economy of words is a statement equally as severe as Gass's, to the effect that the scope of the perceivable world, conventionally understood as history and community, has withered to a degree that will not permit articulate consciousness. Carver's characters are burned out by love, by drink, and by the paralyzing impact of contemporary history since World War II—atomic warfare and the specter of global nuclear holocaust, the Korean stalemate and the Cold War, Vietnam, the Kennedy years that ended in assassination, racial turmoil, the popularization of drugs, record divorce rates, Watergate, economic stagnation . . . Raymond Carver is not an experimental writer in the same category as the later William Gass, Guy Davenport, or Donald Barthelme, but his short stories do take traditional form to an extremity that begins to constitute self-conscious desertion of established esthetics, despite reliance on authentic dialogue and realistic action.

• • •

What emerges from this spectrum is the idea of the contemporary American short story as an index of national consciousness. It takes up as its subjects, however obliquely (for no writers wish to think of themselves as dependent on a daily newspaper for the matter of fiction), the very events that dominate current consciousness. Our contemporary story *is* a historical artifact in and of itself, and in a sense that is by no means unimportant, the writers discussed herein are historians. This means they not only record our history, they anticipate and interpret it, not with an eye toward prediction or evaluation of trends, but for its moral revelation. Today's American short story is a vision, multifaceted as the numbers of its serious practitioners, of American life. It focuses on what it means to be human, and thus becomes an agent of perception with the capacity for influencing moral action in America today.

The short story is well adapted to the development of that vision. As traditional social structures and attitudes crumble, as moral definitions are challenged by the hard realities of American experience in the aftermath of World War II, forms alter to accommodate new visions or old ones in a state of flux. The neat sequence of chronological narration gives way to fragmentation and distortion; the rounded depiction of milieu and character is reduced to a narrow—though no less telling—slice or a vague presence; language and our assumptions about its properties and capacities come under scrutiny.

At the extreme, an author's irony may be so blatant (as with Barthelme or Davenport) as to defy the assumption that either language or the genre can adequately comprehend or contain the seemingly endless variety of contemporary consciousness. This can be seen in several of the stories in Russell Banks's *The New World: Tales* (1978), in which historical characters are dramatized in an effort (perhaps to meet a human need) to re-endow "dead" history with new life transmitted back to the past from the present.

What emerges from the reflection of American history and social upheaval is the inescapable fact that a formal definition of the genre has yet to be articulated. Indeed, the subjects themselves seem to have brought about its division into two formal directions, traditional and experimental (or innovative).

• • •

A short story is only subjectively "short," and what one reader might be able to concentrate on fully at a single sitting (to recall Poe's early definition) could well prove too long for another or not long enough for yet another. If short stories are short, at least shorter than novels, we cannot say just how short they must be, and the work surveyed in the following essays runs the gamut from brief epiphany to long narrative. A purely quantitative scale, exactly distinguishing short story from novel (or novella, to complicate matters) is not possible.

The concept of persona, or voice, is at least a bit more helpful. Every fiction (novel or story) is told by a fictional persona; this is one means of distinguishing it from nonfiction in which the voice is assumed to be that of the author. Although in fiction there may be a first-person narrator who refers to himself or herself as being the author, the reader makes the assumption that this is a device—the persona is always the mask that word's Greek root signifies.

In the traditional story, there is no attempt to confuse the reader as to this distinction. This practice, still dominant, as the authors surveyed here demonstrate, does not call into question the difference between fiction and reality. The experimental mode, however, which has been used more and more in the most recent decade, brings up precisely that question. For example, in self-reflexive fiction, an esthetic assumption appears to be that the work is as real as any other phenomenon in the perceptual and material world, and that fiction is as valid an experience as any other. Perhaps a more basic assumption of such experiments is that language itself is as real as the world it has been heretofore understood only to symbolize.

This contention came into being out of the historical experience since World War II, in which moral and social orders were perceived as bankrupt, as was the language customary to understanding (or reforming or casting aside) them. A new consciousness, perhaps in some sense even a new language, was required to fathom and cope with this situation. Hence a new fiction (or art of whatever sort) was required.

It is also true that any fiction is a statement, however pessimistic or nihilistic about the reality it invokes, that implies, if not some conceivable alternative to the way things are, at least a hypothetical norm or ideal against which its moral criticism can be dramatized. In the end, we have only our language and the conventions of the genre (persona being just a formal feature of fiction), and authors can choose from a range of possibilities that includes taking the conventions as our tradition has transmitted them or altering them to the point at which communication ceases.

One may refer directly to oneself as author, by name, but it does not affect the fact that fiction must have a persona. One can point to the ironic meanings of words in a particular context—in the same sense that one indicates the rhythmic dimension of words in the context of a poem—but words will continue to have significance with respect to the real world. A writer can fragment, distort, or obscure the narrative sequence, but fiction will remain nevertheless narrative, however much of its coherence relies on the reader's reconstruction of it. Thus the distinction between traditional and experimental stories is more surface than substance, and literary experiment, with its roots traceable back to the very sources of our novelistic tradition in the eighteenth century (one thinks again of Sterne), has its own conventions. The history of the short story is a brief one, traceable only to the early nineteenth century in America, and one must conclude that its formal characteristics are in an early, rather than a definitive stage of development.

·   ·   ·

As a commercial enterprise, short stories are a poor speculative venture at best; a mass market for them has all but disappeared. The impact of electronic media and the decline in the numbers of general magazine formats are often cited as among the chief causes; exceptions such as *The New Yorker* and a few other survivors are notable primarily because they *are* exceptions. Unless the author of short stories has a reputation previously established by commercial success with the novel or augmented by the celebrity of television or film, there is little hope of earning a living by practicing the craft.

The interest of large commercial publishing houses in short-story collections (or anthologies) is in equivalent decline. The successful novelist or the writer with a reputation built over several decades (John Cheever, for example, or Peter Taylor) may be assured of the publication of his collected stories, but younger, uncelebrated authors must look elsewhere for an audience.

This void has been filled to a great extent by the profusion of "small" literary magazines. Some of them are well established by university sponsorship and secure now by the sheer fact of survival over many years, although it often seems that as many cease publication each year as are founded. Little magazines have sprung into being in response to the drying up of publishing outlets over the past twenty years. Some of them demonstrate a tendency toward specialization, announcing hard policies with respect to traditional versus experimental writing, or espousing one or another extraliterary policy (gay, black, feminist, etc.) through the vehicle of the short story (and poetry and essay). There are, then, diverse audiences for the short story, all of them small; thus one might be inclined to assume that the extent to which the genre has any real potential for influence on either American policies or sensibility is questionable. At the worst, it might appear that the situation affecting publication of short stories in America presages a medium less and less able to find an audience. Yet it is clear that, nurtured in large part by academia, there is a vigorous creative impulse in our culture that will not be denied, and that prophecies of the death of the short story are as inaccurate as those that have been made about the novel. There is no reason to believe, given our tradition, that serious writers have broken off the practice of the craft because either financial reward was unlikely or appreciative audiences minuscule. There is every reason to believe, ultimately, that the future of the American short story will be as richly productive as it has ever been, and no reason to think—recognizing that art, unlike technology, is not subject to "progress"—that the quality of achievement to be expected is likely to diminish.

• • •

It would be tempting to pronounce definitive judgment on the relative merits of the writers treated in these essays, to rank them as to first, second, or third order of excellence. The critical evaluations of the authors of the three essays are implicit, reflected in terms of the detail and space devoted to an individual writer (although this is also reflective of relative quantity of work), where it is not explicit. We should avoid a commonplace tendency of our culture to declare a "best" or "top ten" when it comes to serious and accomplished literary art. Such sweeping assessments are doubtless easy if we talk of competitive sports or commodities valued in dollars. It is quite otherwise with art, and the authors referred to herein are artists. It is also more difficult to assess the literary achievement of living and recently deceased writers than it is to know the worth of the long-dead, whose creations are fixed and limited for our deliberation.

One premise operative in this book was that only authors of collections of stories would be considered; those whose work through 1980 was published only in periodicals were thus eliminated. Furthermore, although there are a very few (but significant) exceptions, only authors of two or more collections were considered to have produced a canon of sufficient volume to justify consideration.

The reader will notice that, in some instances, reference is quite naturally made to stories published by an individual (John Cheever, for example) prior to 1945; this is for the purposes of coherence and comprehensiveness. Also, some writers (Doris Betts is one) whose collections of stories have appeared at relatively regular intervals over the course of the last thirty-five years are discussed in all three essays. Finally, while in some cases an author's work is restricted to discussion in only one of the essays (see Robison's treatment of Daniel Curley), reference is also made to work produced in a period covered in another essay; this reflects the period in which a writer's major work, or the vast majority of work, was published in collected form. The productivity of short-story writers does not fit exactly, sometimes not even neatly, in arbitrary chronologies.

It is sufficient to say that this study demonstrates that the genre is alive and well, dynamic, as vital and viable a form of literary expression as it has ever been; reports of its demise are not only premature, they are ludicrous.

The selected bibliography of short-story collections gives an indication of just how many stories have been brought, and are being brought, to readers in the last three and one-half decades. They still almost always appear first in commercial and literary magazines, and while publishers are not eager to bring out collections due to the rare chance of making a profit, American university presses and small presses have increasingly chosen to handle them. In addition to the collections listed in the bibliography, the interested reader should consult the *Small Press Record of Books in Print,* 10th edition (Paradise, Calif., 1981—82), edited by Len Fulton and Ellen Ferber, for the most recent complete record of the output of America's small presses.

Of course, the editor accepts the blame for errors or serious omissions in this study, while crediting Jeffrey Walker, E. P. Walkiewicz, and James C. Robison for their achievement and the voluminous reading and research it entailed to produce their essays. The research assistance of William Shute is also greatly appreciated.

Gordon Weaver

Oklahoma State University

1945—1956:
POST-WORLD WAR II
MANNERS AND MORES

The history of the American short story in the decade following the Second World War was not marked by radical changes or startling breakthroughs in style or subject matter. What did occur was a movement toward developing a literature that would mirror the intricacies of life in postwar America. No longer convinced that the journalistic technique that characterized fiction of the depression years was sufficient to interpret contemporary life, and not yet ready to initiate experimental modes that would gain popularity in the early 1960s, the writers of the late 1940s and early 1950s concentrated on the story of manners, a tradition that has characterized the short story since Henry James.

Witty and often satiric, these sketches chronicled the lives of ordinary people. Unlike the naturalists of the 1930s, however, who emphasized broad social issues, writers probed with uncanny insight the manners and mores of the upper, lower, and middle classes; the bedroom, barroom, and drawing room; the city, suburbs, and country. Their stories revealed the inner tensions and conflicts between parents and children, husbands and wives, friends and lovers. They treated such diverse and complex topics as childhood, alienation, old age, disillusionment, and the eternal search for one's identity.

Many writers in this period had published collections of stories before the war and were caught up in the trends developing in the postwar era. John O'Hara, for example, was not only a prolific author in the 1930s and early 1940s, during which time he published five collections, but also in the 1960s when six volumes of his work appeared. The same can be said for James T. Farrell, Eudora Welty, and William Saroyan. Some, like Tennessee Williams and Truman Capote, who as young men began their careers after the war, gained their measure of fame in the 1960s and 1970s. The *New Yorker* cadre of writers, their stories marked by urbanity and wit, and the members of the Southern renaissance, who found fascination in the sometimes grotesque incongruities of character and setting, tended to produce the largest quantity of fiction in the period. Short-story masters such as James A. Michener and Ray Bradbury continued their output in a wide range of fictional areas.

To isolate these writers into stylistic, thematic, or geographic schools, however, would be a mistake. What does characterize them as part of a common literary tradition is their ability to turn tales of local color and social behavior—stories of manners—into metaphors of the American experience.

• • •

A major writer in this tradition is John O'Hara (1905—1970). O'Hara is remarkable in the history of American short-story writers because his career spans five decades and includes twelve collections, plus an anthology of his earlier work. What is even more remarkable is that these collections were published in two different eras, 1935 to 1947, and 1960 to 1972. Although the later stories are probably the best, the earlier tales are characteristic of many of the qualities that were his trademark. Of the five volumes published in the first period, three appeared before the Second World War: *The Doctor's Son and Other Stories* (1935), *Files on Parade* (1939), and *Pal Joey* (1940). Two came out in postwar America: *Pipe Night* (1945) and *Hellbox* (1947).

O'Hara's stories of manners are representative of the style of living exemplified in this period; yet he treats people and their problems in a fashion that is unique. His world is an amoral one, one in which the guilty are not always punished or the innocent always allowed to prevail. The forces of life, whether good or evil, affect everyone, regardless of social position. In fact, social status itself is the motivating factor in many of his stories. O'Hara's method of storytelling borders on the detached fashion of merely reporting the events that occur in the lives of his characters. There is little emphasis on providing psychological insight into motives or methods. The thirty-one stories in *Pipe Night* illustrate this technique.

"Walter T. Carriman," the opening story, narrated by a first-person observer, turns into a "tribute" to his friend, "everybody's friend, Walter T. Carriman." The irony, of course, is the relatively little information the narrator possesses about Carriman's life. He makes this clear in several ways. First, he tells the reader he will report "merely" what he, as one of Carriman's friends, knows about Walter. Therefore he will present "only certain 'highlights'" of his own "arbitrary choosing," leaving others to "elaborate upon or extend these words." Second, in his picture of Walter, the narrator displays a habit for qualifying all his information: "Not having been surrounded in his childhood by great riches, which have been known to disappear overnight . . . Walter, on the other hand, was not raised in poverty and squalor, the details of which can . . . prove equally boresome." Elsewhere in his portrait, the narrator admits that while as a boy, "Walter had been fond of baseball," his participation in sports did not continue "owing to defective vision," and later to training rules that "proved irksome to a lad of Walter's spirit. . . . (The truth is that Walter took his first cigarette at the age of fourteen and from then on was a rather heavy smoker)." Walter, "on the intellectual side," was "somewhere between the studious and the casual." Details like this, as well as the facts of Walter's wandering from job to job, suggest that the narrator's eulogy is not only unconvincing in its sincerity, but consistent in its depiction of a banal and rather lifeless personality.

Not all of O'Hara's characters, however, are banal; rather they are people who survive the bleakness of their isolation. O'Hara makes no attempt to communicate his characters' inner souls; yet they are vividly portrayed as empty people who seek to escape the quiet desperation of routine. Story after story reveals this theme. In "Too Young," a girl uses her affair with a motorcycle cop to fulfill her physical needs; in "Free," a California woman travels all the way to New York for a shopping spree, but spends her time daydreaming about an affair she would like to have but never will; in "Can You Carry Me?" a Hollywood actress verbally abuses a magazine editor because of a story he printed about her, but ends up going to bed with him; in "Nothing Missing," a man just released from prison enters a bookstore to stare at a clerk—just to stare, never to talk; in "A Purchase of Some Golf Clubs," an off-duty mechanic sitting in a bar buys a set of golf clubs from a girl who needs the money to free her husband from jail. In almost all of O'Hara's early stories, nothing much "happens," inner psyches are seldom revealed, and resolutions to characters' problems are never really achieved. In every case, he portrays the everyday affairs of ordinary people in a manner that exposes their failures.

As the author of over three hundred short stories, O'Hara is effective in his vignettes of contemporary manners if only because of the power of redundancy; characters and scenes appear again and again. He has almost made a genre of these sketches, and while the reader may wish for more variety, few can argue with the success of his efforts in *Pipe Night, Hellbox,* and the earlier collections. O'Hara does not have the technical range of other writers, but what he does, he does well. He exposes the worst side of human beings—their greed, stupidity, crassness, and selfishness—and convinces the reader that people cannot escape themselves.

•   •   •

O'Hara was the first of a group of writers who contributed to a literary phenomenon that was to characterize the story of manners in postwar America. Since 1925, *The New Yorker* magazine had been publishing what it considered the best short stories in the country. Most of these were similar in that they relied on brief anecdotes or autobiographical sketches written in a sophisticated style and dealing with contemporary behavior of ordinary people.

Edward Newhouse (1911—   ), for example, like O'Hara, has been a regular contributor. In the six years following the war, Newhouse published two collections of short fiction: *The Iron Chain* (1946) and *Many Are Called: Forty-Two Short Stories* (1951). All but four of the twenty-one stories in the first volume and three of the forty-two in the second appeared in *The New Yorker,* where for years Newhouse was a staff member. He followed what many have called the *New Yorker* formula with stories that are brief character sketches made memorable by their portrayal of cosmopolitan manners and mores rather than by vivid, thoughtful studies of motives and psyches. In some ways, these works are like the magazine's cartoons, with captions that run for half a page instead of one line. Much as O'Hara provides photographic portraits, Newhouse's sketches capture not only the feel of conversation, but ambiance of place.

In "A Gorgeous Number," from *The Iron Chain,* Newhouse describes in five pages a moment in the life of Miss Mae Garvey, a young girl waiting in Jake's Third Avenue saloon for her boyfriend. In her conversation with Jake, she recounts the other men who have courted her, and while sitting there she meets Major Thomas Driscoll, a midget. At the Major's overtures, Miss Garvey breaks into a fit of laughter, and the story ends with him stomping out of the bar. Nothing substantial happens, but the conversation reveals Newhouse's ability to record the vernacular and the habits of a segment of New York society. The other stories in the collection (each averaging ten pages) report similar scenes. Readers can identify with the characters because they are people like themselves captured in moments that show how the commonplace can be both lively and exciting.

•   •   •

Like his *New Yorker* colleague Edward Newhouse, John McNulty (1895—1956) describes the milieu of Third Avenue and the people who frequent its establishments. The best way to describe McNulty's works is to accept his definition in the foreword to *A Man Gets Around* (1951): they are "casuals"; stories "about people here and there and about happenings in New York, N.Y." In this collection, as well as in the earlier *Third Avenue, New York* (1946), McNulty's ear for the nuances of speech and his appreciation of the vitality of life are evident. His stories, including those in *My Son Johnny* (1955) and *The World of John McNulty* (1957) are usually brief, but they treat the commonplace with gusto and the insignificant with originality. In the dedication to *The World of John McNulty,* published posthumously, James Thurber praises McNulty's "unflagging comic spirit." Although not an innovator in the development of the American short story, his stories are characteristic of the fiction about New York City published in the late 1940s and early 1950s.

• • •

A writer of much greater achievement than McNulty who also uses New York City as her milieu is Hortense Calisher (1911—   ). In *In the Absence of Angels* (1951), she describes New Yorkers as a weary lot, beset by the problems of living in a world inhospitable to innocence. They are dreamers and failures, rejects who fail because of their human frailty, their absence of grace, and their inability to establish lasting relationships with the people with whom they work, live, and love.

The title story reflects this failure. The first-person narrator describes the barrenness of her life. She recalls the friends of her youth, her sick mother, and the existence that with hindsight seems to have been a harbinger of her present life, one filled with despair. In her thoughts, she concludes, "finally, that there is no place for people like us, that the middle ground is for angels, not for men. But there is a place. For in the absence of angels and arbiters from a world of light, men and women must take their place."

Many of the other stories echo this theme. Two, "A Box of Ginger" and "The Watchers," recount the youth of Hester Elkin and her response to the death of her grandmother. The chief effect Calisher achieves is failure of the family members because of their inability to share their feelings. Each is isolated by generation, insularity, and unwillingness to resolve the tensions that all of them ironically create and propagate. In "The Woman Who Was Everybody," Miss Abel, who wears "one of the two dresses of the daily requisite black," peers out her window and imagines people like herself asking, "Do you suppose . . . is there anything to be made of me?" She not only seeks a job, but also engages in a depressing affair with a "boy, Max," who would visit and in the "muffled clingings of love-making . . . try again to build up some dark mutual core of unalienable wholeness." Finally, she repeats what she already knows: she is one of the rejected. Equally hopeless are the night riders in the "Night Riders of Northville" who spend their life commuting from home to office and from bar to bar, listening to the sameness of the "ratchety-slat of the pinball machine," than which there is "no more aimless sound in the world."

Calisher's stories are effective not only because of her unremitting portraits of lost souls, but also because of her method of portraying character and place. All of her people are reflections of the places in which they exist. The skies are gray, the trees are gray, the characters and their lives are gray. Every action and response takes place in a middle world in which choices are never clear, and despair, alienation, and confusion reign. These people are never able to escape from this world, because neither they nor the society to which they belong is capable of establishing a lasting set of values. Like Edith Wharton, whose novels of New York manners are compassionate yet hopeless accounts of the human condition, Calisher portrays her world with insight and understanding.

• • •

Louis Auchincloss (1917—   ) creates quite a different fictional world. His stories are concerned almost exclusively with the upper crust of American society: lawyers, business titans, patrons of the arts. In his two collections published in the early 1950s, *The Injustice Collectors* (1950) and *The Romantic Egoists: A Reflection in Eight Minutes* (1954), Auchincloss reports on the contemporary manners of the Eastern seaboard establishment. *The Injustice Collectors* contains eight stories chronicling the lives of people who are "looking for injustice, even in a friendly world, because they suffer from a hidden need to feel that this world has wronged them." In "Greg's Peg," for instance, Auchincloss reveals how social pressure can destroy people. Gregory Bakewell, a misfit in his social class, attempts to gain acceptance by trying to mold his personality to fit the crowd with whom he associates. His efforts, however, are pathetic as he transforms himself into a caricature of the summer colony type. Rebuffed, his company no longer desired, he leaves Anchor Harbor and eventually dies of a heart attack. Auchincloss is successful in rendering the attitudes of Eastern society in this story because he reveals, in more depth than Newhouse, the motives and uncertainties of his characters. Much like Edith Wharton and Henry James, Auchincloss captures the pulse and rhythm of people who pressure themselves to survive in a world that often rebuffs such attempts. These people are deluded into thinking that they must conform: as characters they fall victim to their own insecurities.

The eight stories of the *The Romantic Egoists* follow a similar pattern. "The Fortune of Arleus Kane" details the fortunes and misfortunes of Kane as he makes aborted attempts to enter politics; "Wally" reveals the battle for position in a naval training camp; "The Legends of Henry Everett" exposes the life of a lawyer who is treated with reverence at court and like an "un-housetrained puppy" at home.

All are examples of Auchincloss's technique of using a first-person narrator, and all reveal observers who learn what Henry Everett concludes in his speech to the bar association: ". . . it is one thing to know or even suspect that one knows nothing and quite another to *believe* in nothing—." In this context, Auchincloss's characters are romantic egoists: few believe in anything. He reveals that the ennui and sense of desolation and loneliness usually associated with the middle class is also very much a part of the world of the rich. Whether his setting is a naval base or a lawyer's office, Auchincloss is a master technician who reports the pathos of the upper class.

• • •

Another writer for *The New Yorker* whose best work appeared in the postwar era is Mary McCarthy (1912—   ). Unlike O'Hara, who presented an external view of motives (revealing largely what they did and the effect on others, rather than why they did it) McCarthy investigates her characters' psyches to analyze the reasons underlying their actions. Tailored to reveal many of her own experiences, McCarthy's stories are about incidents in the lives of young women, either her favorite character, Margaret Sargent, or an unnamed "she." In all cases, the stories go beyond O'Hara's photographic realism to provide readers with an inside view of a woman who seeks her own identity and will do whatever is necessary to achieve her ends.

McCarthy objectively exposes the foibles and follies of her young heroines, never by telling us about them, but by showing them in action. Because their portraits are presented dramatically, we come to know their thoughts and the reasons behind what they do. In "Cruel and Barbarous Treatment," collected in *The Company She Keeps* (1942), the reader learns about a young woman who is having an affair and thinking about divorce with the same sense of exhilaration she felt at the time of her engagement. At the beginning of the story, McCarthy tells us that the young wife could "not bear to hurt her husband. She impressed this on the Young Man, on her confidantes, and finally on her husband himself." For her, however, the details are so exciting that she cannot escape what she sees as the glamor of becoming a "young divorcee." She proceeds with the self-centered confidence of one who knows all along that everything will turn out to be socially acceptable. She is not only conceited, but a snob.

This story typically depicts the society in which McCarthy's women roam, always anticipating some excitement, and oblivious to the danger of hurting anyone in the process, sometimes even themselves. Their coldness and lack of conscience mark them as independent as any women in contemporary fiction. The same types appear in McCarthy's next volume of stories, *Cast a Cold Eye* (1950). The title is revealing, for not only do the characters view their lives dispassionately, but the reader is aware of McCarthy's own cold eye in presenting these stories of social relationships. "The Weeds" analyzes the effect of separation on a woman who has left her husband; "Yonder Peasant, Who Is He?" concerns the responses of a young girl to her parents' deaths; "C. Y. E." reports events in a Catholic boarding school. All reveal the coldness of their central characters and form a satiric indictment of urban relationships.

• • •

Jean Stafford (1915—1979) is a writer and chronicler of manners in the McCarthy tradition. Her first and best collection, *Children Are Bored on Sunday* (1953), is diverse in range and subject. From "The Echo and the Nemesis," which describes Ramona Dunn, a terribly obese and pathetic girl who invents a mirror image of herself as a svelte twin sister, to the title story in which a young woman who comes home to New York feels socially insecure among those with whom she thinks she is intellectually inferior, Stafford provides a glimpse into a world characterized by the mildly aberrant to the grotesque. The orphaned Indian boy of "A Summer Day," the Mexican girl in "The Bleeding Heart," the Jewish doctor in "The Home Front," and the American girl in "A Winter's Tale" are characters who, despite their individual situations, have one thing in common: they are all alienated and lonely, living in a world in which anything horrible is possible and usually happens.

Stafford's grotesque world is depicted in "The Home Front." A lonely Jewish doctor, who administers aid to factory workers, has the misfortune of living in a boarding house run by an antisemitic landlady. When he befriends a cat, the landlady and her son kill it. In an unexpected climax, the doctor, dedicated to the saving of lives, kills the son's pet bird in retaliation. The doctor has assumed the cruelty of the environment in which he lives. This is what can happen, Stafford suggests here and in the other stories, when people find themselves in a world to which they are unable to adjust. The fault lies, of course, with a flaw in humanity, not with the environment itself. While some of Stafford's later stories are a bit more encouraging in their portrayal of contemporary life, her best ones suggest the personal agonies of alienation and loss.

• • •

With *New Yorker* writers tending to be masters of comic satire in their chastisement of American manners, it is not surprising that J. F. Powers (1917—   ) has been published frequently in the magazine's pages. Although his stories are concerned with pastors, curates, and parishioners of the Catholic Church, they are not devoted to discussions of theological issues. They are instead brilliantly written comedies of manners using as their province the world of the church with its own intricate code of behavior. Powers's stories reveal the idiosyncratic and unspectacular in the daily lives of his characters and do so in a witty and ironic fashion that gives the tales practical significance.

While some readers might assume that stories peopled with church figures would deal with the good or evil nature of the characters portrayed, Powers's work presents his individuals as victims, often sympathetic and almost always comic, of the passions and petty jealousies that motivate human beings to action. His storytelling methods often help to soften some of those baser human traits he describes. "The Forks," for instance, from the first collection, *The Prince of Darkness and Other Stories* (1947), is representative of the techniques Powers uses to reveal the conflicts between curate and pastor. Monsignor Sweeney, a conservative and materialistic pastor who views his assistant, Father Eudex, as naive for believing that he should act like a Christian, tries to convince Father Eudex of the importance of appearances. He argues for the prudent, practical way of doing things, even going so far as to instruct him about what forks to use at mealtime. At the end of the story, a disillusioned Eudex is almost tempted to believe that the priesthood no longer has any real mission. Such conflicts characterize many of the works in *The Prince of Darkness*. Even the title story presents a priest whose pride and lack of any real religious conviction mark him as an anomaly to those who view the world of the church with unbiased idealism.

In Powers's second collection, *The Presence of Grace* (1956), most of the nine stories continue this theme. Powers's attention to detail and his use of viewpoint are especially noteworthy. Perhaps the best works in the collection are "Death of a Favorite" and "Defection of a Favorite," both narrated by the rectory cat, Fritz. The tone is ironic, and Powers once more is able to parry and thrust satirically through a series of incidents between assistant and pastor. This time, however, the spats are refereed by a cat. In "Defection of a Favorite," Fritz must contend with Father Burner, the same "prince of darkness" central to the earlier story. When Father Malt, the parish priest, slips on the ice and fractures his hip, Father Burner assumes command. Although less proud than before, Burner sees his chance to continue in that office. His new regime produces changes that prompt Fritz to observe that with "Father Burner running the rectory, it was going to be a hard, hard, and probably fatal winter for me." The winter turns out, however, to be fatal for Father Burner's ambition and not for Fritz. The assistant's careful plans backfire when Father Malt resumes his position. Through it all, at least from Fritz's perspective, Burner learns, with Fritz's "good company and constant example," to accept the setback "with grace."

In "A Losing Game," Father Fabre, the parish attendant, finds himself the loser in another of Powers's contests between curate and pastor. Father Fabre is a young man who dreams of doing great works at Trinity, but he soon comes to feel that his pastor is maneuvering against him. Because the story is told from Fabre's point of view, the reader sees the events as Fabre sees them, and quickly discovers that the game under way is being played only by the young assistant. The pastor is completely innocent, and in a series of comic confrontations, Fabre ends up merely frustrating himself and acting the fool.

Powers's stories succeed not only because of his technical expertise, but also because he is a master of comic satire. He has a feel for revealing the foibles of his characters, and with his insight and wit he lampoons many of their battles. In the process, Powers reveals much about the motives and complexities of ordinary men.

• • •

Equally adept at commenting on the American scene is Shirley Jackson (1919—1965). What has probably become the most frequently anthologized modern short story, "The Lottery," first appeared in The New Yorker and later was the title story of The Lottery: or, The Adventures of James Harris (1949). Few readers have failed to recognize the very real elements of human depravity in Jackson's story of the scapegoat on whom all the evils of the community are laid. In this respect, the story is a telling and chilling indictment of American society.

"The Lottery" opens with a realistic portrayal of small-town life. The characters are friendly, neighborly people preparing for an undescribed event that appears to be part of the town's tradition, gathering a pile of stones. This seems innocent enough until the climax of the story when realism is replaced by symbolism, and expectation turns into shock when the townspeople stone to death one of their own. This surprise ending, which contrasts everyday affairs with events that are more comfortably left alone, is an example of Jackson's ability to analyze the feelings and emotions of people caught up in outdated traditions and customs.

• • •

The stories of J. D. Salinger (1919—   ) present excellent examples of people trying to cope with the pressures created by social values and traditions. His novel, The Catcher in the Rye (1951), cemented his reputation as a commentator on the world of adolescents and misfits, but Salinger's short stories are also of importance.

Salinger's first collection, Nine Stories (1953), was selected from thirty stories published between 1940 and 1953. All but two ("Down at the Dinghy" and "De Daumier-Smith's Blue Period") appeared originally in The New Yorker. Like Catcher, the predominant theme is alienation, an alienation that usually ends in reconciliation, but in some cases, death. This sense of isolation is caused by several factors. In "Down at the Dinghy," racial prejudice is the issue when a young boy overhears the housekeeper call his father a "kike." He runs away to the family dinghy, but is finally coaxed home by his mother. Salinger's irony is evident here, for after all that the reader is led to believe about the boy's misery, it turns out that he was disturbed because he thought his father was being called a "kite."

Two other stories in the collection, "Just Before the War with the Eskimos" and "The Laughing Man," deal with broken love affairs, while two others reveal estrangement in marriage, "Uncle Wiggily in Connecticut" and "Pretty Mouth and Green My Eyes." The last is a particularly good example of Salinger's portrait of urban manners. A young executive places two telephone calls to his boss; in each, he wonders aloud as to the whereabouts of his wife. During both calls, she is in bed with the boss.

Although these tales of alienation in love are excellent, Salinger's finest works portray an isolation even more profound. "For Esmé—with Love and Squalor," perhaps his best story, recounts the crisis of a veteran who has suffered a nervous breakdown. The sketch opens with Sergeant X remembering the days preceding the Normandy invasion when a young girl, Esmé, had provided him with a moment of relief to offset the tedium and pressure of preinvasion camp life. Several weeks after the battle, the scene shifts to a civilian home where the sergeant is quartered with other soldiers. As he continues to tell the story, Sergeant X changes to a third-person narrator, a "disguise" rendered "so cunningly that even the cleverest reader will fail to recognize me," he believes. He is suffering from a breakdown, feeling his "mind dislodge itself and teeter, like insecure luggage on an overhead rack," when he looks at his mail and discovers a package that contains a letter from Esmé and her father's watch. Set against the boorish actions of his fellow soldiers and his own spiritually barren and dehumanized state, the letter and watch have the effect of bringing X out of his doldrums "with all his fac—with all his f-a-c-u-l-t-i-e-s intact."

The remaining stories reveal similar people who struggle to reconstruct their lives. "De Daumier-Smith's Blue Period" and "The Laughing Man," both told from a first-person point of view, are stories of young men searching for an identity as they look backward to experiences that had great impact on their lives. The opening story, "A Perfect Day for Bananafish," introduces Seymour Glass, a young man who with other members of his family later appears in *Franny and Zooey* (1961) and *Raise High the Roof Beam, Carpenters and Seymour, An Introduction* (1963). Like Holden Caulfield and Sergeant X, Glass is a typical Salinger character who seeks a resolution to his social maladjustment.

This exploration of the constant search for self was Salinger's major thematic contribution to the short story in the 1950s. In a period when the impact of war and the changing lifestyles of Americans became favorite topics for the short story, Salinger met the challenge and created a fictional world in which patterns of withdrawal and return were prominent. He, and therefore his characters, saw the American scene as a wasteland where only through continual striving and work could the individual maintain himself and survive. His characters' successes were usually small and the process of achieving them painful, but in approaching life slowly and sensibly they were able to transform their suffering into some kind of affirmation.

• • •

The stories of Irwin Shaw (1913—   ) deal chiefly with what people thought and did during the war years and the decade that followed. Although his works do not emphasize the psychological effects of the postwar years with as much clarity as do Salinger's, they portray a range of character types who try to come to grips with problems that seem particularly alarming in modern society. His first two collections, *Sailor Off the Bremen and Other Stories* (1939) and *Welcome to the City and Other Stories* (1942) were followed by *Act of Faith and Other Stories* (1946). *Mixed Company: Collected Short Stories* (1950) contains thirty-seven works selected from earlier editions.

The first story of *Mixed Company,* the often-anthologized "The Girls in Their Summer Dresses," is a good example of a Shaw tale that concentrates on a contemporary problem: the failure of marriage when each partner sees the other as mere convenience. Written in a lighter vein than is typical of Shaw, this story illustrates his tendency to overdramatize. Many of his stories are very effective, especially those concerned with war, but too often his situations are melodramatic. The reader is easily able to discern the "good guys" from the "bad guys," and the resolution of conflicts tends to be clever. "Sailor off the Bremen" is just such a work. Although it contains a good deal of suspense, the action occurs so rapidly and is the product of so many diverse ideologies that by story's end the reader is confused. In addition, Shaw's characters are too often identifiable as types. In "Sailor," Charlie is the agent of justice, Ernest the innocent victim, Lueger the personification of evil. The story may emphasize that the desire for revenge is sometimes justifiable, but Shaw's didactic tone makes the climax almost trivial.

"Act of Faith" is better, if only because it is more moving and convincing in its treatment of racial problems in the context of war. Shaw investigates similar issues in some of his other war stories: "Gunner's Passage," probably the best of these works; "Hamlets of the World"; "The City Was in Total Darkness"; "The Priest"; "Medal from Jerusalem"; "The Man with One Arm," to name a few. In light of the war as a major event in twentieth-century life, Shaw does present a vivid picture of the impact it had on its participants.

• • •

Equally intriguing vignettes of the effects of war on the decade are offered in the short stories of Robert Lowry (1919—   ). If only through sheer volume,

Lowry's stories of the Second World War are impressive. The best and first of these collections is *The Wolf That Fed Us* (1949). Whether Lowry is describing men in action, as in "The Wolf That Fed Us," or the effects that military service and war have had on its observers, as in the story of the wife who must resolve for herself the implications of her husband's impending overseas duty ("Layover in El Paso"), Lowry effectively reveals the feelings and actions of characters set in a specific time and place. The boundaries of Lowry's fictional world expand in later volumes—*Happy New Year, Kamerades!* (1954), *The Last Party* (1956), *New York Call Girl* (1958), and *Party of Dreamers* (1962)—but his best stories are those that deal with war.

• • •

Kay Boyle (1903—   ), too, deals with the impact of war on people. In fact, war and political confrontation provide the bulk of material for her fiction. However, as an early contributor to *The New Yorker,* she published several collections before the war: *Wedding Day and Other Stories* (1930), *First Lover and Other Stories* (1933), and *The White Horses of Vienna and Other Stories* (1936). The best of these prewar sketches were collected in *Thirty Stories* (1946). As a commentator on manners, Boyle has depicted the universal themes of love, marriage, and death. Like Henry James, she spent much of her life abroad so that many of her stories have an international flavor.

"Winter Night" depicts the relationships among a mother, her daughter, and a babysitter, and reveals Boyle's concern with the way in which events can be disrupted by war. In another story from the collection, "Effigy of War," originally appearing in a 1940 issue of *The New Yorker,* Boyle shows the destructive impact war has had on civilians at a seaside resort. Her vision is satiric as she treats two types of victims. The first is an individual who is not officially a part of the "war effort," the second, "the national of an alien country." The leader of the mob who assaults the civilians is ironically portrayed as a likely leader in wartime—the man who vehemently asserts his nationalism. As the story reaches its climax, the man and his mob attack a group of "foreigners" and use their flag with "religious fervor" as a symbol of their nationalism and as an excuse for their actions. Although the story is set in France at the beginning of the Second World War, it is not specifically about that war. Boyle's observations are intended to be universal, as she shows how people are swayed by the tensions and spirit of conflict.

In Boyle's later collection, *The Smoking Mountain: Stories of Germany During the Occupation* (1951), she again demonstrates her understanding of people and their motives by dealing with the aftermath of war. Set in the American zone in postwar Germany, these stories reveal that while winners and losers can superficially adjust to their roles, they can never relate to each other.

• • •

Exploring another group affected by the events and manners of postwar America is Elizabeth Enright (1909—1968). Three collections of stories reflect her interest in the world of children. Her first volume, *Borrowed Summer and Other Stories* (1946), was followed by *The Moment Before the Rain* (1955) and *The Riddle of the Fly and Other Stories* (1959). In "The Playground," from her second collection, Enright describes a day in the life of Nina Bernson, a young girl who encounters the real world with her friends. As she and her friends discuss their mothers' divorces in a matter-of-fact way, three events interrupt their fun. First, they see a couple making love; then they are chased by a potential child molester; and finally, they must save one of their group from drowning. Yet as much as these events have probably wounded them psychologically, Nina's response to her mother's question, "What did you do?" is, "Oh, nothing. . . . Swam. Played. Nothing much." Enright's ability to capture the mind of a child is unerring in this and other stories.

Enright also treats "rebellion in old age," as in "The Moment Before the Rain." Here, Mrs. Dacey and Mr. Kendall discuss the impending marriage of their grandchildren and acknowledge the desolation of old age. Told from Mrs. Dacey's viewpoint, the story reveals the personal anguish of the two as they recognize what age has taken away from them. In "The House by the River," the opening story in *The Riddle of the Fly,* Enright shows the effect on a young boy of hearing from an old woman about the death of her husband. These stories underscore Enright's sensitive appraisal of people and the triumphs and tragedies of their daily existence.

• • •

Mark Van Doren (1874—1972) also writes about childhood or the remembrances of childhood in *The Witch of Ramoth and Other Tales* (1950), *Short Stories of Mark Van Doren* (1950), *Nobody Said a Word and Other Stories* (1953), *Home with Hazel and Other Stories* (1957), and *Collected Stories* (1962).

In the last collection, Van Doren reveals the special qualities of children's imaginations and points up the differences between youth and age. "The Witch of Ramoth" is a tale of the supernatural written for children. Two siblings are frightened by an old woman who they come to realize has supernatural powers. They cannot find their home and soon discover that no one can see or hear them. The ending is equally mysterious as the children appear to be under the witch's spell. "A Wild West Place" contrasts the attitudes between a grandmother and granddaughter; "Grandison and Son" examines alienation between father and son; "Abide with Me" highlights the reconciliation between mother and son. Whether the main characters are children or adults trying to resolve the crises of life by examining the past or looking forward to the future, they are excellent examples of people caught in problems of their own making.

. . .

Like Van Doren, Wallace Stegner (1909—   ) presents the conflict between generations and the ensuing complications in *The Women on the Wall* (1950) and *The City of the Living* (1956). "Chip off the Old Block," from the first collection, is partly autobiographical and is typical of Stegner's ability to comment on the problems that arise when a twelve-year-old Montana boy is made "the man of the house" after his father is struck down with the flu. The boy's decisions, not always prudent, and his bravery in the face of danger, highlight his initiation into manhood. Similar themes surface in the other seventeen tales in this volume and in the eight stories of *The City of the Living*.

"The Blue-Winged Teal," for instance, reveals tension and conflict between a father and son in their attempts at reconciliation after the death of the boy's mother. Henry Lederer has had to quit college to take care of his father, whom he hates. He makes the older man a peace offering of nine blue-winged teals. It is not enough, however; the gift can neither salvage the present nor recapture the past. When he decides there will be no change in the relationship, Henry leaves "with the feeling he might have had in letting go of the hand of a friend too weak and too exhausted to cling any longer to their inadequate shared driftwood in a wide cold sea."

. . .

More prolific than Stegner, Warren Beck explores a wide variety of subjects in his four collections: *The Blue Sash, and Other Stories* (1940), *The First Fish, and Other Stories* (1947), *The Far Whistle, and Other Stories* (1951), and *The Rest Is Silence, and Other Stories* (1963). Beck concentrates on satiric depiction of the responsibilities men and women must face to offset prejudice, violence, and misunderstanding in the postwar years.

. . .

The stories of Charles Jackson (1903—1968) and William Goyen (1915—   ) explore these same themes. In two volumes published in the early 1950s, *The Sunnier Side: Twelve Arcadian Tales* (1950) and *Earthly Creatures: Ten Stories* (1953), Jackson uncovers the illusions of youth and shows how people destroy themselves when these illusions are shattered. Goyen's *Ghost and Flesh: Stories and Tales*

(1952) emphasizes the conflict between youth and age. His people seek ways of freeing themselves from the ghosts of the past so that they can understand the meaning of the present. Ironically, their attempts are often self-destructive.

• • •

While this group of authors was at work delineating American manners, others were writing about changes taking place in the South. Nowhere in the geography of American letters in the last thirty-five years has more fresh and original fiction surfaced than in the South, where writers have created a body of work that is the equal of any written in the postwar era. Following the example of William Faulkner, and inspired by the fragmented social landscape of a region that was still steeped in the traditions of the past, they portrayed the rural, and hence largely conservative, manners of a new generation of Southerners. Unlike their Northern counterparts, Southern stories of the decade tend to be tragic, rich in legend and myth, often populated by grotesque characters, and softened by the cadences of Southern speech. Of this new wave of short-story writers, few are the equal of Peter Taylor.

Although Taylor's stories detail the urban, middle-class world of his native Tennessee, they also mirror many of the tensions and complications that give shape and substance to the genre as it applies to all of contemporary America. Like his fellow storytellers, Taylor (1917—   ) focuses on a world torn by its reverence for traditions of the past and its necessary adherence to pretensions of the present. No longer able to survive through an allegiance to old-fashioned notions, no longer able to order their lives according to old loyalties, Taylor's people find themselves caught up in a world where blacks seek their freedom, women assert their independence, and children express their unwillingness to be seen and not heard. These new values that his Southerners are hesitant to accept are responsible for the disintegration of family structure and social order. Taylor's first two collections of stories, *A Long Fourth and Other Stories* (1948) and *The Widows of Thornton* (1954), reflect these changes.

All seven stories of *A Long Fourth* reveal a growing urban, industrial South. The title story is characteristic of the collection and brilliantly explores this changing world. Harriet Wilson, "just past fifty," her ineffectual doctor-husband "Sweetheart," their two tipsy daughters, Helena and Kate, and their son, together with Mattie and BT, the Negro servants, make up the household. The story tells the events surrounding the son's return to Nashville for a long weekend before he enters the army. The family crises that take place during this time are explosive, and they reflect the not-so-engaging side of Southern manners.

Taylor achieves his vivid portrait by concentrating on Harriet. As the story opens, she has to handle a number of emergencies. Mattie's son BT threatens to move away from Nashville to work in a factory, a move that upsets Mattie and turns the household upside down. Matters are not helped by the two daughters whose drunken behavior threatens plans for the weekend. Then Son arrives and brings with him a New York girl, whose ideas seem radical to the Wilsons and who seems to have too much influence on Son. Instead of a genteel weekend, complete with appropriate social amenities, the "long Fourth" becomes a forum for the discussion of inflammatory social and political ideas. The argument, for example, over the place of Negroes (Kate believes that "Southern white people have a great responsibility" toward blacks; Son counters with his newly formed idea that the people in the South "cannot expect to progress with the rest of the nation until they've forgotten their color line") is symptomatic of the changes that are taking place, and no one in Taylor's stories is immune from their effects. The portrait of the Wilson household vividly reveals the turmoil between the old and new South.

Because Taylor's South is uncertain of itself, it becomes a place where old values are fair game for skeptics and spokesmen for radical ideas. "A Spinster's Tale" and "The Fancy Woman" are especially good examples of these personal and social conflicts. Like "A Long Fourth," these are stories about women who appear to react most strongly to and are most affected by the changes in their society. Josie of "The Fancy Woman" and Elizabeth of "A Spinster's Tale" are, like Harriet, women whose ambivalence and wonder at these shifts in values give Taylor's stories their depth. Their inability to resolve conflicts and their ambiguous relationships with men are typical of Taylor's keen insight. Taylor suggests that women more than men are sensitive to the ironies of life that affect them profoundly.

In Taylor's next collection, *The Widows of Thornton,* the best-drawn characters are again women. In the opening story, perhaps the most compelling and skillful of the collection, Taylor continues to address the issues of old and new, tradition and innovation, order and change, past and present. "Their Losses" introduces three women, two of whom are spinsters and the third a married woman. Returning to Thornton with her aunt after a holiday, Miss Patty Bean decries the fading away of the old South—its values, its farmland, its towns—to her two traveling companions and former classmates, Ellen Louise Watkins and Cornelia Weatherby Warner. At breakfast, all three discuss the bleak landscape, the end of the old South, and death. Cornelia doesn't believe in mourning. For Miss Patty, this is sacrilege, as she feels mourning is an obligation, part of a tradition that represents a "prosperous and civilized existence," and taking her aunt to Memphis is therefore an act quite noble and natural. Ellen Watkins, the third member of the party who is bringing home the body of her mother for burial, falls somewhere between the conservative Patty and the liberal Cornelia in her allegiance to past values. Despite their differences, these women have one thing in common: all reflect a sense of melancholia for their unfulfilled lives. Their reunion on the train is neither beneficial nor pleasant. Like the other people in Taylor's stories, they are alone in an alien and unfriendly world.

The other characters in *The Widows of Thornton* are also affected by change. In "Cookie," for instance, Taylor portrays a wife comfortably settled in middle-aged stasis with a husband who no longer finds their relationship (chiefly characterized by a stiff, formal evening meal) either stimulating or rewarding. He comes home, eats his dinner, engages in what becomes a tedious and routine conversation, and then escapes. At the end of the story, Taylor uses the husband's car to suggest his disenchantment with the studied world of his wife and their servant, Cookie: "He began walking with light, sure steps, over the grass—their ugly, old voices. In the driveway, his car, bright and new and luxurious, was waiting for him." For the husband, his marriage is not bright, new, or luxurious.

In "A Wife of Nashville," the characters find it more difficult to escape the past. The Lovell household, for years beset by a series of servants who leave them for one reason or another, is faced, after long devoted service, with the loss of Jess McGhee, the very best of the lot. Taylor constructs the story using a series of flashbacks, each of which describes the virtues and idiosyncrasies of the departed servants, to concentrate on his major theme: the loneliness and isolation that affect both blacks and whites in the new South. He establishes with great poignancy the special kinship that develops over the years between Helen Ruth Lovell and Jess. At the end of the story, when the men of the Lovell family are shocked at the inexplicable departure of Jess, Helen Ruth alone understands.

"A Wife of Nashville" is an excellent example of how Taylor's style creates interest and meaning. Robert Penn Warren describes Taylor's method of storytelling in his introduction to *A Long Fourth*. He states that it is a "natural style, one based in conversation and the family tale, with the echo of the spoken word, with the texture of some narrator's mind." Warren's evaluation suggests that unlike some Southern and Northern contemporaries, Taylor finds his subjects in the quieter, though no less tragic, dramas of domestic situations and family affairs. Because of his style, vivid character portrayal, and command of form, Taylor is one of the masters of the contemporary story of manners. His representation of middle-class values and standards of conduct exposes their hollowness in an ironic and significant way.

• • •

Even more compelling than Taylor's study of the effects of the changing American scene are the stories of Eudora Welty (1909—   ). Welty combines elements of comedy, pathos, myth, horror, and fantasy to reveal the conflict in a character's ability to distinguish appearance and reality, a sense of the past and perception of the present, and obligations to the social world and to self. Like Taylor's *The Widows of Thornton,* Welty's *The Golden Apples* (1949) describes the lives of various family members in her fictional Morgana, Mississippi. Perhaps not as effective as her two earlier collections, *A Curtain of Green* (1941) and *The Wide Net* (1943), *The Golden Apples* nonetheless illustrates Welty's methods of storytelling.

In "Shower of Gold," the first story in the collection, Welty introduces the history of King MacLain, one of the most compelling characters in her fiction. A traveling salesman who also fancies himself a great lover, he is presented as a figure of Southern lore whose exploits are both mysterious and legendary. Cast as a comic version of Jove, MacLain also appears in two other stories, "Sir Rabbit" and "The Wanderers," the latter describing his homecoming after years of roving. King's two sons, Randall and Eugene, appear in "The Whole World Knows," a soliloquy by Randall dealing with the effects of his wife Jinny's infidelity, and in "Miser from Spain," a story about Eugene's life in San Francisco. The other stories in the collection recount the lives of other Morgana citizens, but the MacLain sketches are the best.

The Golden Apples is unified by Welty's use of the mythical quest for the golden apples. Just as King MacLain is a wanderer searching for gold of his own, so, too, are other residents searching for meaning in their lives. Some may leave Morgana for a time, but eventually all return in an attempt to understand their ties with the town. Even more important than Welty's sense of place in these stories (most of them take place in Mississippi) is her emphasis on individual identity. She is interested in probing the enigma of people caught in traps created by their inability to solve life's mysteries. The events in her stories are simple, but the people and their responses to these events are complex.

In her fourth collection, *The Bride of the Innisfallen and Other Stories* (1955), three stories take place in the contemporary South, another is set in the Civil War era, and two more are based on her European experiences; the final story takes place on a mythical island in the Mediterranean. While her four Southern pieces—"Ladies in Spring," "Ken," "No Place for You, My Love," and "The Burning"—are quite in the Welty tradition of revealing her characters' limitations, mortality, and cosmos, the other three are not as effective. Even though they appear to lack the force of her earlier work, they are successful because Welty brings to them the same unerring quality she brings to all her stories: she is a master of analyzing the human condition, whether the people live in rural Mississippi or in Cork, Ireland, the setting of "The Bride of the Innisfallen."

In this story, the bride, a girl who has been lost in the frustration of an unsuccessful marriage in England, comes to realize the possibilities of a new life as she walks about the streets of Cork seeing vegetation flowering and children in confirmation dresses running up and down the street.

The key to Welty's success and skills lies in her willingness to take chances. In an essay, "How I Write," she explains that often the "most exacting and sometimes the simplest appearing work is brought off (when it does not fail) on the sharp edge of experiment, not in dim, reneging safety." Regardless of place and time, Welty's stories of dying husbands, cosmetic saleswomen, aging men, and simple field hands, blacks and whites, Southerners and Northerners, work because of her amazing diversity of subject, style, and technique.

•   •   •

Of Eudora Welty's contemporaries who also liked to take chances, certainly Flannery O'Connor (1925—1964) is the most fascinating. Like Welty, she uses the South as her province, but her characters are more grotesque than Welty's. They are a collection of misfits and pariahs, characters who assume abnormal and bizarre attitudes toward each other and themselves. Her first and best collection is *A Good Man Is Hard to Find and Other Stories* (1955). In these ten stories, O'Connor blends comedy and tragedy in her depiction of people whose problems are not caused solely by their social or family upbringing, but by a basic flaw in their characters. "Good Country People," for instance, portrays people's physical and mental infirmities. Everyone in the tale suffers from some degrading, crippling condition that distorts and demeans their human dignity. Hulga's maimed body is symbolic of her maimed soul. Because she has an artificial leg, she has changed her life to reflect the change in her body. She has a doctoral degree in philosophy, has announced herself an atheist, and has changed her legal name from Joy to Hulga. When she meets a Bible salesman who proclaims himself to be a "country boy," Hulga decides to seduce him. In their rendezvous in the barn loft, Hulga's assumed superiority is revealed to be spurious. Not only is the salesman a false Christian—as he disappears down the hayloft ladder with her artificial leg, he shouts to her that he has "believed in nothing" ever since he was born—he has turned out to be more than her match. O'Connor reveals Hulga's pride and intellectual posturing to be only gullibility and ignorance.

The conclusion to "Good Country People" illustrates O'Connor's method of composition. Because she records the events in her stories in such a casual manner, the reader is lulled into believing that little is happening. This flow, however, is characteristically broken by an explosive ending, delivered with such ironic impact that it forms a startling climax to O'Connor's portrayal of distortions in modern life.

Distortions are also the subject of "The Artificial Nigger," a story about the estrangement and reconciliation of two Georgians, an old man named Mr. Head and his grandson Nelson, who go to the city for a visit. Nelson has never seen a black man, and the opening pages show his first encounter with one. He expresses awe for a huge Negro man wearing a ruby stickpin and an unexpected affection for an enormous black woman. His response is contrasted with an incident in which he knocks down a white woman carrying groceries. The grandfather in a moment of shame denies his grandson's existence when he says, "This is not my boy . . . I never seen him before." This causes a rift between the two, and O'Connor's reconciliation comes when they see a plaster statue of a Negro (eating watermelon) who is supposed to represent God's grace: "They could both feel it dissolving their differences like an action of mercy." Both exclaim, "An artificial nigger." This communication transforms them, as Mr. Head is described as an "ancient child" and Nelson as a "miniature old man." The dramatic ending is a surprise, and it achieves the effect of shocking both the characters and the reader into an awareness of their infirmities.

The remainder of the stories are not as effective, for they fail to create a balance between O'Connor's grotesque vision and her imaginative power. They reveal her too frequent tendency to end a story with death. "The Baptism" concludes with a drowning, "A Late Encounter with the Enemy" with a corpse, and the title story, "A Good Man Is Hard to Find," with the murder of an entire family. Such gratuitous violence is a reflection of her tendency to deal in extremes.

· · ·

Another Southern woman writer uses the grotesque even more boldly than Flannery O'Connor. Carson McCullers (1917—1967) in her collection, *The Ballad of the Sad Cafe* (1951), presents a cast of characters who are failures and outcasts in a world in which traditional values are no longer visible. Three of the selections in the book are novellas *(The Heart Is a Lonely Hunter, Reflections in a Golden Eye,* and *The Member of the Wedding); each is a brilliant, longer version of the perversities McCullers presents in the short stories, reflecting the themes of loneliness, alienation, and frustrations of love that have become her trademark.

"The Ballad of the Sad Cafe" best illustrates her technique. Here McCullers creates a gruesome trio of caricatures. Amelia, a six-foot bootlegger, lives in a decrepit shack with two men who are equal to those in any horror story: Macy, her husband who supposedly carries in his pocket the severed ear of a man he once killed in a fight; and Lyman, a sinister-looking four-foot dwarf. This threesome forms an unusual "family" whose adventures reveal their almost inhuman behavior and make-up. Despite such features as a macabre love triangle, a bone-cracking wrestling match between Amelia and Macy, and a violent ending, McCullers avoids turning the story into a gruesome melodrama by injecting folk humor from time to time. Throughout, she uses ballad motifs to humanize her characters and to make their behavior less morbid.

When Lyman the dwarf arrives at Amelia's house, she takes him in, offers him food and drink, and sets up a relationship, that although strange, begins to transform both of them into more likeable human beings. Eventually Amelia's house becomes a cafe to which customers come to escape their melancholy. This lasts only six years, however, just until Macy arrives. Years before, Amelia and Macy had been married for ten stormy days, and with his reappearance the story moves toward what the town sees as an inevitable battle. The description of this final match of two "epic" combatants is presented with a combination of humor and realism. At the end, when Lyman, the appointed referee, announces Macy the winner, the two men break up Amelia's possessions, exit town together, and leave the woman a recluse.

McCullers's use of ballad motifs (dreams, superstitions, music) creates an atmosphere that makes the tale mirror the rituals of romance. By turning the story and its characters into something almost allegorical, McCullers comments on the choices inherent in every lover's affairs. She suggests that passion is the dominant element in human relationships, and that to be both the lover and the beloved is part of the ideal every human being seeks. Even though that love is distorted, there is no reason for it not to exist in the lives of misfits and outcasts. To transcend spiritual isolation in love, then, becomes her most haunting theme.

• • •

Another of the writers belonging to the Southern renaissance, Truman Capote (1924—   ) achieved his fame in the 1960s and 1970s, but was recognized as an important writer in the early 1950s. His early stories, collected in *A Tree of Night and Other Stories* (1951), reveal his talent for short fiction. Capote not only emphasizes the decadent and macabre aspects of Southern gothic fiction, but reveals his ability to treat such major modern themes as loneliness, the search for individual identity, and alienation. In "Jug of Silver," for instance, he blends psychological realism with comic vision to tell the story of a search for the pot at the end of the rainbow. Narrated by a small-town observer, the story introduces Appleseed, a twelve-year-old boy (thought by some to be eight) who guesses the correct amount of nickels and dimes in a jug. This "jug of silver," a gimmick thought up by Ed Marshall, the Valhall druggist, becomes the object of controversy by story's end. Young Appleseed, a stranger who appears in the town with his sister, is said to have psychic powers because he was "born with a caul" on his head. When he correctly guesses the amount in the jar (to the very nickel), the townspeople cry foul, but are never able to solve the mystery of how he did it. This mystery becomes a legend that is retold by Marshall every Christmas day to the Baptist Bible class.

Capote's fictional world, peopled by vivid characters, the events of which are told from the point of view of a town representative, is a key element in his stories. There are actually two worlds portrayed in "Jug of Silver" and many of his other stories: one, a realistic and humorous daytime world, the other a nocturnal place often characterized by its illusory nature. Capote's characters fade in and out of the action thereby providing the stories with an eerie quality much like those tales of his fellow Southerners. The humorous touch of Appleseed's sister, for instance, joyously announcing that the money her brother won will be used to buy her a new set of white false teeth, is offset by Appleseed's mysterious powers and the pair's eventual disappearance.

This atmosphere is also found in "Miriam," another of his stories of children. A middle-aged woman, Mrs. Miller, is frightened by her meeting with a strange child. Mrs. Miller moves throughout the story as through a dream. Objects lose shape, strange sounds emanate from rooms in her apartment, and she becomes increasingly terrified by Miriam's appearances and disappearances. In this story, as in "The Headless Hawk," "Master Misery," and "Shut a Final Door," Capote elucidates in a much more vivid manner than in "Jug of Silver," the contrasts between illusion and reality, the forces of good and evil, light and dark. The people in these stories, whether adults or children, are obsessed by their fear of the unknown.

"A Tree of Night" is an especially good example of Capote's dreamlike world. Unlike other gothic writers, he uses gothicism to evoke a sense of evil rather than to provide psychological portraits of characters. This story is disturbing because it presents so many possible answers to the questions it asks. Kay, the main character, is a college student riding alone on the train back to college after her uncle's funeral. The tension surfaces when she meets a weird couple who pay an undesired amount of attention to her. As if through a sense of déjà vu, Kay thinks she recognizes them, but is terrified by the thought. When the man leans over and touches her cheek for no apparent reason, the contact between them is established. As the story rapidly reaches its conclusion, Kay is slowly mesmerized and at the end, as they take her purse and draw her raincoat over her head, the reader is stunned. Capote's dreamlike atmosphere has a psychological effect on the action as it draws the reader into a surrealistic world of dreams and the supernatural. The effect is both compelling and unsettling.

Capote's second collection, *Breakfast at Tiffany's: A Short Novel and Three Stories* (1958), however, is quite different in tone and effect. Of the short stories, "A Christmas Memory" (the other two are "House of Flowers" and "A Diamond Guitar") is considered one of Capote's best. A seven-year-old tells the story of a young man and his "sixty-something" cousin. As best friends whose battles with relatives are portrayed as comic impediments to their goal of gathering the ingredients for baking Christmas fruitcakes, the two provide a lighthearted look at the last Christmas they spend together. The mirthful quality of this story is quite different from the somber tone of Capote's other works.

• • •

The four collections of short stories by Tennessee Williams (1914—   ) reveal worlds very similar to those of Capote and O'Connor. His characters resemble those in his plays. In fact, many of the stories were early versions of the ideas he later used in works for the stage: "Portrait of a Girl in Glass" for *The Glass Menagerie;* "Three Players of a Summer Game" for *Cat on a Hot Tin Roof;* "Man Bring Up This Road" for *The Milk Train Doesn't Stop Here Anymore;* and "The Night of the Iguana" for the play of the same name. In all of his work, Williams portrays both adolescents and adults who are disillusioned and frustrated. They are men and women who are different, and because of their eccentricities have a need to see the world clearly. They succeed, but end up recognizing the horror that is present. As characters lost in time, they tend not to belong to their own world or to any other. Like his Southern contemporaries, Williams's stories become portraits of a generation that views itself as displaced.

One Arm and Other Stories (1948) is Williams's first collection. "Portrait of a Girl in Glass" exemplifies the people in his fictional world. Laura is a girl who "made no positive motion toward the world but stood at the edge of the water so to speak, with feet that anticipated too much cold to move." She needs to be "shoved . . . roughly forward" to overcome her fear of the world. As the story comes to a climax, she never does. Similar tales of meandering in and out of life make up the major stories in *One Arm*. In "The Field of Blue Children," two loners briefly meet, love, and drift away from each other into their own world; in the title story, a young man finds himself penned "in a corner and only waiting for death"; in "The Malediction," Lucio finds a cat, Nitchevo, wounded and dying. He sees in the cat's eyes a reflection of his own life: "They were full to the amber brims with all the secrets and sorrows the world can answer our ceaseless questioning with loneliness—yes. Hunger. Bewilderment. Pain. They wanted no more."

In *Hard Candy: A Book of Stories* (1954), Williams's second collection, similar themes and techniques appear. Throughout, the individual's confrontation with a truth too painful to bear is the highlight of the action. In "Three Players of a Summer Game," Brick Pollitt, former athlete and current alcoholic, is driven by his wife Margaret to a condition that turns him into a wreck of a man. Margaret controls Brick: "It was as though she had her lips fastened to some invisible wound in his body through which drained out of him and flowed into her the assurance and vitality that he had owned before marriage." By the end of the story, Brick has given in to Margaret's hammerlock on his life and is "no longer a human, but a babbling and goggling wreck." He has become her "boy" and she his conqueror. Other stories reveal the same emphasis on the unlived life that is not worth living. In "The Vine," "The Important Thing," "The Resemblance Between a Violin Case and a Coffin," and "The Mattress by the Tomato Patch," Williams's protagonists are all afflicted by their loss of innocence and inability to face reality.

By the time his third collection, *The Knightly Quest: A Novella and Some Short Stories* (1961), was published, Williams's craft had diminished. His best fiction by this time had already been written, his best plays already produced. *The Knightly Quest,* the novella, is a strange story of Gewinner Pearce, who returns home after years of travel to discover that great changes have taken place. The Project, a top-secret government plan, obsesses the town, and the Laughing-Boy Drive-In has been built directly across from the Pearce family mansion, having been given a ninety-nine-year lease by Gewinner's brother. The story is almost farcical as it follows the antics of Gewinner and the townspeople responding to these changes. Gewinner, for instance, is launched into space on a knightly quest, a part of the story made unbelievable by Williams's treatment of the entire incident. The other stories are more vintage Williams as they explore earlier themes.

It is clear that Williams's reputation as a major American literary figure rests in his dramatic achievements. Yet the early stories are important, too, especially as the best of them mirror the themes of his most remarkable plays, for they establish his place in the Southern renaissance.

. . .

With the stories of Robert Penn Warren (1905—   ) in *The Circus in the Attic* (1948), the theme of individual dignity is again dominant. Warren was born a Southerner, and has remained one spiritually, but his allegiance has been complex. Perhaps because of the diversity of his experiences with academic and nonacademic people, Northerners and Southerners, intellectuals and laborers, his stories tend to comment not only on regional values, but on universal ones as well. Like the work of his best counterparts, his tales become more than local color; they mirror the manners of an era in America.

Most of his short fiction is a painful celebration of young men's first steps into the real world. Perhaps the most outstanding is "Blackberry Winter." Here a man in his early forties recalls his initiation into manhood. As a boy, he had been attracted to a stranger who had come to work on his family's farm during a period of torrential rains and severe flooding. When the man left the farm because of an argument, the boy went with him vicariously. At the end of the story, the narrator, remembering the incident with chagrin, realizes he never could accept the devastation and the poverty of his youth, and thus tried to escape that world and its responsibility by not being an active part of it. In telling the story from the point of view of a man looking back in time to his youth, Warren accents the effect of change, not just on the young man in particular, but also on the South and young men in general. The narrator has been overcome with guilt, everpresent in Warren's stories, and he is not sure how to respond to it after so many years.

"When the Light Gets Green" also illustrates Warren's thematic and narrative techniques. Once again the story is told from the viewpoint of an adult looking back to his childhood. The speaker wants to discuss his relations with his grandfather as they were when they existed, and not reveal what he has thought about them as an adult. To accomplish this, Warren has his narrator show what he understood during the actual time of the relationship without comment from his present self. This technique discloses that the boy was mature enough to understand his feelings, but too immature to comprehend what they meant for either his grandfather or himself. This technique has the advantage of telling the story from a series of random recollections, rather than having to include details that are not germane to the effect Warren wants to achieve. The boy recollects only those incidents that had meaning for him in his youth. Warren therefore provides the reader with a sense of sharing and understanding life, instead of merely giving information. Like Warren's other initiation stories, this style enables him to emphasize the young man's guilt. The grandfather had waited years for love, but the grandson cannot love. As an adult, he feels guilty about his inability to comprehend this deficiency.

The other stories in *The Circus in the Attic* contain similar recognition scenes. In "Christmas Gift," "Testament of Flood," and "Her Own People," Warren shows characters who create guilt as a response to their sense of imprisonment. Like the misinformed Jack Burden of *All the King's Men,* Warren's major novel of the period, his characters search for an identity in the present only to discover that they cannot escape their past.

•   •   •

The short stories of Caroline Gordon (1895—1981) also celebrate the stability to be found in the past. Like Warren, she stresses the need for individual responsibility in coming to grips with the social disintegration of the modern North and South. Specifically, her stories reveal the contrast between the agrarian society whose values reflect the hierarchy of the early South, and the urban society in which skepticism and impersonal relationships are characteristic of the industrial age.

As a disciple of Henry James and believer in his theory of psychological realism, Gordon concentrates on the conduct of people in their relationships with others and the changes that must and do take place in these relationships. For Gordon, the need to reveal the subtle shifts in people's attitudes toward each other, and to do so in a way that describes their emotions, is of prime importance. Gordon also realizes that James's use of a restricted third-person point of view is the most effective technique. By filtering the events of the story through a single narrator, she can disclose the feelings of the narrator toward himself, others, and his place in the world. This information is not always reliable, but it does serve to enhance form and spiritual authority in her work.

Almost any of the stories in *The Forest of the South* (1945), her first collection, illustrate her use of point of view. "Old Red," one of the stories in which Gordon uses Aleck Murray as the central consciousness, is the tale of a man who values his freedom above all else. We understand his limited view of other characters and come to know his thoughts on everything: his food, his family, the nature of time. As these thoughts are filtered through the character, Gordon's themes surface. First, the reader learns that fishing is Aleck's life; it is an obsession, a passion, in many ways an art for him. He fishes not as a hobby, but as a way of finding himself. Also, for him, time is the measure of a man's life. Everyone else in the story is afraid of time, and according to Aleck, wastes it. His son-in-law Stephen is for Aleck a "Poor boy, dead to the world," who leads a disordered, abstract life. Ironically, as the story progresses, it is Aleck who realizes, "It was he, not Steve, that was the queer one!"

Throughout the action, Aleck is aware that he is fighting a battle against those who disapprove of his philosophy of life. The central moment comes when Aleck remembers "Old Red," the wily fox that eluded capture because of his ability to escape every hunter's ploy. Aleck like the fox is a hunted figure. From Old Red he learns two lessons: first, that freedom is most important to him; and second, that like the fox hunt, his family's attempts at trapping him are sport. At the end of the story, he wins his race against time and the hunters.

Caroline Gordon's story is effective and provocative in several ways. Aleck Murray and his family symbolize the essential conflict between the individual and a society that tends to departmentalize life and make a man feel guilty over whatever freedom he can salvage. Gordon's narrative technique effectively allows her main character to define his basic values. She uses similar techniques and themes in the rest of the stories of *The Forest of the South.*

In "The Last Day in the Field," another Aleck Murray story, Gordon creates a vivid portrait of the character's philosophical cast of mind, his stoicism, and his nature, by revealing the internal conflicts between him and his fishing companion. These differences, when played out against the action, create the dramatic tension that ultimately reveals Aleck's failing health and his almost ritual farewell to the hunt.

Elsewhere in the volume, Gordon charts the disillusionment of her central characters. In "The Brilliant Leaves," love disintegrates into frustration when a young girl realizes an affair has changed with the passage of time; in "Her Quaint Honour," the narrator watches a barn full of tobacco spoil because the man in charge yields momentarily to his passion for the black wife of a hired hand; in "The Forest of the South," one of Gordon's Civil War stories, a girl is ruined by those who, like herself, fought for an ideal the consequences of which they were unable to foresee. In all of these stories, Gordon compares the grandeur of the early South and its diminished present with men and women whose past has also diminished over time.

As a regionalist, she stands with the best of her contemporary Southern writers, but her major contributions to the short story come from her portrayal of character. For the most part, her stories seem to have little plot, but on second glance they reveal the manners of the South in the middle of the twentieth century and the dynamic quality of human relationships between ordinary men and women.

．　．　．

Similar tales of Southerners undergoing the rigors of daily life are found in *The Black Prince and Other Stories* (1955) by Shirley Ann Grau (1929—   ) and in the first collection of stories by Doris Betts (1932—   ). Although neither has the range of Gordon, Betts is especially astute at revealing character. In "The Sympathetic Visitor," the opening tale from *The Gentle Insurrection and Other Stories* (1954), she describes the trauma of a white woman as she travels to a black household in Rabbittown to learn the details of a murder. Because "Niggers always left her feeling tired," a refrain sounded several times throughout the story, the traveler leaves Rabbittown, not with warmth or sympathy, but with "nameless horror" at what she has learned.

Like the best stories in the collection ("A Sense of Honor," "Mr. Shawn and Father Scott," "The Gentle Insurrection," "The Very Old Are Beautiful"), "The Sympathetic Visitor" reveals Betts's ability to write stories that exhibit a diversity of characters and reactions to everyday pressures. Whether the characters are young or old, black or white, girls having babies or old men facing death, she unmasks their personalities in a realistic and unsentimental fashion.

．　．　．

Jesse Stuart (1907—   ) also emphasizes the commonplace in his stories collected in *Tales from the Plum Grove Hills* (1946) and *Clearing in the Sky and Other Stories* (1950). Stuart sketches life in the hills of Kentucky and describes days in the lives of people who face trauma with an unyielding spirit. Unlike some of his Southern contemporaries, Stuart's characters are not grotesque, nor does he rely on the bizarre. His families are simple people who recall the past with affection (as in "Grandpa Birdwell's Last Battle" or "I Remember Molly"), the manners and superstitions of the countryside with humor ("Fitified Man," "Frog-Trouncin' Contest"), the place of nature in their lives ("Thanksgiving Hunter," "The Storm"), and death with respect ("Death Has Two Good Eyes"). Stuart is not on a par with Taylor, Welty, or Warren as a technician. He is primarily a local-color writer, yet his stories of hill people, told as though they were being shared with neighbors over the local crackerbarrel, have an intimacy and immediacy that is appealing.

• • •

Although Southern writers produced most of the important short fiction in the postwar decade, others belonging to no distinct school were just as prolific and made significant contributions in their portraits of local manners. The best of them escaped the pitfalls of producing work that was a product of regional dialects, habits, and traditions only. Their sense of milieu enabled them to turn the regional into the archetypal, the specific into the universal.

The short stories of James T. Farrell reveal a vivid portrait of life in Chicago. Farrell (1904—1979) published four collections in the dozen years after 1945: *When Boyhood Dreams Come True* (1946), *The Life Adventurous and Other Stories* (1947), *French Girls Are Vicious and Other Stories* (1955), and *A Dangerous Woman and Other Stories* (1957). Although he is a prolific writer of novels, novellas, short stories, poems, and literary criticism, and although his cycles of novels starring Studs Lonigan, Danny O'Neill, and Bernard Carr have created a mythology of their own, he has never received much serious critical attention. For the most part, like John O'Hara, he is a photographic realist who presents a literal report of life as seen from the outside. He traces the personal destinies of his characters as they wander from one church parish to another, from one job to another, or from one woman to another.

Despite their lack of narrative variety, his short stories do achieve something that O'Hara's fail to accomplish. With his characters, many of whom are drawn from his novels and appear in story after story, Farrell creates a fictional world composed of types brought together by common problems. Like Chekhov, Farrell concentrates on character rather than action, and it is this emphasis that makes his stories vivid portrayals of urban manners.

• • •

Also writing about life in the Midwest is Jessamyn West (1907—   ). Although she spent most of her life in California, her first collection, *The Friendly Persuasion* (1946), depicts the world of a Quaker family in Indiana. These fourteen stories of the Jess Birdwell family are sympathetic treatments of family problems. "Shivaree Before Breakfast" is interesting for its use of the initiation theme in which a young boy is shocked by his glimpse into the adult world. West's method of allowing the family boys to understand and respond to an unexpected discovery is well-handled. They begin by arranging a shivaree (wedding serenade) for Alf and Molly. When they realize the two are not married, they are shocked and find it hard to accept. West avoids the sentimental with a good bit of irony and turns what could have been a pathetic situation into a humorous one.

She continues her portrait of Quaker life in the other stories. Again, she uses irony to reveal the intricate customs and traditions of a religious group infrequently fictionalized. Her rendering of the rural atmosphere in this collection and in the later *Love, Death, and the Ladies' Drill Team* (1953) is effective.

• • •

Texas is the scene of many of William Humphrey's (1925—   ) stories. In *The Last Husband and Other Stories* (1953), Humphrey's concern is with small-town manners and mores. In a typical story, "Quail for Mr. Forester," a young boy reveals his family's experience when Mr. Forester, a member of an antebellum, aristocratic family who has gone into the hardware business in the postwar South, comes for dinner. Conversation is principally concerned with the decline of the old world and contrasts the values of the past with those of the present. At story's end, the boy, impressed deeply by Mr. Forester's tales, feels with his parents that "there is no hope for him in these mean times." The difference in social class portrayed through the boy's eyes is characteristic of the Texas Humphrey displays in *The Last Husband*. Lost in the glory of the past, his characters find little solace in their improved but unromantic place in the present.

• • •

The stories of William Saroyan (1908—1981) are filled with bursts of local color. In addition to plays and novels, Saroyan published eight volumes of short fiction. His first collection, *The Daring Young Man on the Flying Trapeze* (1934), introduces the major themes and articulates the style used in most of his later collections: *The Assyrian and Other Stories* (1950), *Love* (1955), *The Whole Voyald and Other Stories* (1956), *My Kind of Crazy Wonderful People* (1966), and *The Man with the Heart in the Highlands and Other Stories* (1968).

With the publication of *The Daring Young Man* at age twenty-five, Saroyan established his reputation as a serious writer. Although most of the stories are autobiographical and lack traditional plot, they do establish his philosophy of writing and reveal his background. Unlike other social realists writing in the 1930s, many of whom emphasized the dismal aspects of the period, Saroyan, while certainly evoking the setting and tone of the period, does so to highlight the people and their problems rather than to comment on the causes of the depression. With this emphasis on character and action, Saroyan deals effectively with loneliness, alienation, and the inability of people to achieve lasting relationships.

Later stories written after the Second World War are different in both tone and style, although they continue to be autobiographical. Characteristic of these collections are prefaces written to justify and sometimes to apologize for his writing.

• • •

James A. Michener (1907—   ) is recognized today more as the author of epic-length novels than of short stories. Yet his stories, collected in *Tales of the South Pacific* (1947) and *Return to Paradise* (1951), were his first ventures into fiction. Not a major innovator or technician in the short story tradition of the decade, Michener is important for his depiction of place, time, and mood. In these postwar years, his stories played to the romantic tastes of his readers. Rather than Farrell's seamy Chicago dives, O'Hara's New York streets, or Auchincloss's upper class mansions, Michener's exotic and faraway places appealed to an American audience seeking to escape the war years. Yet, ironically, Michener's stories are not always escape. Like the best writers since Henry James, Michener combines the elements of romance and realism to portray contemporary society. The settings may be romantic, but the action is always real. His war stories ("Coral Sea," "The Sea," "The Milk Run," "Alligator," among others) in *Tales of the South Pacific* are realistic in their portrayal of fighting and death. His other stories of the war years are equally vivid in their disclosure of men and women caught up in history.

• • •

America's love affair with Michener's tales of the South Seas was matched after the war by the rising popularity of a new genre: science fiction. Like those tales of romance that allowed people to live their daydreams and momentarily escape problems, pressures, and pollution, science fiction created a similar release. Published at a time when the advances of science were fashionable topics of conversation, these tales of fantasy stimulated interest, especially among the young. Of the science fiction writers in the period, Ray Bradbury (1920—   ) is certainly the best.

In his five collections of stories published within an eight-year period—*Dark Carnival* (1947), *The Martian Chronicles* (1950), *The Illustrated Man* (1951), *The Golden Apples of the Sun* (1953), *The October Country* (1955)—Bradbury treats the achievements of science as fable, prophecy, and nightmare. In his satiric delineation of American society, he sees the dangers emerging from its dependence on machines. His stories satirize those who are ecologically irresponsible, smug, and materialistic, and he projects the alienation and loneliness he fears will be a result of these attitudes. Bradbury's fictional realm is one in which doubt and fear of death produce irrational behavior.

In the opening of *The October Country,* he describes what becomes for him an eerie world, a country "composed in the main of cellars, sub-cellars, coalbins, closets, attics, and pantries faced away from the sun . . . whose people passing at night in the empty walks sound like rain . . ." It is apparent in the tattoos of the Illustrated Man that this country is the product of our unmasked fears. In this collection of stories, probably Bradbury's best, the narrator meets a man whose tattoos are illustrations that "predict the future." As the narrator gazes at the illustrations, eighteen of them take on life of their own, and from them stories emerge, each one revealing glimpses of the future. In the epilogue, when the tales are complete, the narrator sees on the man's back a final scene: "I saw only enough of the Illustration to make me leap up. . . . The picture on his back showed the Illustrated Man himself, with his fingers around my neck, choking me to death." The collection ends with the narrator running toward town, never looking back.

The rise of science fiction in this period is important in helping shape the short story of the 1960s and 1970s. Because it created new myths of America, and because it relied on satire as its chief mode, later writers used many of its techniques in their innovative fiction.

•　•　•

Besides science fiction, literature written by blacks was to have a profound impact on the stories of later decades. One of the most promising black writers was Langston Hughes (1902—1967). His collection, *Laughing to Keep from Crying* (1952), is a series of sketches portraying the black experience in America. Hughes's tales are short and autobiographical, and they reveal a sensitivity to issues that were beginning to take hold of the national conscience in the 1950s.

In "Who's Passing for Who," the first of the twenty-four sketches, Hughes begins by writing, "One of the great difficulties about being a member of a minority race is that so many kindhearted, well-meaning bores gather round to help." This opening is symptomatic of the misunderstanding and tensions Hughes portrays as blacks began their quest for equality. Throughout the collection, "well-meaning bores" are contrasted with intolerant and activist whites and blacks. In "African Morning," Maurai, a mulatto boy, realizes that "nobody wanted him" because he is neither white nor black; in "Something in Common," a black and a white soldier join ranks to fight against their common enemy, prejudice; in "Who's Passing for Who," a man and wife pose as whites, then blacks, then whites again in a comedy of errors. All the stories reveal Hughes's satiric attempts to reconcile the differences between the races. His portraits mark him as one of the important writers of the postwar ear.

• • •

For writers such as Langston Hughes and others who had their start in the decade following the war, the critical reception today is mixed. In part, it is because some of them are seen as imitators of the short story tradition of the first half century or as unsuccessful innovators who were perhaps ahead of their time. Yet the very best of them were and are models of the technical and stylistic virtuosity that mark the development of the twentieth-century short story as a distinctive American achievement. Whether these postwar storytellers used the city or the country as their milieu, the urbane witticisms of New Yorkers or the colloquialisms of Southerners to delineate character, or simply the diversity of American regionalisms and rituals to create their own fictional settings in or out of this world, no simple classifications or generalizations can be applied to any of these major contemporary writers. The individuality of their styles and approaches makes each a special problem in analysis and appreciation.

Yet each of these writers has one thing in common. Each wrote fiction to seek positive values to take the place of those lost in the chaos of the Depression and the Second World War. They recognized that the individual, confronted by the myriad changes that were taking place, was losing his identity and his importance as a person. This search certainly contributed to the starkness and reality of their short stories. For some, this meant writing fiction without departing from the traditional plot framework and creating interest through the interaction of character and incident. For the majority of others, however, the challenge of presenting a portrait of the human scene with sharpened insight and with individually developed styles of their own enabled them to produce stories ranging in mode from the realistic to the allegorical and grotesque. In breaking new ground, these postwar writers worked in the

characteristic American vein, which has always been innovative and explor-
atory, in their attempt to portray the manners of a changing American society.

Jeffrey Walker

Oklahoma State University

1957—1968:
TOWARD DIVERSITY
OF FORM

The period from 1957 to 1968 was an extremely significant and productive one for American practitioners of the art of short fiction. It saw the literary maturation of such major figures as John Cheever, Flannery O'Connor, Isaac Bashevis Singer, and Peter Taylor. It witnessed the emergence of the new and important voices of John Updike, Bernard Malamud, and John Barth.

In the tradition of Hawthorne, James, and Twain, American short-story writers continued to evoke a sense of place in their fiction. Authors such as Cheever, Updike, and Hortense Calisher began to explore what was rapidly becoming a Northeastern megalopolis. The Southern renaissance was in full swing. Other writers in the Midwest and Southwest drew heavily on the cultural background of their regions.

Ethnic heritage was also becoming a very important element in the creative process. In the late 1960s, a number of young writers initiated a black literary renaissance, reconciling their particular concerns with the demands of their craft. It was a synthesis that had already been achieved by Jewish-Americans such as Singer, Malamud, and Saul Bellow who, from the 1950s on, became not only the voices of their own ethnic ties but also ethical spokesmen for American society as a whole.

While it drew on such a variety of backgrounds, the American short story remained, for the most part, a vehicle for the exploration of contemporary society. Indeed, in the 1950s and early 1960s it became apparent that the main purpose of the genre was to create a fiction of manners. This was emphasized by the continued preeminence of periodicals such as *The New Yorker* and the popularity of authors such as Cheever and Updike. Whether they were Easterners or Southerners, Jewish or black Americans, writers in the period contributed to the Jamesian goal of rendering even the "simplest surface" in order "to guess the unseen from the seen, to trace the implication of things, to judge the whole piece by the pattern" (Henry James, "The Art of Fiction").

This is not to suggest that they chose to express contemporary conditions and mores in ways that were completely or even primarily realistic. For, as Richard Chase has suggested in *The American Novel and Its Tradition,* the American imagination "seems less interested in redemption than in the melodrama of the eternal struggle of good and evil, less interested in incarnation and reconciliation" than in "the aesthetic possibilities of radical forms of alienation, contradiction and disorder." Embodying these tendencies, the American short story, like the American novel, has often fused realism and romance, something that is particularly evident in the period we are considering.

Faced with the radical changes of the previous few decades, with the growing complexity of contemporary life, the increasingly perplexing relationships between the individual and society, short-story writers in the late 1950s and the 1960s began more and more to discover the limitations of realistic or naturalistic fiction. Thus while some continued to focus on the everyday and the usual, others came more and more to explore the grotesque, the fantastic, and the supernatural. While some continued to employ traditional narrative forms, others began not only to reject conventional realistic narrative but also to expose and question the conventions of fiction in general. This blend of realism and romance, of traditional and innovative, characteristic of the fiction of the period as a whole, is manifested even in the work of artists, such as John Cheever, who have somewhat fallaciously been labeled as celebrators and historians of the usual.

• • •

John Cheever (1912—1982) has long been regarded as one of the most astute observers and recorders of contemporary American society. With the publication of *The Stories of John Cheever* (1978) his short fiction won even wider consideration. So polished is his prose for the most part, that it is easy to miss his experimentation with narrative technique and to conclude that he is a mere chronicler of everyday events. So felicitously does he capture the seriocomic essence of metropolitan and suburban angst that one may fail to notice the mythic and fantastic elements interwoven with his observations on contemporary mores.

Raised in Quincy, Massachusetts, and having resided in New York and New England, Cheever has much in common with those other products and portrayers of Northeastern culture, Henry James and Nathaniel Hawthorne. Like James he is interested in capturing the intricate vagaries of interpersonal relationships and in exploring the possibilities of fictional narration. While he is not above celebrating the simple joys of life, Cheever, like both these predecessors, is also concerned with that deeper, darker, Puritan aspect of the American psyche, the realm of the moral, mythical, and supernatural. As he himself put it in the Preface to his collected stories: "The constants that I look for in this sometimes dated paraphernalia are a love of light and a determination to trace some moral chain of being. Calvin played no part at all in my religious education, but his presence seemed to abide in the barns of my childhood and to have left me with some undue bitterness." Although Cheever may thus be seen as working within a tradition, both the method and milieu of his short stories are unique and modern, something readily discernible in his first major collection, *The Enormous Radio and Other Stories* (1953).

The differences between the stories in *The Enormous Radio* and his first volume, *The Way Some People Live* (1943), are significant. Impressive as first efforts, the earlier pieces are nonetheless sketchy and sometimes banally realistic (Cheever has called them "embarrassingly immature"). By contrast, the works in his second collection are in every sense more complete and distinctive. Cheever's perennial topics—loneliness, the vanity of human wishes, the evil that conceals itself behind a commonplace facade—are given fuller and more complex treatment. Cheever's mature method, his subtle obfuscation of the realistic and the romantic, is here evident for the first time. Because he has narrowed his geographic compass to New York and its environs, he develops that rich sense of place so crucial to his purpose.

The title story is in many ways illustrative of the book as a whole. Like Paul Hollis of "The Summer Farmer" and the narrator of "The Season of Divorce," Jim and Irene Westcott, the apartment-dwellers in "The Enormous Radio," have purchased happiness with ignorance and self-deception. "The kind of people who seem to strike that satisfactory average of income, endeavor, and respectability that is reached by the statistical reports in college alumni bulletins," the Westcotts become characters in a modern gothic tale, their shallow complacency annihilated by the acquisition of a minor technological marvel. Whether it is a supernatural agent or an objective correlative for the evil and meanness lurking behind the metropolitan mask, their malevolently glowing radio plays out the cruel and shabby dramas that actually are being enacted in the apartments about them. Although they have the radio repaired, they themselves remain permanently attuned to what is "horrible," "dreadful," and "depressing" in their neighbors' lives, aware now that their own life is no different.

Most of the pieces in the collection follow this pattern, the gradual stripping away of illusion, innocence, and ignorance. For many of Cheever's characters, greater awareness brings pain, or even horror, and a heightened sense of futility. In "Torch Song," Jack Lorey discovers too late that a "handsome," "healthy" girl is in reality an Angel of Death with an uncanny, almost supernatural ability to attach herself to men who, like him, are self-destructive and dying. In one of the alternative endings for "O City of Broken Dreams," the Malloys, having been disillusioned by and made to feel ridiculous in New York, head stolidly for California, where presumably they will be disillusioned and made to feel ridiculous once more.

Knowledge is not always a liability, however, and there are moments of light here as well. In "The Pot of Gold," Ralph Whittemore, thwarted in his attempts to acquire wealth, discovers in his wife the treasure he has been seeking. In one of Cheever's best stories, "Goodbye, My Brother," the narrator, maintaining his sense of life in the face of his brother's dark negativism, speaks to us directly and calls our attention to the "surface beauty of life" manifested in a single instant of brightness and perfection.

Cheever's third volume of stories, *The Housebreaker of Shady Hill* (1958), is marked by even greater geographic focus and thematic unity. All of the major characters are residents of the banlieue of Shady Hill, rich or apparently rich suburbanites who "travel around the world, listen to good music, and given a choice of paper books at an airport, will pick Thucydides, and sometimes Aquinas." Most of their stories are expressions of Cheever's belief that "we are still experimenting. This is a haunted nation. Haunted by a dream of excellence."

In Shady Hill the experiment seems to have gone awry; the dream has taken on the qualities of nightmare. We meet a respectable citizen who pilfers cash from his neighbors' homes to keep up appearances, a former track star compelled to relive "his brillant past" by hurdling living room furniture, a "country husband" who discovers Venus in his children's babysitter, and an alcoholic father who cannot understand why his twelve-year-old daughter failed to find "that home sweet home was the best place of all." Excellence has been replaced by status or materialism or security; the power of the dream remains, but Cheever's people seem unable to discover how to embody it.

Cheever's own experimentation, however, is more successful. Many of the stories are characterized by shifts in point of view and by narrative complexity. Reading "The Country Husband" for the first time, for example, we may recognize that something unusual is going on in the first line ("To begin at the beginning . . ."), may even realize that we are to think in terms of oral storytelling. Only when we have read the story through and have experienced Francis Weed's frustration at being unable to recount the crash landing he has survived do we understand that his desire to tell his story in his way has infected the text, making what first appeared as objective narration into something very different.

Whereas Cheever's tapestry of Shady Hill is tightly woven, *Some People, Places, and Things that Will Not Appear in My Next Novel* (1961) is, as the title of one of its pieces suggests, "A Miscellany." Developing a sense of place seems not as important as exploring a variety of reactions to the absurdity and dislocations of contemporary life, and Cheever employs a number of different settings, European as well as American. Most critics citing "A Miscellany of Characters" agree that this is a transitional volume in which Cheever in a sense exorcises unsatisfactory responses to and treatments of the modern condition. Although this may indeed be true, the book as a whole makes clear what will happen in his future work. We find in these pieces a great deal of narrative intrusion and play, a disregard for the restrictions of genre (is "A Miscellany" an essay, a short story, or a blend of both?), and an increasing emphasis on the fantastic and fabulous, all characteristics of the work that follows.

In the closing line of "A Miscellany" Cheever, by implication, makes a commitment "to celebrate a world that lies spread out around us like a bewildering and stupendous dream." In his next book of stories, *The Brigadier and the Golf Widow* (1964), we travel through an America in which the real and the unreal, suburban and dream landscapes, coexist and interpenetrate. In "The Swimmer," for instance, Cheever cleverly confounds internal time, clock time, and mythic time. To Neddy Merrill, his cross-country swim through backyard swimming pools seems to take but an afternoon. There is much textual evidence that suggests, however, that his "heroic journey" begins in midsummer and ends in autumn, and we cannot even be certain whether the seasons through which we move are those of a single year or a lifetime. The reader seeking a rational explanation may find one in the deterioration of Merrill's psychological state, but the mythic structure makes possible another, not necessarily contradictory, reading: Merrill's suburban *nostos* is an ironic odyssey that results in loss of social status and concludes with his return to a locked and deserted home.

Cheever's use of apparently realistic narration to achieve surrealistic effects is also evident in this collection. In two stories, the dream world intrudes in the form of seemingly supernatural agents who offer assistance to his afflicted suburbanites. In "The Angel of the Bridge," a hitchhiking angel intercedes to help the narrator overcome his phobia about bridges, a fear linked to his hatred of modern life. In "The Music Teacher," a modern-day witch provides a harried husband with a musical formula that converts his wife from shrew to slave. In the four sketches that comprise "Metamorphoses," he concocts a playful mixture of fantasy and irony, matter-of-factly describing a series of modern ovidian transformations that comment not only on the diminution of humans but also on the deflation of myth itself.

If *The Brigadier and the Golf Widow* is dominated by one impulse in Cheever's fiction, the reaction to calvinism, the descent into bitterness, then *The World of Apples* (1974) contains some of the clearest expressions of that other, contrary impulse, the celebration of living, the ascent into light. This is not to say that Cheever has put failure, frustration, and loss behind him; they are still inextricably bound up in the contemporary condition. But one may discover in several of these stories a change in tone, an aura of affirmation. Perhaps the best example of this is the well-crafted title story, which recounts the struggle of a poet to overcome the fading of inspiration and the feeling that his work has been unjustly overlooked. Although he succumbs for a time to the downward pull, indulging in suicidal thoughts and scatological verse, he checks his fall, purifies himself through nature and memory, and begins "a long poem on the inalienable dignity of light and air." It is a fitting conclusion to the final story in the final volume that Cheever produced in the period.

•   •   •

Born in Shillington, Pennsylvania, and educated at Harvard, John Updike (1932—   ) is, like Cheever, a Northeasterner whose fiction ostensibly records the everyday lives of ordinary people in small-town, urban, and suburban America. Also like Cheever, Updike is a master craftsman, a novelist as well as a short-story writer, whose short fiction has most often appeared in *The New Yorker*. Whereas Cheever's genii are James and Hawthorne, Updike's genius is clearly James Joyce.

In his childhood reminiscences, "A Dogwood Tree," Updike presents an approach to art which he tells us he has never outgrown:

I reasoned thus: just as the paper is the basis for the marks upon it, might not events be contingent upon a never-expressed (because featureless) ground? Is the true marvel of Sunday skaters the pattern of their pirouettes or the fact that they are silently upheld? Blankness is not emptiness; we may skate upon an intense radiance we do not see because we see nothing else. And in fact there is a color, a quiet but tireless goodness that things at rest, like a brick wall or a small stone, seem to affirm. A wordless reassurance these things are pressing to give. An hallucination? To transcribe middleness with all its grits, bumps, and anonymities, in its fullness of satisfaction and mystery: is it possible or, in view of the suffering that violently colors the periphery and that at all moments threatens to move into the center, worth doing?

It is a statement of purpose that has much in common with the esthetic theory in Joyce's own book of reminiscences, *Stephen Hero*.

Updike's commitment "to transcribe middleness," then, is a commitment to seeing clearly and fully, to capturing all of the complex "pirouettes" of life in order ultimately to apprehend that radiant goodness that brings reassurance. Thus the typical Updike story, like the typical *Dubliners* story, is dependent for its effect not on overt action but on the accumulation of details and perceptions leading to that moment of epiphany when we see beyond the chaotic surface of things. There is, however, a distinctive difference between Joyce's short fiction and Updike's.

In Joyce's dark Dublin, to see clearly is usually to apprehend folly, frustration, or loss, to become aware of the tangled snares woven by self and circumstance. Although this is true of many of Updike's pieces as well, his epiphanies are occasionally more positive. For him, *claritas* sometimes truly is *quidditas,* and the light does shine through.

This careful balancing of the delineation of life's grits and bumps with intuition of its satisfactions and mysteries is found in Updike's first volume of stories, *The Same Door* (1959). In this collection we discover characters who exhibit an entire spectrum of responses to revelation. In "Tomorrow and Tomorrow and So Forth," Mark Prosser makes a conscious effort to disregard his moment of insight, to hold on to the illusion of self-importance rather than admit to himself that he, like his more ordinary colleagues, has been ridiculed by two of his high school students. In another story, "Sunday Teasing," a somewhat similar character does permit himself to see a bit more clearly, allowing one day's events to coalesce into the realization that he doesn't "know anything." Although it is unclear whether or not he will act on the self-knowledge he has gained, move beyond tolerance of his wife's ignorance to an acceptance of her difference, we cannot help but feel that his reaction is in some way more positive than Prosser's.

Finally, in "Dentistry and Doubt," an American cleric visiting England possesses a moment that qualifies as an epiphany in its fullest sense. Sitting in the dentist's chair and feeling disoriented and isolated, Burton is troubled by his own skepticism and by the presence of evil in the world. Overcoming difficulties of communication, however, he reaches out to the dentist and is rewarded, in this most incongruous of settings, with a vision of universal harmony: "Outside the window, the wrens and starlings, mixed indistinguishably, engaged in maneuvers that seemed essentially playful."

Updike's next two volumes of stories, *Pigeon Feathers* (1962) and *Olinger Stories: A Selection* (1964), make clear something that is perhaps not initially apparent in *The Same Door:* for Updike, experience is not only a balance of positive and negative discoveries, but a mixture of "memory and desire." Updike chose as the epigraph for *Pigeon Feathers* a passage from Kafka's "A Report to an Academy," which reads, in part: "In revenge, however, my memory of the past has closed the door against me more and more. I could have returned at first, had human beings allowed it, through an archway as wide as the span of heaven over the earth, but as I spurred myself on in my forced career, the opening narrowed and shrank behind me; I felt more comfortable in the world of men and fitted it better."

Viewed in terms of this epigraph, Updike's early stories fall into two basic categories, those that are products of an attempt to recapture, through memory, the innocent joys and gropings of youth, and those that describe the efforts of older individuals to reach outward into "the world of men" in search of mature joys. A careful reading of *Olinger Stories,* which collects all of the Olinger pieces from the first two volumes (Olinger is Updike's fictional shadow of Shillington, Pennsylvania), reveals an increasing distancing from that child-hood world. The epigraph to *Pigeon Feathers* and the Olinger collection both emphasize not only the importance to Updike of recapturing the past, but his growing difficulty in sustaining that nostalgic impulse in the face of more so-called adult concerns.

This becomes especially significant when one realizes that the majority of positive epiphanies in *Pigeon Feathers* take place in the past, a past that is as much recreated through art and conscious effort as it is recollected. The epiphanies recorded in stories such as "A Sense of Shelter" and "Pigeon Feathers" seem more temporary, become moments of insight and satisfaction that mark a journey outward. At the same time, the stories with more contemporary settings ("Walter Briggs," "Dear Alexandros," "The Doctor's Wife") become increasingly marked by a perception of separation and an awareness of the gulfs between past and present, self and others.

"The Persistence of Desire" is in many ways the most characteristic story of this stage in Updike's career. A young man, changed by the world (a magazine article he reads proclaims, "the cells of the human body are replaced in toto every seven years"), returns to Olinger. In an optometrist's office, amid a stopped grandfather clock and "other imitation antiques," he encounters a former sweetheart. He tells her that he is happily married, "but happiness isn't everything," and filled with the memory of past desire, he attempts to arrange an assignation. When he leaves the office, however, he discovers that he cannot read the note she has passed him, for time has dismissed him "into a tainted world where things evaded his focus." His desire remains unfulfilled in the present; only in an imagined past can he find satisfaction and clarity of vision: "The maples, macadam, shadows, houses, cement, were to his violated eyes as brilliant as a scene remembered; he became a child again in this town, where life was a distant adventure, a rumor, an always imminent joy."

The initial piece of *The Music School* (1966), the last Updike volume to appear in the period, contains a farewell to Olinger. The tone of "In Football Season" is consciously nostalgic, and the story concludes with the narrator grudgingly pulling himself forward in time: "Now I peek into windows and open doors and do not find that air of permission. It has fled the world. Girls walk by me carrying invisible bouquets from fields still steeped in grace, and I look up in the manner of one who follows with his eyes the passage of a hearse, and remembers what pierces him." One world has died for him, and he must find what he can in another.

As many of the stories in *The Music School* emphasize, that other world, the adult one of marriage and social interaction, is harder, less tolerant, and marked to a great extent by divorce in all its forms. Updike's contemporary characters sleep in separate beds ("Twin Beds in Rome"), suspect each other of infidelity ("The Rescue"), and purchase what happiness they have with blood ("Giving Blood"). Speaking of his earlier work in the Foreword to *Olinger Stories,* Updike noted that the point of them was that *"We are* rewarded *unexpectedly.* The muddled and inconsequent surface of things now and then parts to yield us a gift." In *The Music School,* there are few such gratuitous gifts; whatever has been gained has usually been paid for.

Updike does not, however, permit suffering permanently to usurp the center. In the title story, for example, we share with Alfred Schweigen an epiphany in some ways fuller and more significant than those that dot the enchanted landscape of memory. Surrounded by indifference and diffidence, Schweigen is a writer who cannot write, adrift in a modern limbo: "We are all pilgrims, faltering toward divorce. Some get no further than mutual confession, which becomes an addiction, and exhausts them. Some move on, into violent quarrels and physical blows; and succumb to sexual excitement. A few make it to the psychiatrists. A very few get as far as the lawyers." Technology, the substitute for religion, provides him with no solution, for it has merely replaced one kind of acolyte with another, the "typical specimen of the new human species that thrives around scientific centers, in an environment of discussion groups, outdoor exercise, and cheerful husbandry."

Yet in spite of all this, Schweigen, with the aid of the synthesizing power of music, experiences a moment of satisfaction through a hard-won acceptance of life as it is: "The world is the host; it must be chewed. I am content here in this school. My daughter emerges from her lesson. Her face is fat and satisfied, refreshed, hopeful; her pleased smile, biting her lower lip, pierces my heart and I die (I think I am dying) at her feet."

The intensity and the holistic quality of Schweigen's experience here illustrate why there is little of the supernatural in Updike's short fiction. For him, the natural and supernatural are not coexistent. The spiritual is bound up with the material; the luminous essence of things shines through them to be perceived in instants of heightened perception. Whether Updike's stories culminate in major epiphanies or conclude with lesser, more equivocal ones, their success or failure depends, therefore, not solely on the development of patterns of images, but on his ability to convey a flash of intuition in a few highly charged words.

This may be one of the things responsible for what some perceive as an unevenness in his work. When we feel that the *mots justes* have evaded him at the crucial point, the story as a whole may strike us as on the one hand artificial or on the other prosaic. When Updike succeeds, however, the effect is as wonderful as any to be found in the genre.

•   •   •

The two collections published by Peter Taylor (1917—   ) in the late 1950s and early 1960s attest to his continued mastery of the form. The sense of place remains strong in these stories, most of which are set in the country towns and cities of contemporary Tennessee. Taylor is certainly more than a regional writer, however. Less of an experimentalist than Cheever, less a modernist than Updike, he is nonetheless their equal in technical artistry, and he shares with them some basic concerns: the subtleties of interpersonal relationships, the difficulty of communication, and the effects of urbanization on individuals and their culture.

The title of Taylor's third volume, *Happy Families Are all Alike* (1959), taken from *Anna Karenina* ("Happy families are all alike; every unhappy family is unhappy in its own way"), emphasizes once more his preoccupation with home life as mirror of the contemporary condition.

In "Heads of Houses," he adroitly manipulates point of view to delineate the intricacies of familial stratagems and alliances. Although Taylor's technique here is certainly not innovative, the story is a tour de force, a smooth and masterful evocation of the manner in which preconceptions and failed communication may negate good intentions and blind a household to its potential sources of strength and harmony. Whereas here the combatants are male heads of houses, in "Guests" it is the women, Henrietta and her country cousin, Annie, who engage in warfare with social convention for weapons, making it impossible for the men to reach out to one another in hope of discovering "what it is people keep alive for."

Taylor's characters may be ordinary people and the world they inhabit the everyday world, but there is an undercurrent of evil and a trace of the supernatural in many of his stories that place them in the tradition of Southern gothic. "A Walled Garden," for example, is a cameo of evil incarnate, reminiscent in setting of Hawthorne's "Rappaccini's Daughter" and in technique of

Browning's "My Last Duchess." Through dramatic monologue, Mrs. Harris reveals to us how her insane desire for control and order led her cruelly and unfeelingly to prune her daughter's spirit and individuality so that she, too, might fit into the scheme of her mother's walled garden. In Taylor's 1959 O. Henry Award winner, "Venus, Cupid, Folly, and Time," narrative complexity, intimations of incest, and careful development of atmosphere contribute to an eerie yet poignant portrayal of decay.

Taylor's fondness for the supernatural, the slightly surreal, and the grotesque is further evident in three of the previously uncollected pieces that appear in *Miss Leonora when Last Seen* (1963), a volume of sixteen stories, ten of which appeared in *The Widows of Thornton* and *A Long Fourth*. One of these stories, entitled, appropriately enough, "A Strange Story," deals overtly with the apparently supernatural, with the narrator's recollections of a period in his childhood when the world was a magical place in which mysterious, quixotic, and sometimes prophetic voices spoke to him. In another, "At the Drugstore," Matt Donelson, "back home on a visit," wakes up one morning and walks, apparently unconsciously, to a neighborhood drugstore where he seems to step back in time: "It was as if this very morning he had run all the way from home with his school books under one arm and his yellow slicker under the other and was now afraid that the streetcar—the good old Country Day Special—would pass before he could get waited on." The face behind the drugstore counter is "indisputably the face of old Mr. Conway as it had been forty years ago," the now modern drugstore threatens "to turn back into the place it had been once," and Matt feels trapped "in a dream from which he could not wake himself."

There are, of course, psychological explanations for the occurrences in both these stories. The narrator of "A Strange Story" merely thinks he heard voices, something not uncharacteristic of certain children at a certain stage of development. Matt sees what he wants to see in the drugstore so that he can fulfill a subconscious need to clarify his roles as son and father. Taylor's skillful use of point of view, however, makes it difficult for us to be satisfied with such analysis. So clever is he at making us imagine that we hear what a character hears or see what he sees, that even after the fact, when the common-sense alternatives become apparent (the figure behind the counter is Conway's son), we are still left with the feeling that we have experienced something unusual. Like Cheever in "The Swimmer" or James in "The Turn of the Screw," Taylor leaves us suspended somewhere between the rational and the supernatural.

In the title story Taylor plays on our conceptions of what is realistic or normal in a slightly different manner. Miss Leonora Logan appears at first to be a type—the small-town eccentric, regarded by other townspeople as slightly peculiar in behavior and dress. The last surviving member of "a family that for a hundred years did all it could to impede the growth and progress" of her town, she is a living anachronism, the final existing specimen of an outmoded way of life.

Again, Taylor makes us uneasy in our attempts to categorize and define. Miss Leonora is a grotesque only in the eyes of those around her, among whom we cannot count the narrator. His ambivalence toward her, in fact, leads us to consider the inherent relativism of concepts such as conformity and sanity. Even more than that, his inability or unwillingness to tell us her whereabouts calls into question our very notions of reality itself. All we have are a few tantalizing documents, a half-dozen postcards, to trace her existence in space and time, and the narrator's belief, perhaps the product of his need to believe, that she is still alive behind the wheel of her 1942 Dodge convertible, "orbiting her native state." She remains, finally, an intuited but unseen presence somewhere "out there," and readers may consider, if just for a moment, to what extent their own sense of people and things is based on similarly dubious bits of evidence.

If we are even slightly unsure about something that fundamental, can we wholeheartedly agree with the narrator that "times do change, and the interests of one individual cannot be allowed to hinder the progress of a whole community"? Can we be certain that Miss Leonora's opposition to the condemnation of Logana and the community's plans for "a new consolidated high school" is the product of individual interests alone? We most likely cannot, and Taylor here, as elsewhere, is asking us to consider the nature of change, the relationship of the past to the present. These are complex matters, and his awareness of relativism prevents Taylor from presenting us with facile formulations. As a native of a state that is neither Southern nor Midwestern, a member of a society that is a mixture of the old elegance and the new commercialism, he can do no more or less than convey to us what it means to be, like Miss Leonora and Thomasville itself, suspended between.

・　・　・

Although Tillie Olsen (1913—   ) shares with Taylor a profound interest in the complexities of familial relationships, her approach is significantly different. Taylor is extremely adept at using the conventional tools of third-person narrative and dialogue to create the illusion of intimacy with his characters, but something is always withheld from us. Even when he occasionally employs first-person narrative, we are still being "told" a story, and we are never actually privy to his characters' innermost thoughts and impressions. In contrast, Olsen's technique is an innovative combination of third-person narrative, dialogue, and interior monologue that reveals her characters' thoughts, memories, and perceptions. Many of Taylor's stories expand outward from dialogue to atmosphere; all of Olsen's move from dialogue inward, focusing on individual instants of experience.

The extreme care with which Olsen practices her art is attested to by the fact that her complete fictional oeuvre consists of four short stories and one short novel. Although this might lead one to assume that she is a limited writer, nothing could be farther from the truth. Each of the stories in *Tell Me a Riddle* (1961) is a minor masterpiece, and the characters whose inner lives are explored are vastly different individuals, similar only in their preoccupation with isolation and regret. Whether depicting a mother's attempts to rationalize her neglect of her daughter ("I Stand here Ironing"), a merchant seaman's self-destructive ambivalence toward family and security ("Hey Sailor, What Ship?"), or a young girl's initiation into the cold truths of social reality ("O Yes"), Olsen time and again discovers the universal in the particular.

The method of the title story is typical. Dying of cancer, an old woman stubbornly resists the half-selfish efforts of her family to convince her to go quietly and peacefully. Refusing to play the role of transmitter of tradition, she recoils, folds in on herself:

Blows, screams, a call: "Grandma!" For her? Oh please not for her. Hide, hunch behind the dresses deeper. But a trembling little body hurls itself beside her—surprised, smothered laughter, arms surround her neck, tears rub dry on her cheeks, and words too soft to understand whisper into her ear (Is this where you hide too, Grammy? It's my secret place, we have a secret now).
And the sweat beads, and the long shudder seizes.

When she does begin to speak, it is to spew out a torrent of "stained words" that "betray" her "youth of belief" and indict the times in which she has lived. Although her husband tries not to listen to her, he is forced into an awareness of her suffering and his own:

The cards fell from his fingers. Without warning, the bereavement and betrayal he had sheltered—compounded through the years—hidden even from himself—revealed itself,
    uncoiled,
    released,
    sprung

and with it the monstrous shapes of what had actually happened in the century.

For Olsen, to be conscious is to live with pain; she captures one individual's private agony, and through it portrays the torment of a generation.

•   •   •

Like Olsen, John Knowles (1926—   ) published only one collection in the period, but the six stories in *Phineas* (1968) are also worthy of note, and he manifests a good deal of variety in his treatments of contemporary individuals and society. Two of the stories take place at Devon School, the setting of his popular novel, *A Separate Peace*. (Indeed, "Phineas" is a different version of the central incident in that novel.) The others are set in such widely divergent places as West Virginia; Wetherford, Connecticut; Cairo; and St. Jean de Luz, France. Through their day-to-day interactions, Knowles's characters reveal their self-centeredness, jealousy, and potential for evil.

Knowles is at his best when he injects an almost vicious irony into his character sketches, and plays on the reader's expectations. In "The Peeping Tom," for example, Paul Marowski's antisocial behavior is motivated by his inability to replace his father and fit into the female-dominated universe of his own home. Brought to trial, he views his public humiliation as a form of salvation, a means of "getting out" of "the trap" his life has become. "A Turn with the Sun," perhaps the best piece in the volume, hinges on a stunning reversal. Wanting desperately to fit into the society of Devon School, Lawrence Stuart first attempts to win the respect of the school's elite. Failing miserably, he tries to satisfy his egotism by excelling in his studies and playing the contemptuous loner to become "the greatest, and the most inaccessible." Gradually, he begins to realize his folly, to discover the finitude of life, the transience of fame. The universe remains as indifferent to him as it ever was. In the fullness of his new-found self-knowledge he drowns, while the seasons move on, and "the earth, turned full toward the sun," brings "forth its annual harvest."

· · ·

Whereas Olsen and Knowles are examples of the writer who can exhibit a good deal of versatility in a few short pieces, John O'Hara (1905—1970) is a prime example of the veteran writer who, settling into a style, can play a seemingly infinite number of variations on a limited number of themes and character types. Following a fourteen-year hiatus, during which time he wrote novels, plays, and essays, but no short stories, O'Hara rediscovered the genre, producing a body of work that attests to his incredible prolificacy. Between 1960 and his death in 1970, he published six large volumes of stories: *Assembly* (1960), *The Cape Cod Lighter* (1962), *The Hat on the Bed* (1963), *The Horse Knows the Way* (1964), *Waiting for Winter* (1966), and *And Other Stories* (1969). Two other volumes, *The Time Element* (1972) and *The O'Hara Generation* (1972), a retrospective, were published posthumously.

Turning his reporter's eye on the society of the 1960s, O'Hara updates the chronicle of American life begun in his short fiction of the 1930s and 1940s. His themes are the perennial ones of loneliness, the war between the sexes, difficulties of aging, and the ephemerality of success. His characters usually survive as best they can, considering their diminished potential, in a society that is indifferent to individual wants and intolerant of individual differences.

O'Hara has often been criticized as being a formula writer, a popular author whose work is essentially nonliterary. It may be partially true, as Albert Erskine suggests in the Introduction to *The O'Hara Generation,* that this evaluation is a fiction concocted by reviewers and members of the academic community who are unable to recognize excellence in any popular writer. There is no denying that what O'Hara does, he does well. Nonetheless, anyone who reads a significant number of his stories cannot help but begin to notice a remarkable sameness to them. Coming to know O'Hara is coming to know what to expect.

• • •

Irwin Shaw (1913—   ) is another popular writer who was quite productive in the period, publishing three collections: *Tip on a Dead Jockey and Other Stories* (1957), *Love on a Dark Street and Other Stories* (1965), and *Short Stories* (1966). At his worst, Shaw vacillates between the banal and the sensational, and the strings he pulls are often too obvious. At his best, in stories such as "Love on a Dark Street" and "Circle of Light," he effectively evokes the anomic nature of contemporary life in the big cities and affluent suburbs of Europe and America.

• • •

The characters we encounter in Gilbert Rogin's *The Fencing Master* (1965) are, like many of O'Hara's and Shaw's anti-heroes, unexceptional men who feel put upon by existence itself, and are unable or just barely able to cope with the daily pressures of making a living and maintaining social relationships. Whether the setting is New York, Miami, Las Vegas, Los Angeles, or even the South Pacific, when we read one of Rogin's stories we are thrust into a neurotic universe in which even dreams are indictments. Constantly psychoanalyzing himself and evaluating his own motives and deeds, the typical Rogin protagonist is incapable of acting. Many of the most important literary works of the century have dealt with this aspect of the modern condition.

For Shaw and Rogin, the significant elements of urban existence are the same everywhere. Their characters move through a paradigmatic metropolis that bears many names. In the works of Richard Yates, Louis Auchincloss, and Hortense Calisher, the city is more specifically New York.

• • •

The New Yorkers to whom Richard Yates (1926—   ) introduces us in *Eleven Kinds of Loneliness* (1962) are members of the middle and lower middle class—cab drivers, newspapermen, school teachers, young couples starting out in life. All experience some kind of loneliness; some attempt to find self-definition and overcome their isolation by reaching out to others, acquiring possessions, or pursuing what they think of as success. In one story, "The B.A.R. Man," the search for self-esteem, following a pattern that has become increasingly common, leads to an act of irrational violence. John Fallon, a clerk for an insurance company, is a man "nobody had even thought much about" until "he got his name on the police blotter, and in the papers." Aging, his job and home life dull routines, Fallon still wears his "serviceman's identification bracelet, the relic of a braver and more careless time," and his only source of pride is the memory that he had been pronounced "a damn good B.A.R. man" during the war. Thwarted and mocked in the present, he strikes out at a political figure who becomes, purely by accident, the focus for his rage and frustration.

• • •

In *Powers of Attorney* (1963) and *Tales of Manhattan* (1967), Louis Auchincloss (1917—   ) introduces us to a different class of people—the patrons of "the ancient auction gallery of Philip Hone & Sons," members of the respected law firm of Arnold & Degener, society matrons who hold court in Manhattan and Oyster Bay. Auchincloss's work is perhaps the clearest example of the short fiction of manners to be produced in the period. Although he has been taken to task for the uniformity of his approach and the triviality of his subject matter, *Tales of Manhattan* demonstrates his ability to manipulate point of view and his willingness to inject a touch of the bizarre or supernatural into his urbane universe. Exhibiting his characteristic wit and sophistication, both these collections contribute significantly to Auchincloss's objective of fully dissecting a particular stratum of society in the manner of an American Trollope or Galsworthy.

• • •

In some ways, the stories of Hortense Calisher (1911—   ) present a more complete portrait of New York and its inhabitants than we find in the work of either Yates or Auchincloss. In *Tale for the Mirror* (1962) and *Extreme Magic* (1963), her second and third collections, we encounter the surviving members of a genteel society that has become anomalous and anachronistic, and the representatives of a younger, urban middle class who discover success, values, and even human relationships to be ephemeral and contingent. Moreover, the city we visit is not only the impersonal contemporary metropolis of the 1960s but the more human and comfortable New York of the 1910s and 1920s.

Through the accumulation of details and the description of objects, places, and everyday rituals, Calisher develops a full and rich sense of place in her fiction. This is particularly true of the Hester-Kinny Elkin stories, which appear in all of her collections and which are based in part on memories of her childhood. Calisher, however, aspires to a good deal more than careful observation of external detail. As she herself notes in the preface to *The Collected Stories of Hortense Calisher* (1975), the "very duration" of the short story, "too brief to make a new mode in, verges it always toward that classical corner where sits the human figure. And perhaps the genre flourishes best during those periods of life—both for authors and eras—when the human drama is easier accepted as the main one going. . . . A story may float like an orb, spread like a fan or strike its parallels ceaselessly on the page—as long as its clues cohere. Language itself may *be* the idea."

Some readers may feel that at times Calisher focuses on scenes of human drama that are too minor to warrant serious consideration. In other stories, her love and mastery of language cause her to approach a kind of verbal preciosity, and the medium of telling threatens to overwhelm the tale. In her most successful pieces, however, she presents full and human characters in fitting and elegant language, elevating the apparently trivial and local to the significant and universal.

· · ·

The development of a sense of place is also an important element in the short fiction of a number of other writers active in the period. This is not to suggest that these authors should be viewed as local colorists, a term that has been applied in the past to such major figures as Hawthorne, Twain, and Faulkner. The evocation of locale should be considered in its relationships to other aspects of their work. Indeed, as we shall see, many of the Midwesterners, Southwesterners, and Southerners contributing to the genre in the years 1957—1968 share the major concerns of those Northeastern regionalists, Cheever and Updike.

The blankness, provinciality, and hermetic family structure of the Midwest figure prominently in the stories of R. V. Cassill (1913—   ), Calvin Kentfield (1925—   ), Evan S. Connell, Jr. (1924—   ), and William H. Gass (1924—   ). The strongest stories in Cassill's *The Father* (1965) and *The Happy Marriage* (1965) are set in Iowa or other parts of the region. "Larchmoor is Not the World," for example, traces with gentle irony the seduction of an English professor by a literary type. Deluding himself, Dr. Cameron ventures out of the safe physical and emotional retreat he has created on a small Midwest campus, enticed by a vision of "the gold-embroidered princess, the beautiful lady without mercy and hope." Drawn out of his "warmer corner," he concludes that he will "die in the real cold," defending himself "against self-ridicule, self-obloquy." In "The Father," a story that is vastly different in both tone and impact, Cassill plays on our superficial conceptions of Midwestern farm life, creating a powerful drama of guilt and obsession that truly qualifies as American gothic.

Kentfield's *The Angel and the Sailor* (1957) and *The Great Wondering Goony Bird* (1963) illustrate both the variety of ways in which a writer can make use of regional heritage and the inadequacy of regionalism as a critical concept. In "The Rose of Sharon" and the stories that highlight the Garrett family ("Chip Canary," "River Stay 'way from My Door") the accurate depiction of small-town life is crucial to Kentfield's exploration of the trials of youth and adolescence. In his fine ghost story, "The Angel and the Sailor," on the other hand, we are made to distrust our sense of place as much as our sense of reality. Merging the real and the supernatural, Kentfield turns a Midwestern farm into a backdrop against which the Strap family plays out its fears and anxieties, wrestling unsuccessfully with mysteries of heredity, until the Iowa landscape and some past ocean appear to coexist in a kind of non-time. Finally, in Kentfield's sea stories, place becomes indistinguishable from character. There is a good deal of Kansas in Davy Humble, the naive merchant seaman who appears in many of these tales, and in "Windmills," another character, drawing on the Midwest that lives in his memory, transforms a waterspout into a tornado and Palermo into the expanses of his boyhood.

Several of the stories in Connell's *The Anatomy Lesson* (1957) satirize Midwestern sterility and provinciality. The title story, for instance, presents the painful and apparently futile attempts of an art professor to awaken his dull, practical students to the sweetness and bitterness of life, while "The Beau Monde of Mrs. Bridge" effectively, if a bit archly, dissects a Kansas City matron who in her innocence, hypocrisy, and pretension has much in common with E. E. Cummings's "Cambridge Ladies." Other pieces in *The Anatomy Lesson* and in Connell's later collection, *At the Crossroads* (1965), however, take place in New York, Rome, Paris, a Nevada desert that could be the set for a Beckett play, and a universe that to all intents and purposes exists only in dialogue.

Although it may seem now to be a bit dated, in retrospect a bit too much a product of the 1960s, W. H. Gass's *In the Heart of the Heart of the Country* (1968) had a significant impact when it was first published and probably influenced a number of young writers. The title story is an excellent example of how far one can progress from the simplistic approach of the nineteenth century local color tale without abandoning, as other contemporary writers have, the sense of a specific place. Using a style that is more lyrical than narrative, and employing the modernist techniques of fragmentation and repetition, Gass obliterates the distinction between inner and outer landscapes. The wintry emotional and mental state of Gass's love-sick narrator is projected onto the environment:

"For we're always out of luck here. That's just how it is—for instance in winter. The sides of the buildings, the roofs, the limbs of the trees are gray. Streets, sidewalks, faces, feelings, they are gray. Speech is gray, and the grass where it shows." At the same time, the weather has its effect on the inner climate: "In the Midwest, around the lower lakes, the sky in the winter is heavy and close, and it is a rare day, a day to remark on, when the sky lifts and allows the heart up." Exploring the possible relationships between the observer and the observed, Gass raises a number of ontological questions while still managing to capture what he considers to be the sterile, mechanical aspects of Midwestern society. Although one may question whether the form he has chosen is adequate for its philosophical content, one must admire the effort.

• • •

In new collections published in the 1960s, William Humphrey (1925—   ) and William Goyen (1915—   ) manifest different approaches to their Southwestern legacies. The title of Humphrey's second collection, *A Time and a Place: Stories of the Red River Country* (1965), reemphasizes the importance of temporal and geographic location in his fiction. All of the stories take place in the Red River Country, the border between Oklahoma and Texas, in the 1930s, the period which marks the death of frontier existence and the birth of the new Southwest. Humphrey focuses on individuals who are affected by the changes in their environment: farmers driven insane with greed by the discovery of oil or native Americans faced with cultural extinction. While some of Humphrey's plots and his use of biblical tone and diction are at times obvious, his work is redeemed by his ability to maintain contact with the "red Oklahoma Earth."

Goyen's *The Faces of Blood Kindred* (1960) is, like his earlier work, characterized by the exploration of different kinds of frontiers—the blurred borders between narrative and lyrical, realistic and mythic or fantastic, material and spiritual. As he points out in the Introduction to the *Selected Writings of William Goyen* (1974), the world of Trinity, Texas, "its countryside, its folk, its speech and superstitions and fable, was stamped into" his senses during his first seven years of life. Although he has lived outside of the region for most of his adult life, his "writing life" has focused upon ways of "giving shape to what happened, of searching for meanings, clarification, Entirety."

Less overtly fantastic than those in *Ghost and Flesh* (1952), the stories in Goyen's second volume examine the claims of the dead on the living, past on the present. Employing a style that melds objective description, lyricism, and personal symbolism, Goyen traces the physical and spiritual ties that bind the individual to something greater than himself. It is a process that does indeed lead to meaning and a sense of "Entirety," for as one of his characters notes, it is "the effect of what was" that "is the long-lastingness in us. . . . The same patterns do exist all over the world. . . . And a sudden sight of this human pattern in one place restores a lost recognition of it in another, far away, through an eternal image of a simple flower, in the hands and care of both . . . "

·   ·   ·

While such writers were discovering the fictional possibilities in their Midwestern or Southwestern heritage, others were contributing in remarkably varied ways to the development of what has been called a Southern literary renaissance. John Bell Clayton's *The Strangers Were There* (1957) was published posthumously in the period, as was Flannery O'Connor's *Everything that Rises must Converge* (1965). The year 1963 saw the publication of works as different as *Old Red and Other Stories,* a volume of earlier pieces by Caroline Gordon (1895—1981), and *The Names and Faces of Heroes* by the North Carolinian Reynolds Price (1933—   ). Tennessee Williams's third book of stories, *The Knightly Quest,* appeared in 1967.

·   ·   ·

The significance of his Southernness for Florida's George Garrett (1929—   ) is emphasized by the passage from *Jeremiah* 12:8 that serves as the epigraph for one of his pieces: "Mine heritage is unto me as a lion in the forest; it crieth out against me; therefore have I hated it." Many of the stories in *King of the Mountain* (1957), *In the Briar Patch* (1961), and *Cold Ground Was My Bed Last Night* (1964), probe this heritage in its multiple forms: the knowledge and memories a son inherits from his father ("The Test," "The King of the Mountain"), the gentleman's code of behavior that forbids masculine sensitivity ("In the Briar Patch"), and the Southern legacy of violence ("The Last of the Spanish Blood," "Comic Strip"). Although Garrett's heritage may at times cause him anguish, his response never takes the form of lament. His characters, like Professor B. of "Comic Strip," may discover in history a sense of shame, guilt, disgust, and confinement, but Garrett is protected from self-hatred by language and humor.

·   ·   ·

Like Garrett, Doris Betts (1932—   ) is very skillful at demonstrating the influence of her cultural milieu on the psychology of ordinary Southerners. Many of the characters in *The Astronomer and Other Stories* (1965) are unremarkable people who, confined by their small-town or rural environments and by their own ordinariness, make pathetic, ludicrous, and futile attempts to escape what and where they are. A bored housewife fantasizes about a road crew; a small-town lawyer tries to "make the most of what he has" by orchestrating an

"Egg Day" celebration; a retired mill worker becomes a self-proclaimed astronomer. Through precise prose and careful selection of tone, Betts manages to expose the sexual energy, violence, and despair underlying the surfaces of their lives, while avoiding the cliched sensationalism of the genre to which one of her characters is addicted—those books "about plantations, lusty octoroons, and dueling pistols fired through curtains of Spanish moss."

• • •

The short stories of two other writers, Jesse Stuart (1907—   ) and Donald Windham (1920—   ), once again call into question the concept of regionalism, for they not only exhibit widely different approaches to place, but they also depict two different Souths. An incredibly prolific Kentuckian, Stuart published four collections of stories in the period: *Plowshare in Heaven* (1958), *Save Every Lamb* (1964), *A Jesse Stuart Harvest* (1965), *My Land Has a Voice* (1966). Telling simple tales simply, he has confined himself to the task of celebrating all aspects of his own particular section of rural America. Whereas Stuart writes of the relatively unchanging world of the Kentucky hills in a style that exhibits some of the qualities of oral folklore, Windham writes of the modern urban South in a manner that is a good deal more literary. His Atlanta, recreated in *The Warm Country* (1962) and *Emblems of Conduct* (1963), a book of reminiscences, is probably the farthest thing possible from Stuart's nurturing, responsive land. It is a place that leaves people "deserted, stranded, spent" ("The Warm Country"), and where honor, beauty, and love are elusive ("The Seventh Day"). Failed communication is a major theme in Windham's work, and his characters have difficulty contacting their environment as well as each other. When they do, it is often to read in the landscape a reflection of their own internal condition, as in "Life of Georgia," in which the city sends (in the form of an insurance company sign) a message that seems to mock a young woman's empty, stagnant life.

• • •

Ernest Gaines's South is yet a different place. Although Gaines (1933—   ) has until now produced only a single volume of stories, he has made a significant contribution to the genre. Focusing on the black experience in rural Louisiana, his work is more than history, sociology, or psychology.

Bloodline (1968) is an extremely varied and consistently excellent collection in which Gaines draws on elements of his ethnic and regional heritage and uses a number of different narrative techniques to develop universal themes. In "A Long Day in November," for example, his mastery of first-person narrative (we view things through the eyes of a young boy) and his fine ear for dialogue and dialect combine to produce a strong, unnerving, yet sensitive portrayal of family relationships. In another piece, "Just Like a Tree," he employs multiple points of view, turning the depiction of a single, apparently simple episode into a commentary on the tensions and differences between young and old, past and present, whites and blacks, city-dwellers and country-dwellers.

Gaines's treatment of racial matters is always subtle and complex. "Three Men" is a moving evocation of one individual's discovery of the nature of human dignity, while "Bloodline," exploring the influence of heredity and environment on identity, questions the very concept of race. "The Sky Is Gray," a story that is coming to be considered a classic, presents several different responses to discrimination. One is that of a black preacher who trusts in God to right all wrongs; another is that of his younger, more educated antagonist whose initiation into the ways of the world has turned him into a cynic: "I'm not mad at the world. I'm questioning the world. I'm questioning it with cold logic, sir. What do words like Freedom, Liberty, God, White, Colored mean? I want to know. That's why *you* are sending us to school, to read and to ask questions. And because we ask these questions, you call us mad. No sir, it is not us who are mad." In contrast to these philosophical stances, which are both abrogations of personal responsibility, the young narrator learns from his mother a way of life based on individual integrity and a sense of self-worth.

Gaines, together with other young writers, helped to initiate a new black literary renaissance in the late 1960s and 1970s that was to rival and perhaps exceed in scope and impact the Harlem renaissance of the 1920s. While these newer voices were beginning to be heard, some older voices were still commanding our attention. *Eight Men,* a book of earlier pieces by Richard Wright (1908—1960) appeared in 1961, and in 1963 Langston Hughes (1902—1967) published *Something in Common and Other Stories,* containing a selection of stories from *The Ways of White Folks* (1934) and *Laughing to Keep from Crying* (1952), as well as some previously uncollected works. Whereas Wright's fiction is marked by the use of broad symbolism and characterized by what is sometimes a heavy didacticism, Hughes's is markedly different in style and tone. As a poet who knows the value of conciseness and precision and is well versed in the potential of satire and irony, Hughes manages in his short vignette-like pieces to give full humor and artistic treatment to many of the same major issues raised by Wright.

• • •

The most distinctive voice of the generation between those of Hughes and Gaines is that of James Baldwin (1924—   ). Although Baldwin is primarily a novelist, he has, like Hughes and Wright, demonstrated his ability to work well in several genres, and *Going to Meet the Man* (1965) is a most noteworthy book of short fiction. Two of the stories, "Sonny's Blues" and the title piece, have been widely discussed and anthologized. The former, set in Harlem, celebrates the ability of the individual to discover in art a means of personalizing, expressing, and transcending his own suffering and that of his people: "For, while the tale of how we suffer, and how we are delighted, and how we may triumph is never new, it must always be heard. . . . And this tale, according to that face, that body, those strong hands on those strings, has another aspect in every country, and a new depth in every generation." The latter, set in the South, is one of the most controversial short stories of the postwar period. Going to meet "the man," entering the warped and tormented mind of a Southern sheriff, we discover the effects of his racism not only on the objects of his hatred and violence but also on his own psyche. The story is a chilling testament to the dehumanizing power of bigotry and its capacity for warping reality and turning all parties involved into inhuman grotesques. Carefully crafted and exhibiting a remarkable control of tone and image, "Going to Meet the Man" is evidence that Baldwin, like Gaines and Hughes, is capable of reconciling what he called the "all but irreconcilable war between [the black writer's] social and artistic responsibilities."

. . .

The conflict between social and artistic responsibility, or between maintaining a sense of ethnic identity and creating literature of more universal significance, was also successfully resolved by a number of Jewish-American short-story writers in the period following World War II. Literary artists such as Malamud, Bellow, and Singer proved themselves to be most adept at drawing on the linguistic, customary, ethical, and philosophical elements of their cultural backgrounds and at depicting the position of the Jewish-American in society. Although these particular concerns set them apart from the other writers discussed, their interest in examining interpersonal relationships, their skill at developing a sense of place, and their fascination with dream and fantasy place them within the main tradition of American short fiction.

. . .

This ability to synthesize traditions is manifest in the works of Brooklyn-born Bernard Malamud (1914—   ). His first volume of short stories, *The Magic Barrel* (1948), won the National Book Award and is regarded by critics as his best and most even collection. Several of the stories take place in Italy; some have non-Jewish protagonists. While these pieces attest to Malamud's range and are far from failures, he is strongest when focusing on the struggles of Jewish protagonists to ensure their economic, social, or spiritual survival in a New York that is part naturalistic wasteland and part fantastic dreamscape.

Malamud's most successful stories depend on the careful maintenance of dynamic tension in both voice and tone: the voice of the Yiddish storyteller, the oral fabulist, framing, breaking through, and playing against realistic description; the serious treatment of serious matters, supported by biblical allusion and patterns of symbols, blended with humor and undercut by irony. In addition, he is often successful dealing with particular and universal themes. Viewed in one light, his New York stories exhibit the naturalist's concern with the impact of environmental and cultural factors on a segment of society. Looked at another way, they are structured by the basic tragic and comic pattern of myth: the individual's quest for identity, his alienation from and reintegration with society.

The first two stories in *The Magic Barrel,* "The First Seven Years" and "The Mourners," are illustrative. Although there are intervals of impersonal, literary narration in both stories—"The shoemaker shrugged and continued to peer through the partly frosted window at the near-sighted haze of falling snow"—we hear the distinctive voice of the storyteller constantly breaking through, particularly in the inversions of syntax that are characteristic of Yiddish-American dialect: "Who he was the shoemaker for a moment had no idea. . . . " Both voices are often made to serve naturalistic ends, such as demonstrating the dehumanizing effect of urban social and economic deprivation: "In the tenement, although he had lived there ten years, he was more or less unknown. The tenants on both sides of his flat on the fifth floor, an Italian family of three middle-aged sons and their wizened mother, and a sullen childless German couple named Hoffman, never said hello to him, nor did he greet any of them on the way up or down the narrow wooden stairs."

The mythical and biblical allusions in "The First Seven Years" are rendered incongruous by context. Although he possesses a flute, Max is not Mozart's Tamino or even Papageno, but a seedy student, "tall and grotesquely thin, with sharply cut features, particularly a beak-like nose." His birdlike appearance emphasizes not his magical abilities but his mute rapaciousness, and is not mythic amplification but parody. Although Sobel labors seven years for Feld's daughters, the two men are not Jacob and Laban, but poor shoemakers, and the legacy at stake is not Abraham's patrimony but a meager shop that barely provides its owner with a living. "The Mourner" is also marked by contrary patterns of amplification and diminution. Elements of Jewish ritual act to expand the scope of Kessler's mourning; he grieves not only for himself but also for his people and for those who have killed themselves by closing their eyes to suffering. At the same time, however, his lamentation has taken on the quality of obsession, turning him into a grotesque, something less than a complete human being.

Focusing on the particulars of both stories, one can read them as sociology, documents that record and analyze the economic hardships and problems of acculturation that faced the Jewish immigrant. Viewed in this way, the stories, at least initially, present contrasting responses: Feld, desiring a better life for himself and his daughter, buys the American dream of success and social advancement at the cost of other values; Kessler, on the other hand, steadfastly retains his values at the price of isolation and ostracism. To read them solely in this way, however, is to miss another dimension, for both explore in more general terms the roles played by love and suffering in the individual's quest to discover his own identity and his relationships to others.

Still another dimension is added to Malamud's work by his introduction of characters and events that are overtly or faintly supernatural. In "Angel Levine," a tailor named Manischevitz aids and is aided by "an angel from God"; while in "The Magic Barrel," probably Malamud's best story, Leo Finkle, a rabbinical student, is assisted by Salzman, a mysterious marriage broker whose office is "in the air" and who seems at times to be an agent of fate. Yet in Malamud's world, even the supernatural is tainted by the naturalistic, and the sense of wonder generated by seemingly magical transformations or resolutions is undercut by cynicism. Displaying human weakness and a fondness for the pleasures of the flesh, "Angel Levine" is as much in need of help as he is capable of offering it, and Manischevitz discovers him not in some ethereal habitat but in a sleazy Harlem cabaret. Salzman provides Leo with his ideal bride, but she is as much whore as virgin, and his desire for her is as much a product of self-delusion and a need for self-mortification as it is of love.

The fantastic element apparent in these two pieces reappears in two of the stories in Malamud's second collection, *Idiots First* (1963), which many critics consider to be less consistent than *The Magic Barrel.* In the allegorical title story, Mendel struggles to protect the life of his idiot son, fighting time and an antagonist, Ginzburg, who symbolizes death, upholder of the "cosmic universal law," the law of entropy. Mendel's conditional victory over Ginzburg is won through selflessness and compassion, through an assertion of his basic humanity in the face of universal indifference. In "The Jewbird," Harry Cohen is visited by a talking "longbeaked bird" named Schwartz who torments him by exhibiting all of the qualities of the Jewish stereotype. Driven "bats" by the fact that Schwartz is "there always, even in his dreams," Cohen finally attacks the bird and tosses him out onto the sidewalk. Cohen's victory, unlike Mendel's, is delusory, for he has won by stubbornly denying what he is. The fantastic elements in these stories prevent us from reading them as anything but allegory, and our apprehension at the author's seriousness is balanced by his use of humor.

Reprinting the Fidelman stories from the first two volumes and presenting three new ones, *Pictures of Fidelman: An Exhibition* (1969) reveals another Malamud: the literary artist self-consciously examining the difficulties and paradoxes of his vocation. The protagonist of all these pieces is an unsuccessful painter whose situation is summed up by the epigraphs to the volume:

Not to understand. Yes, that was my whole
occupation during those years—I can assure
you, it was not an easy one.
R. M. Rilke

The intellect of man is forced to choose
Perfection of the life or of the work . . .
W. B. Yeats

Both.
A. Fidelman

Choosing both, Fidelman continues to botch his life and his art until he is forced to understand that he must accept both on less grandiose terms. Grouped together, Malamud's portraits of the artist cease to be independent short stories, forming instead what the author himself has called a picaresque novel.

Whether he is completely successful or not, Bernard Malamud exhibits in his short fiction an admirable propensity for treating a variety of themes in a variety of manners. A quick glance at some of the stories in his most recent volume, *Rembrandt's Hat* (1973) reveals once again his range and his potential for developing new forms. "The Silver Crown," for instance, is a reexamination of the vagaries of belief, cast in the mold of the earlier fables, while the title story is a more realistic piece which, in its treatment of artistic self-consciousness and failed communication, is in some ways reminiscent of the earlier Fidelman stories. "Talking Horse" is not only different from both of these, but significantly different from anything else Malamud has written. Combining traditional narrative with the kind of question-and-answer format that Joyce employed in *Ulysses* and *Finnegans Wake,* he presents us with a talking horse whose absurd condition ("Am I a man in a horse or a horse that talks like a man?") embodies all of the apparent dualities of human existence.

Looked at as a whole, Malamud's short stories are expressive of the totality of his heritage, of the mystical, ethical, and intellectual impulses that together define the Jewish-American character. This is not to suggest, however, that he is merely a Jewish-American writer. For, as he has indicated: "I handle the Jew as a symbol of the tragic experience of man existentially. I try to see the Jew as universal man. Every man is a Jew though he may not know it" (interview in *Jerusalem Post* [Weekly Overseas Edition], April 1, 1968, p. 13).

· · ·

The Jew as universal man preoccupied with existential questions is also a central figure in the fiction of Saul Bellow (1915—   ). Although Bellow was awarded the Nobel Prize in literature primarily on the basis of his novels, his facility with shorter works is demonstrated in *Mosby's Memoirs* (1968), a collection of three short stories from *Seize the Day* plus three newer ones. Like the protagonists of his novels, Bellow's Jews are men who think continuously about themselves and about other men who think. At times, like Rogin in "A Father-To-Be," they may be rescued from the neurotic isolation and cold frustration of their thoughts by a simple act of compassion:

"But there's absolutely nothing wrong with you," she said, and pressed against him from behind, surrounding him, pouring the water gently over him until it seemed to him that the water came from within him, it was the warm fluid of his own secret loving spirit overflowing into the sink, green and foaming, and his anger at his son-to-be disappeared altogether . . .

At other times, as when Dr. Braun contemplates death and the past in "The Old System," the sense of futility that is the product of their tendencies to over-intellectualize may make impossible any emotional rescue from without:

And Dr. Braun, bitterly moved, tried to grasp what emotions were. What good were they! What were they for! And no one wanted them now . . . once humankind had grasped its own idea, that it was human and human through such passions, it began to exploit, to play, to disturb for the sake of exciting disturbance, to make an uproar, a crude circus of feelings. . . . And these tears! When you wept them from the heart, you felt you justified something, understood something. But what did you understand? Again, *nothing!* It was only an intimation of understanding.

Tone is always extremely important in Bellow's fiction, something made clear by the narrator's description of the central consciousness of the title story: "Mr. Mosby—Dr. Mosby really; erudite, maybe even profound; thought much, accomplished much—had made some of the most interesting mistakes a man could make in the twentieth century. He was in Oaxaca now to write his memoirs. He had a grant for the purpose, from the Guggenheim Foundation. And why not?" The irony of this description, really the unconscious irony of self-description, fixes Mosby from the start, directing us in our reading of his "Memoirs." Mosby's "interesting mistakes" (such as displeasing "the institutional gentry" by suggesting "that however deplorable the concentration

camps had been, they showed at least the rationality of German political ideas")
have made him an exile in Oaxaca where he sits drinking mescal and beer,
searching for a way "to put some humor" into his memoirs.

He finds it in the story of Hymen Lustgarten, a Jewish one-time Marxist
whose grandiose business plans failed miserably because, "strangely meek,
stout, swarthy, kindly," he was hampered further by "a traitorous incompe-
tence." Lustgarten's schemes for stealing a fortune out of the ruins of postwar
Europe are deserving of censure. But in using Lustgarten's life story for his own
purposes, turning him into a stereotype of bungling failure and greed, Mosby
exhibits the intellectual detachment that led to that destruction in the first
place. "Having disposed of all things human," exiled himself to the rarefied
atmosphere of his own thoughts, he ends up gasping for air like those other
victims of twentieth-century rationalism, the Jews of Auschwitz and Dachau.

• • •

Whereas Bellow's characters endlessly cogitate on what it means to be human,
the Jews we encounter in Philip Roth's *Goodbye, Columbus and Five Short Stories*
(1959) are preoccupied with what it means to be Jewish. Neil Klugman's
confrontation with the world of American-Jewish aristocracy in the novella
Goodbye, Columbus is a rite of passage with which many readers and moviegoers
are quite familiar. Three of Roth's short stories, however, present differing
versions of the process of self-discovery.

In "The Conversion of the Jews," a pesty young student, annoying because
he asks the wrong questions, forces his hypocritical elders to break through the
walls of stale dogma and intolerance and admit what should be considered
truths by Jew and Christian alike, that "God can do Anything" and that "You
should never hit anybody about God." In "Defender of the Faith," Sergeant
Nathan Marx must see through another kind of hypocrisy, that of an army
recruit who plays on Nathan's sense of kinship, using his Jewishness as an excuse
for escaping duties and gaining favors. While Ozzie Freedman recovers the basic
religious tenets of his culture by pretending to become a Christian savior,
Nathan Marx discovers its ethical basis by rejecting a certain type of Jew.
Finally, in "Eli, the Fanatic," a practical suburban lawyer changes clothes with a
religious fanatic and reclaims the lost consciousness of suffering that is a part of
his heritage, saving himself from the pretenses of his shallow community and
becoming a madman in the eyes of his neighbors and family.

Although in all of these stories Roth teaches us important lessons about
ethnic and individual identity, he avoids didacticism by employing his excellent
comic skills, demonstrating why *Goodbye, Columbus* won a National Book Award.

• • •

The voices of Malamud, Bellow, and Roth were, of course, not the only Jewish-American voices to be heard in the short fiction of the period. Grace Paley's (1922—   ) first volume of stories, *The Little Disturbances of Man,* published in 1959 and reissued in 1968, exhibited for the first time to a large audience her unique treatment of description and dialogue. In "The Loudest Voice," for example, she evokes a sense of the past by focusing on the sounds of childhood: "There is a certain place where dumb-waiters boom, doors slam, dishes crash; every window is a mother's mouth bidding the street shut up, go skate somewhere else, come home. My voice is the loudest."

Elsewhere, as in "Goodbye and Good Luck," a tale of love lost and regained in the Yiddish theater, she is very adept at capturing the rhythms and diction of Jewish-American dialect:

I was popular in certain circles, says Aunt Rose. I wasn't no thinner then, only more stationary in the flesh. In time to come, Lillie, don't be surprised—change is a fact of God. From this no one is excused. Only a person like your mama stands on one foot, she don't notice how big her behind is getting and sings in the canary's ear for thirty years. Who's listening?

•   •   •

Herbert Gold (1929—   ) explored love, isolation, and responsibility, in his collection *Love and Like* (1960), and 1965 saw the appearance of a noteworthy first collection by Hugh Nissenson, *A Pile of Stories.* In the same year, Stanley Elkin published *Criers and Kibitzers, Kibitzers and Criers,* the title story of which employs Jewish folk philosophy to demonstrate the emotional and ethical blindness that results from reducing complex human matters to facile formulations.

•   •   •

One of the most distinctive writers of the period, however, is Isaac Bashevis Singer (1909—   ). Singer is something of an anomaly. Amazingly prolific, he has nonetheless proved himself consistently excellent, winning a National Book Award in 1973 and the Nobel Prize for Literature in 1978. A Polish Jew who has lived in the United States since 1935, he has continued to write in Yiddish, often assisting in the subsequent translation of his work into English. Describing his method in the Author's Note to *An Isaac Bashevis Singer Reader* (1971), he points out, "Because of this, I can call myself a bilingual writer and say that English has become my 'second original.'"

In the late 1950s to late 1960s Singer published four volumes of short stories—*Gimpel the Fool* (1957), *The Spinoza of Market Street* (1961), *Short Friday* (1964), and *The Seance* (1968)—and several illustrated books of stories for children. The latter are remarkable in their similarity to his tales for adults, manifesting the same concern with the supernatural and taking place in the same wonderful world in which the past survives, coloring and informing our sense of the present. As Singer notes in the Foreword to *Zlateh the Goat* (1966):

Children are as puzzled by passing time as grownups. What happens to a day once it is gone? Where are all our yesterdays with their joys and sorrows? Literature helps us remember the past with its many moods. To the story-teller yesterday is still here as are the years and decades gone by. In stories time does not vanish. Neither do men and animals. For the writer and his reader all creatures go on living forever. What happened long ago is still present.

The majority of Singer's stories are set in the recreated past, in the late nineteenth-century and early twentieth-century hamlets and cities of his native Poland, in Frampol, Chelm, Lublin, and Warsaw. It is a past recaptured not only through recording the physical details of landscape, dress, and daily activity, but also through evoking the mood of the people who inhabited it, as embodied in their philosophy, their customs, and their rituals. Defined in this way, mood becomes more important to Singer than character and setting—or, rather, mood becomes character and setting. Even Singer's contemporary Jewish-Americans, residing in New York and Florida, share to a large extent the same sense of reality that shapes and informs the lives of Gimpel, Zlateh, or The Spinoza of Market Street.

The view of reality that they share is a product of their cultural heritage and of the memory, dreams, and imagination of the storyteller. What Gimpel says of himself could also be applied to his creator:

I heard a great deal, many lies and falsehoods, but the longer I lived the more I understood that there were really no lies. Whatever doesn't really happen is dreamed at night. It happens to one if it doesn't happen to another, tomorrow if not today, or a century hence if not next year. What difference can it make? Often I heard tales of which I said, "Now this is a thing that cannot happen." But before a year had elapsed I heard that it actually had come to pass somewhere.

Going from place to place, eating at strange tables, it often happens that I spin yarns—improbable things that could never have happened—about devils, magicians, windmills and the like.

Singer's stories are filled with improbable events—mysterious transformations, occurrences that defy the principle of causality—and populated with human grotesques and supernatural beings, dwarfs, giants, crones, imps, devils, and angels.

The voice of the storyteller, heard through impersonal narrative or speaking through the voices of his various personas, entrances us. Once captivated, taking things on his terms, we are subject to his remarkable skill at depicting full, human characters. Discovering human qualities in even the most strange and fantastic creatures, we end up by willingly suspending our disbelief to the point of accepting the entirety of Singer's bizarre universe.

Singer does more than convince us to suspend our sense of reality; he questions it. At the conclusion of "Gimpel the Fool," Gimpel notes, "No doubt the world is entirely an imaginary world, but it is only once removed from the true world. At the door of the hovel where I lie, there stands the plank on which the dead are taken away. . . . When the time comes I will go joyfully. Whatever may be there, it will be real, without complication, without ridicule, without deception." Although the storyteller's universe is admittedly a fiction, so too, he indicates, is ours. "What difference does it make?" Gimpel asks us. What real difference is there, Singer seems to suggest, between viewing ourselves as creatures composed of id and superego or as creatures controlled by devils and angels, between conceiving of the cosmos as patterns of waves, forms of energy, or as a thought in the mind of God?

This is not to say that Singer considers human actions to be meaningless. While he almost never moralizes, he is a moralist, and his stories are intended to serve, at least partially, as instruction. At first glance, however, it may be difficult for us to determine exactly what it is that we are expected to learn from the stories, for they appear to present us with a world characterized as much by injustice as justice, one in which good and evil are equally powerful forces, and in which men are both governed by fate and possessed of free will.

In a story such as "The Gentleman from Cracow," for example, we get what we expect. The people of Frampol, succumbing to their passion for gold, place themselves in the hands of a stranger, in reality Ketev Mriri, Chief of the Devils. As a result, everything is turned topsy-turvy, demons dance in the streets, all the first-born of the village die, and the townspeople become perpetual paupers, preserving always a hatred of wealth. The moral here seems clear. But what are we to make of "Under the Knife," in which Leib rewards a prostitute's kindness by killing her, or "Fire," in which a man is assumed to be guilty of a crime he only imagined committing? What of Singer's dwarfs, cripples, witches, and fools, condemned to be what they are by accidents of birth or the perceptions of others?

The answer lies, again, in recognizing our limitations. "The world is full of puzzles," Singer tells us. "It is possible that not even Elijah will be able to answer all our questions when the Messiah comes." Although the results of our actions in this world may seem contradictory, although we may see kindness punished and cruelty rewarded, our choices do, ultimately, matter. For, as one of Singer's characters puts it: "There is a God. There is a purpose in creation. Copulation, free will, fate—all are part of His plan." Not knowing the plan and being unable to judge our own deeds solely on the basis of the fruits they bear, we must rely on something like common sense, our intuition of what is proper and natural.

In "Big and Little," a man who has been ridiculed during his entire life for his smallness forces his wife to marry a giant when he himself dies. After describing the disastrous consequences, the storyteller comments: "As I was saying—spite. . . . One shouldn't tease. Little is little, and big is big. It's not our world. We didn't make it. But for a man to do such an unnatural thing! Did you ever hear the like of it? Surely the evil one must have gotten into him. I shudder every time I think of it."

•   •   •

It may initially seem extremely capricious to compare the short fiction of Singer, a Polish Jew, with that of Flannery O'Connor (1925—1964), a Southern Catholic. Certainly, the particulars of time and place and the cultural backgrounds on which they draw are quite different, as are their narrative techniques. Moreover, whereas there are often overt supernatural elements in Singer's stories, O'Connor's fiction is always firmly rooted in the physical. Yet there are similarities that balance out the differences. Like Singer, O'Connor is deeply concerned with ethical questions but never didactic or moralistic, and her work, like his, often focuses on human limitation and deformity.

O'Connor's second, and last, volume of short stories, *Everything that Rises must Converge* (1965), exhibits once again her preoccupation with the grotesque, with individuals who are physical, emotional, mental, and spiritual cripples. Unlike writers such as John Cheever, who may discover the bizarre in the usual, Flannery O'Connor is an artist for whom the everyday *is* bizarre. In a lecture at Notre Dame University (quoted in the Introduction to *Everything that Rises must Converge*), she noted: "I doubt if the texture of Southern life is any more grotesque than that of the rest of the nation, but it does seem evident that the Southern writer is particularly adept at recognizing the grotesque; and to recognize the grotesque, you have to have some notion of what is not grotesque and why . . ." It is this awareness, this acuity of vision, that permits her to turn the description of a doctor's office in "Revelation" into a catalogue of distortion and ugliness:

Next to her was a fat girl of eighteen or nineteen, scowling into a thick blue book which Mrs. Turpin saw was entitled *Human Development*. The girl raised her head and directed her scowl at Mrs. Turpin as if she did not like her looks. She appeared annoyed that anyone should speak while she tried to read. The poor girl's face was blue with acne and Mrs. Turpin thought how pitiful it was to have a face like that at that age. . . . Next to the ugly girl was the child, still in exactly the same position, and next to him was a thin leathery old woman in a cotton print dress. She and Claud had three sacks of chicken food in their pumphouses that was in the same print. . . . And at right angles but next to the well-dressed pleasant lady was a lank-faced woman who was certainly the child's mother. She had on a yellow sweat shirt and wine-colored slacks, both gritty-looking, and the rims of her lips were stained with snuff. Her dirty yellow hair was tied behind with a little piece of red paper ribbon.

There are difficulties with reading symbolic content into any of O'Connor's descriptions, for things usually become symbols only when her characters see them as such. This description, however, coming in one of her best stories, may be viewed as something close to a metaphor for the world of her fiction in which all are ill, all are patients awaiting cure. Their sickness lies not only in the fact that they are spiritual beings trapped within physical prisons, but also in the fact that, although obviously limited, they presume completely to understand that condition and the means by which they may transcend it. Thinking that she is better and different, Mrs. Turpin is just as deformed as the acne-scarred young girl, and in the girl's eyes, just as ugly, just as much a parody of human development.

As many critics have noticed, the title of O'Connor's second collection is taken from Teilhard de Chardin, the French Jesuit who viewed human evolution as a teleologic physical and spiritual process. Looked at in the light of her comment that the book contains "nine stories about original sin," her choice of title must be viewed as at least partially ironic, which is borne out by careful reading of the stories.

Indeed, in O'Connor's universe man is not Teilhard's totally unique being, evolving in time toward physical and spiritual perfection, but a limited creature incapable of completely comprehending the mechanism of salvation and embodying two aspects of the Fall: the descent into flawed physicality that resulted from it and the sinful pride that led to it.

Focusing purely on the physical, O'Connor's characters find that they and others are not products of Teilhard's separate human line of development, but very much members of the animal kingdom. Parker's ugly wife is "a giant hawk-eyed angel" with "a terrible bristly claw" ("Parker's Back"). Tanner, we are told, "had looked like a monkey" when he was young, "but when he got old, he looked like a bear" ("Judgement Day"). Having been called "a wart hog from hell" by the blue-faced young girl, Ruby Turpin, her own face turned greenish blue from a bruise, stands confused before her "pig parlor": "How am I a hog and me both? How am I saved and from hell too?"

Just as the physical condition of O'Connor's characters belies Teilhard's notion of developing perfection in the "biosphere," so too does their social interaction contradict his notion of positive evolution in the "nousphere."

Most of the pieces in this volume present twisted relationships between parents and children. Julian sees his mother only as an ignorant and ridiculous bigot and toys with "ways by which he could teach her a lesson" ("Everything that Rises must Converge"). Asbury, a similar character, looks on his mother as a literal-minded fool whose sole purpose is to suffocate him ("The Enduring Chill"). Thomas, feeling helpless before his mother, acts on the perverted concept of manhood that is his father's legacy to him ("The Comforts of Home"). If this represents continuity between generations, if this is the quality of inheritance, what are we to think of the concept of spiritual evolution? Where are we to find the human difference?

One place we clearly cannot find it is in any human rational faculty. It is when O'Connor's characters feel they have things figured out that they are most in trouble. Believing that he knows how to appease his wife, Parker has a portrait of Christ tattooed on his back, only to have her accuse him of idolatry and attack him with a broom ("Parker's Back"). Relying on his notion of psychology, Sheppard (another version of Rayber in her novel, *The Violent Bear it Away*) attempts to rehabilitate a lame juvenile delinquent ("The Lame Shall Enter First"). Not only does he fail to change the boy, who ends up making a fool of him, he fails to understand and love his own son, who ends up committing suicide.

Is there, then, a solution to Mrs. Turpin's dilemma: "How am I a hog and me both? How am I saved and from hell too?" For O'Connor, the answer seems to be that as imperfect creatures we are like animals, condemned to physicality, suffering, and ignorance. Yet we are different because we may ultimately be saved. Looking up to heaven at the end of "Revelation," Mrs. Turpin sees

. . . a vast swinging bridge extending upward from the earth through a field of living fire. Upon it a vast horde of souls were fumbling toward heaven. There were whole companies of white-trash, clean for the first time in their lives, and bands of black niggers in white robes, and battalions of freaks and lunatics shouting and clapping and leaping like frogs. And bringing up the procession was a tribe of people whom she recognized at once as those who, like herself and Claud, had always had a little of everything and the God-given wit to use it right. They were marching behind the others with great dignity, accountable as they had always been for good order and common sense and respectable behavior. They alone were on key. Yet she could see by their shocked and altered faces that even their virtues were being burned away.

We are different, but to assert this difference or to attempt fully to comprehend it is to lose sight of it. To O'Connor the prideful person and the self-proclaimed prophet both suffer from blindness, for the one fails to see that all are equal in purgation, and the other pretends to see something beyond our perception.

In another statement reprinted in the Introduction to *Everything that Rises must Converge,* she says, "The serious fiction writer will think that any story that can be entirely explained by the adequate motivation of the characters or by a believable imitation of a way of life or by a proper theology, will not be a large enough story for him to occupy himself with. . . . The fiction writer presents mystery through manners, grace through nature, but when he finishes, there always has to be left over that sense of Mystery which cannot be accounted for by any human formula." Everything that rises must converge, but for O'Connor as for Singer, not necessarily in this world or in a manner we can ever understand.

. . .

O'Connor's sense of the usual as bizarre is shared by James Purdy (1923—   ). In *Color of Darkness* (1957) and *Children Is All* (1962), he creates characters who are marked by physical deformities and behavioral aberrations, victims of indefinite horrors and compulsions. Trapped within themselves, his people seek absurdly futile ways out. One tries to assert his identity by shaving his beard ("The Cutting Edge"); another attempts to alter hers by refusing to be called by her married name ("Don't Call Me by My Right Name"). Most often, what we see are people mechanically performing meaningless rituals, and as the title of one of his stories indicates, what we almost always hear is nothing but the "Sound of Talking." Unlike Singer and O'Connor, Purdy does not even suggest that there may be a purpose to what he sees as the absurd condition of contemporary society, nor does he offer any hope for his human grotesques. As the protagonist of one of his disturbing modern horror stories puts it: "There isn't anything to say about such private sorrow. You just wait till the lights go out and then reach for your hat" ("You Reach for Your Hat" in *Color of Darkness*).

. . .

There are, of course, possible responses to the absurdity and surrealism of contemporary existence other than to suggest that such things are aspects of man's fallen condition or that they simply are. One such response is to consider progress and technology as possible contributors to alienation and dehumanization. Since the time of H. G. Wells, examination of this causal relationship has served as subject matter of works by the best practitioners of science fiction. Living in the age of Sputnik and in the shadow of the bomb, a number of competent short-story writers in the late 1950s and early 1960s chose to work with this fictional form (which has its roots in romance), contributing pieces to the plethora of science fiction publications that arose in the period, and which increased the respectability of the genre. Although Kurt Vonnegut (1922—   ), for example, is now considered a mainstream, if experimental, author, he began by writing short stories that must be classified as science fiction, exploring in *Welcome to the Monkey House* (1968) the possible effects of technological advances on ethics, politics, and human sexuality. A similar concern with the implications of scientific progress characterizes the work of Ray Bradbury (1920—   ), a science fiction writer who has exhibited an admirable degree of literary artistry in several fine volumes of stories in the period: *A Medicine for Melancholy* (1959), *The Machineries of Joy* (1964), *The Vintage Bradbury* (1965), *The Autumn People* (1965), and *Tomorrow Midnight* (1966).

· · ·

Another possible response to absurdity, one very much evident in O'Connor's work, is to emphasize the contradictory and the mechanical through humor. Confronted with what is obviously absurd and irreconcilable, the contemporary writer may find that the only justifiable reaction is laughter in the dark. So intrinsic is this attitude to the twentieth-century American zeitgeist that it has given rise to a tradition of black humor that is seen in the novels of Nathanael West, Joseph Heller, and Thomas Pynchon, and the short stories of Jean Stafford (1915—1979) and Bruce J. Friedman (1930—   ).

Several of the pieces in Stafford's second collection, *Bad Characters* (1964), are anything but humorous. "Cops and Robbers" is a chilling portrait of parental cruelty, while "A Winter's Tale" is a subdued but relentless story in which Stafford carefully draws a character sketch that not only exposes one individual's capacity for evil, but evokes the Evil unleashed in Germany in the 1930s and 1940s. Most of the other pieces, however, range in tone from the bizarrely comic to bitingly ironic. Whether she is using a child protagonist to mock the doctrine of alienation ("Bad Characters"), satirizing the modern cult of youth and beauty ("The End of a Career"), or dissecting the academic mentality ("Caveat Emptor"), Stafford creates a universe that is at once absurdly ludicrous and convincingly real. As the Author's Note to the collection makes clear, her world is populated by characters who are either victims or possessed of "wicked hearts." Encountering this rogue's gallery and finding our own portraits there, we have no recourse but self-consciously to laugh.

Friedman's sense of humor is even more outre and in its extravagance, even more characteristic of the black humor of the 1950s and 1960s. In *Far from the City of Class* (1963) and *Black Angels* (1966), he not only wickedly satirizes many facets of contemporary culture—our commercialism and media addiction, our fascination with psychoanalysis, our growing inurement to death and violence—he mocks our willingness to believe and our gullibility as readers. "Yes, We Have No Ritchard" burlesques the banality and ludicrousness of the traditional concept of heaven, ridiculing as well our need to believe in an abstract system of rewards and punishments that will ultimately determine our worth. "The Mission" is nothing more than a shaggy dog story that plays on the reader's desire to discover significance, and "The Night Boxing Ended" is really an extended joke at the reader's expense. In a mock-serious tone, Friedman realistically describes a dull prizefight, sets us up by depicting the reactions of the crowd, recording one of the spectator's cries for more violence, and delivers the punchline: one of the fighters *does* knock the other's head off, and it floats out over the arena.

. . .

This kind of play, based on the assumption that writer and reader are engaged in a contest of wits, is also typical of the fiction of Vladimir Nabokov (1899—1977), the Russian-born novelist, poet, playwright, translator, and short-story writer. As Page Stegner notes in the introduction to *Nabokov's Congeries* (1968), referring to one of Nabokov's favorite analogies:

Certainly one of the most characteristic aspects of Nabokov's art is the composition of riddles, word games, sleights of hand, false bottoms that drop out from under a reader like the trap door in a gallows. . . . The contest in chess, he says, is between the composer and his hypothetical solver, just as in fiction the contest is between the author and his reader, and the value of a problem lies in the number of "'tries'— delusive opening moves, false scents, specious lines of play, astutely and lovingly prepared to lead the would-be solver astray." The author establishes certain rules to which he adheres, creates barriers which he tries to hurdle, takes the most devious and difficult route from point A to point B, and invites the reader to follow.

Most of the collections which were published by Nabokov in the period or issued after his death consist of stories that first appeared much earlier or were English translations of earlier Russian stories. Although his work therefore does not strictly speaking lie within the province of this study, it is worthy of mention because of its influence on and similarity to the innovationist literature of the 1960s. In his adoption of the role of a conjurer who exposes his tricks, and in his love of parody, puns, mazes, and mirrors, he anticipated the later work of writers such as Barthelme and Barth.

The "Vane Sisters" from *Nabokov's Quartet,* one of the few entirely new stories Nabokov wrote during the period, is an excellent case in point. The narrator, a professor of French literature at a small girls' college, begins by describing the day on which he heard of Cynthia Vane's death, a day of glittering icicles and surreal parking meters:

And as I looked up at the eaves of the adjacent garage with its full display of transparent stalactites backed by their blue silhouettes, I was rewarded at last, upon choosing one, by the sight of what might be described as the dot of an exclamation mark leaving its ordinary position to glide down very fast—a jot faster than the thaw-drop it raced. . . . The lean ghost, the elongated umbra cast by a parking meter upon some damp snow, had a strange ruddy tinge. . . .

Contemplating the parking meter, the narrator runs across D., who informs him of Cynthia's death, and we plunge into a series of reminiscences of the two sisters: Sybil, who had committed suicide months before, and Cynthia, a spiritualist who had professed to be in contact with her dead sister.

Following Cynthia's own death, the narrator discovers that his attitude has changed, that he no longer finds Cynthia's "ridiculous fondness for spiritualism" to be another of her "ingenious fancies." He begins to detect her spiritual presence everywhere and, as the final paragraph indicates, is obsessed by the notion that she has sent him a message that he cannot decipher: "I could isolate, consciously, little. Everything seemed blurred, yellow-clouded, yielding nothing tangible. Her inept acrostics, maudlin evasions, theopathies—every recollection formed ripples of mysterious meaning. Everything seemed yellowly blurred, illusive, lost." The reader who is alert to Nabokov's own evasions will have discovered earlier the key to this last paragraph: "And I wish I could recollect that novel or short story (by some contemporary writer, I believe) in which, unknown to its author, the first letters of the words in its last paragraph formed, as deciphered by Cynthia, a message from his dead mother."

Containing such a mysterious acrostic, the ultimate paragraph of "The Vane Sisters" causes us to doubt the fictional principles of verisimilitude and narrative integrity. If the narrator is unaware of the message, who has composed it?—the Vane sisters; or a godlike author who is toying with his reader, testing his powers of recall and observation? It also calls into question our tacit acceptance of the notion that art is derived from experience and that it comments on it in some significant way. Playing Nabokov's game, we may ask ourselves the same question posed in the verse by Frederic Meyers, which is quoted in the story:

What is this—a conjuror's rabbit,
Or a flawy but genuine gleam—
Which can check the perilous habit
And dispel the dolorous dream?

. . .

The propensity for game playing and tendency toward parody apparent in most of Nabokov's work are also evident in other short fiction of the period. Many of Shirley Jackson's short stories, collected in *The Magic of Shirley Jackson* (1966), take place in a fictional universe that appears to be governed by its own physical laws and its own logic. The title story of George P. Elliott's *Among the Dangs* also plays on our expectation of truth by presenting us with a narrative that is similar to the autobiographical anthropology of a writer such as Margaret Mead, and with a narrator who comes to believe in the role he has adopted to carry out his studies.

•   •   •

The most thorough and innovative manipulation and exposure of literary convention in the period, however, is to be found in *Lost in the Funhouse* (1968) by John Barth (1930—   ). The first piece in the volume, "Frame-Tale," is an emblem of the whole. It consists of a strip of paper, which is to be cut out, twisted, and fastened end to end, and which reads "ONCE UPON A TIME THERE WAS A STORY THAT BEGAN." "Frame Tale," like *Lost in the Funhouse* itself, is a Möbius strip that appears to be three-dimensional but is in actuality a two-dimensional, single surface that twists in on itself endlessly. Like an imaginary traveler on such a strip, the reader of Barth's book may for a time be deceived by the illusion of progress or development, only to discover that he has returned to where he began. Lost in the funhouse of fiction or of any other conceptual model of the universe, the reader has his desire for significance repeatedly frustrated on a number of different levels.

Persisting in the belief that the "senselessest babble, could we ken it, might disclose a dark message, or prayer" ("Glossolalia"), the reader who has been trained to search the text for clues will find a profusion of them here. Several of the pieces, for example, are filled with freudian symbolism, sexual puns, and oedipal relationships. Others treat mythological subjects or invoke mythic parallels, and the sequence as a whole follows the pattern of heroic quest described by Lord Raglan and Joseph Campbell.

Like Nabokov, however, Barth makes a farce of freudianism. His use of language that is psychosexually charged is gross, cliched, obvious, and ludicrous, a joke at the expense of both the assumed author of his pieces and the reader who may feel that he has discovered the meaning of his heavy-handed symbolism. The mythic parallels are similarly farcical—Barth's artist-hero becomes bogged down in language, in the manner of telling his tale, and his quest for self-expression concludes, like Tristram Shandy's, with much "left unsaid, much" which "must be blank."

The reader who puts aside any desire for significance, settling for plot and character development, will be equally frustrated. "Lost in the Funhouse," for instance, makes intermittent reference to the conventional pattern of narrative development and to its own inability to follow it: "A long time ago we should have passed the apex of Freitag's Triangle and made brief work of the *denouement;* the plot doesn't rise by meaningful steps but winds upon itself, digresses, retreats, hesitates, sighs, collapses, expires. The climax of the story must be its protagonist's discovery of a way to get through the funhouse. But he has found none, may have ceased to search."

In another piece, "Menelaiad," Barth creates a mirror-maze such as Borges might devise, a structure of tales within tales that thrusts the reader into a state of confusion in which it is impossible with certainty to determine who is saying what:

" " " " " " 'Why?' I repeated," I repeated,' I repeated," I repeated,' I repeated," I repeat.
" " " " " "And the woman, with a bride-shy smile and hushed voice, replied: 'Why what?'

The narrator of "Life-Story," which purports to be autobiography, discovers that he is "in a sense his own author, telling his story to himself." The main "character" of "Autobiography," we are told, is a monophonic recorded authorial voice that calls itself "a fiction without real hope," a "halt narrative: first person, tiresome." If we cannot read for plot, characterization, or extra-textual significance, "for what discreditable motive" ("Life-Story") do we go on?

We continue to read because, while denying our conventional expectations, Barth manages to satisfy our hunger for language and to create intricate and often pleasing literary artifacts. As he himself noted:

Contemporary writers can't go on doing what's been done, and done better. I revere Flaubert and Tolstoy, Hemingway and Faulkner; but they're finished as objects of interest to the writer. My God, we're living in the last third of the twentieth century. We can't write nineteenth-century novels ... Beckett is moving toward silence, refining language out of existence, working toward the point where there's nothing more to say. And Borges writes as if literature had already been done and he's writing footnotes to imaginary texts.

But my temperament is entirely different . . . I start with the premise of the "end of literature" and try to turn it against itself. I go back to Cervantes, Fielding, Sterne, the *Arabian Nights,* to the artificial frame and the long connected tales. I'm interested in the *artifices* of narrative, in what can be done with language.

For Barth, language and literature are both meaningless and ultimately significant. As products of the mind, they are obviously artificial; as the intrinsic forms of human perception and understanding, they may be all we have.

· · ·

The self-conscious artificiality of *Lost in the Funhouse* was to prove characteristic of one kind of short fiction written in the late 1960s and the 1970s—the experimental stories of Donald Barthelme, Joyce Carol Oates, and others. Barth's refusal to play the Jamesian game was not reflective, however, of a universal attitude toward the genre. For in the subsequent decade many short-story writers continued to rely on the traditional elements of narration, description, plot, dialogue, and characterization.

E. P. Walkiewicz

Oklahoma State University

1969—1980:
EXPERIMENT AND
TRADITION

Short fiction of the 1960s and 1970s was heavily influenced by the intellectual turbulence caused by such forces as the civil-rights movement and the Vietnam conflict. The amount of experimental work being written increased markedly during this era, and once the styles became better defined, a debate developed between traditionalists and experimentalists.

Traditional fiction proceeds on premises solidified with the rise of the novel in the eighteenth century: there is objective reality, and the best way to involve the reader's thoughts and feelings is to use convincing characters in believable situations. The experimental style grew from the belief that post-World War II civilization had undergone such radical changes that old forms no longer met new needs of expression. In their writing, experimentalists question the existence of objective reality. Although the possible forms of experimentation are by definition unlimited, the most common ones are metafiction (as in Curley's "Who, What, Where, When—Why?") surrealism, and discontinuous narrative (as in Barthelme's "Views of My Father Weeping").

Although the stories cited herein occasionally mention civil rights and the war, the effects of those times reach much deeper into the outlook of a writer than merely into subject matter. The world view of the individual writer shapes style and makes a philosophical statement, however muted it may be, and the frame of reference within which characters are placed determines the focus of the work. Writers are discussed here in the context of themes that they use most frequently (or most successfully) to establish the identity of their characters: society at large, ethnic or religious group, or the family. Of course, no writer fits exclusively into one category, but this format will serve as a foundation for the study.

Characters who are presented primarily in relation to the mass of society, and not in relation to a smaller group within it, are inevitably and severely alienated. Either they utterly reject their family or ethnic ties, or struggle with shifting contexts. They tend to relate to society as a whole, although they may find solace in temporary romances. Typical examples are stories by Donald Barthelme, Ann Beattie, Doris Betts, Ray Bradbury, Herbert Gold, Shirley Ann Grau, James B. Hall, Joyce Carol Oates, and Irwin Shaw.

There is also a logical extension of these alienated characters: outcasts. They are defined by the society in which they live, but to which, in fact, they do not belong. Some are outcasts because their vision places them beyond the limits of one society and into history itself. Such characters dominate the stories of Guy Davenport and appear in some by Russell Banks. Others are foreigners or pariahs, as is usually the case with characters in stories by Paul Bowles, H.E. Francis, and Paul Theroux. The styles of these writers are diverse.

A more personal context than society is the ethnic or religious group. The struggles of characters who are caught inside these more confining limits (social, racial, or religious) are often more intense than those of people standing up to society at large. Along with more violent conflict, however, comes greater hope that their actions will make a difference, since the arenas of personal battles are smaller. Louis Auchincloss, James Alan McPherson, Leonard Michaels, Hugh Nissenson, Flannery O'Connor, J. F. Powers, and I. B. Singer fill their stories with the cadence and vocabulary of the social groups of which they write.

The most intimate context of anybody's identity is the family—the easiest to recognize and the hardest to escape. The closeness of family members offers countless opportunities for writers to portray dramatic conflicts that exemplify basic human problems. People feel alienated from each other in any of the three contexts mentioned, but alienation within the society is the most bewildering, while within the family it is the most painful. Regardless of this, however, the family is the most consistent source of consolation in American short stories of the 1960s and 1970s. Writers relying primarily on family matters are Frederick Busch, Raymond Carver, Daniel Curley, Grace Paley, Richard Stern, Barry Targan, Peter Taylor, and John Updike.

Looking at such writers in terms of the broad scope of their fiction reveals a sense of similar purposes and shows some parallels of style and theme.

·   ·   ·

From the prominence of *The New Yorker,* Donald Barthelme (1931—   ) exerted a formidable influence on the short story of the two decades. Of recent writers of short experimental works (such as John Barth, Robert Coover, and Ronald Sukenick), Barthelme has had the most visible and enduring impact on American fiction.

A virtue he shares with most successful experimental writers is a piercing eye for the absurdities of conventional behavior, an awareness that seems to have been the starting point for most experimentalists. He has a fine ear for language and can make trenchant social criticism by his use of idiom and vernacular.

Barthelme's stories can be classified according to clarity: the obscure stories ("The Piano Player," "Views of My Father Weeping," and "City Life"), which are amusing, coherent, subtle, and clear; and the didactic stories ("A Shower of Gold," "The Glass Mountain," and "Kierkegaard Unfair to Schlegel"), which proclaim theme at the expense of subtlety. These classifications that straddle either side of the so-called balanced story contain difficulties that often trip writers of new fiction. Experimentalists tend to reduce coherent action and depth of character in favor of manipulating form and word-play. When they fail, they can either land in the hole of meaningless obscurity or in the safety net of flat didactic statements.

Come Back, Dr. Caligari (1964) contains stories that contributed substantially to Barthelme's reputation, and are representative of tales found throughout the body of his work. "The Piano Player" presents much of what Barthelme's critics have attacked: deteriorating absurd conversation, repeated incantation of a key term ("ugliness" in this case), incongruous and incoherent action, and a chaotic conclusion (the daughter's piano strikes the father dead). The story is fragmented and strained by clashes of images and ideas.

Quite different from the obscure stories is "A Shower of Gold," in which the sculptor Peterson conducts a TV talk show that the producers have determined should be a platform for expressing twentieth-century alienation. After playing along for a while, he rebels and announces his credo to the audience: "In this kind of world . . . absurd if you will . . . there are opportunities for beginning again . . . How can you be alienated without first having been connected?"

Balanced stories, such as "Me and Miss Mandible" and "Marie, Marie, Hold on Tight," find the middle ground and effectively combine incongruity and commitment to theme. The first appears as the diary entries of a thirty-five-year-old who has been unaccountably put back into the sixth grade. The story points out the arbitrariness of social convention and the necessity of conformity as the narrator learns that he must "pick up the clues" to prosper in a baffling society. The second story tells the agony of three men who "demonstrate against the human condition" by picketing a church, asking, "Why does it have to be this way?" After they are beaten by thugs, one returns and delivers a speech the next night. The narrator explains, "He was very eloquent. And Eloquence, Henry Mackie says, is really all any of us can hope for." In this allegory of the modern writer performing his role, human warmth conveys humor and makes a resonant statement.

City Life (1970) is generally a weaker collection than *Caligari*. "The Tolstoy Museum" and "Brain Damage" are presented through words and illustrations, and they achieve an occasional sharp stroke of satire. "The Glass Mountain," a didactic first-person-absurd story of a man scaling a skyscraper, appears in the form of one hundred brief entries (mostly single sentences) that are the allegory of a romantic hero's quest for excellence in a corrupt society. "City Life" is the story of two young women suffering various hardships of involvement in society, deciding that they dislike city life, but surrendering to it at last. The final despair is clear. "Views of My Father Weeping" is told by a bewildered first-person narrator, and the story is obscured by a montage of incongruous elements: a mixture of nineteenth-century and twentieth-century images and motifs from cowboy movies and freudian psychology. By contrast, the meaning of "Kierkegaard Unfair to Schlegel" is clear because it is a philosophical discourse rather than a conventional story. The reader is finally led to believe that irony is not satisfying, but it is acceptable, rather like the eloquence mentioned in "Marie, Marie, Hold on Tight." Here there is less of the dramatic texture of the earlier story.

As such stories illustrate, Barthelme tends to use either the coldly objective third-person narrator or the bewildered first person. Both techniques keep the reader at a distance from the characters and, to use Wayne C. Booth's term from *The Rhetoric of Fiction,* at a distance from the "implied author." When the author strikes an indifferent pose toward his characters, it is hard for the reader to care about them.

"Daumier," from *Sadness* (1972), is one of Barthelme's finest stories, complex but ultimately rewarding. Daumier complains of his "hankering" and "rapacious" feelings. He proposes to compensate for his imbalance by creating a world in which everyone's flaws are balanced out by his surrogate form. This world is made of Western-movie characters and plot devices. The counterpart of Daumier's real-life Amelia is Celeste (a parody of a Corinne Calvet character from a Western about mail-order brides), who is voluptuous and speaks in broken English and French. A narrative voice describes her:

> Then Daumier looked at Celeste and saw that the legs on her were as long and slim as his hope of Heaven and the thighs on her were as strong and sweet-shaped as ampersands and the buttocks on her were as pretty as two pictures and the waist on her was as neat and in-curved as a fiddle and the shoulders on her were as tempting as sex crimes and the hair on her was as long and black as Lent and the movement of the whole was honey and he sank into a swoon.

The repeated "on her" has an authentically crude sound, but the specific descriptions are breathtaking and amusing at the same time. The parody has mocked and surpassed the tone of the original film. The story is written in brief titled sections through which the "real" and created narratives run parallel and finally mix. By an act of will, Daumier rescues Celeste from the substitute world and ends up with both her and Amelia, the moral to the story being, "The Self cannot be escaped, but it can be, with ingenuity and hard work, distracted." As in earlier stories, Barthelme offers eloquence and irony as stays against futility.

In *Great Days* (1979), the title story and many others are unnarrated dialogues, a form seen earlier in "Kierkegaard Unfair to Schlegel." In a sense, Barthelme is writing one-act plays, and the influence of Samuel Beckett, whom he admires, is not far beneath the surface. A major difference between the two, however, is that at his best Barthelme is more concerned with the nobility of his characters than with their absurdity. At their weakest, these stories are bitterly glib, such as "The Crisis." At their strongest, they become a mixture of lampoon and paean. "The Leap" subjects Kierkegaard's "leap of faith" to the kind of argument Beckett might raise; it echoes lines from *Waiting for Godot*:

—God is good and we poor are wretches who—
—Wait.

As the argument deepens, Barthelme is at his seriocomic best: "He who hath not love is a sad cookie." The nameless characters finally resolve not to act today, but soon. "Great Days" continues the focus on struggling with dignity and the importance of doing "our damnedest." The subject of this conversation-story is the agony of doing the right things while facing daily discouragement. Amid the undertow of despair and lines that bring the tension of police distress calls, come words that are both self-mocking and sincere: "I find you utterly delightful. Abide with me. We'll have little cakes with smarm, yellow smarm on them." Borrowings from a hymn title and the slang of the society set bring the speaker's aspirations down to reality and suggest that dreams for the future are not based on naivete but on sobering experience. At the conclusion, the man and woman remain, as do most of Barthelme's characters, dissatisfied. They have the only hope that Barthelme offers throughout his fiction: the solace of eloquence, the relief of irony, and the comfort of each other.

Donald Barthelme has influenced contemporary fiction, but unfortunately, he has also too often been praised for the wrong reasons. The obscurity of his work is readily visible and therefore has drawn critical praise under the label of inventiveness. His surface innovations work best when they are supported by a narrative energy and ironic humor that would strengthen any type of fiction, from the most radical to the most conservative.

· · ·

The stories of Ann Beattie (1947—   ), many of which were also first published in *The New Yorker,* generally combine the realistic surface of traditional fiction and the bitter outlook typical of experimental work. Often her stories are set in New York City, or the characters are indirectly influenced by city life, but her style is not so clipped as that of other New York writers such as Grace Paley and Leonard Michaels. Her narratives flow, although in a lurching, commuter-train rhythm, and the long and short bursts finally create an underlying motion suggestive of restrained hysteria beneath a smooth surface.

Without the city, her stories tend to lose immediacy and reflective irony, which is a major problem in *Distortions* (1976). "Snake Shoes" is a good case in point. The story opens with a scene in which a character who has been telling nature myths insists, "Imagination is better than reality." Human experience is discouraging and defeating. With apparent satisfaction, Beattie's narrative voice shows none of the controlled self-mockery that often saves the work of equally bleak but more mature writers.

In *Secrets and Surprises* (1978), Beattie achieves a much more sophisticated effect in restating her themes of the need for companionship and the inevitability of alienation. "The Vintage Thunderbird" traces the on-and-off relationship of Nick and Karen through several years. They are basically symbiotic, responding to each other's weaknesses and coming back together after affairs with others. From the account of Nick's being robbed by a boy on the street prior to this story and then by two men during the story, it becomes clear that he is alone and afraid. He seeks solace in Karen's company and in her fine possessions that seem to have escaped time and danger. Thus the Thunderbird becomes enmeshed in his image of her because it is nostalgic and timeless.

When Karen says that she has sold the car, Nick becomes desperate to buy it back, as desperate as if it were his youth. The childishness of his trying to hide from the brutality of the world and the relentlessness of time is handled with humor and makes Nick likable, even pitiable. The character speaks eloquently of the urge to escape from the world into the womb of nostalgia.

"Secrets and Surprises" shows similar effective characterization and more complexity of conflict and theme. The first-person narrator is a divorcée who has moved from New York City to Connecticut. The story shows Beattie at her best in creating a sense of barely checked emotions as the narrator channels her despair between the order of language and the relief of humor. Her insecurity shows when she works through two drafts of a letter to her former husband, finally sending him a "short, funny postcard" instead. She is desolate in the country but afraid of the city. An important undercurrent of plot is the story of her retarded brother; he is a figure of human isolation, although she is even more alone. The couple who visit her also seem alone, even within their relationship. Thus life becomes a maze of secrets, with people unwilling or unable to be honest with each other, and surprises like that of her husband having left her. Her lover pleasantly surprises her when he releases a jar of lightning bugs in their bedroom, but he also tells her that he is going on tour in Europe, which will surely end their relationship. Surviving secrets and surprises is the recurrent challenge for Beattie's characters.

• • •

For the characters of Doris Betts (1932—   ), the predominant problem is lack of love. Their alienation stems from a variety of sources, but the most common solution is redemption through another human being; whereas society as a whole obliterates people, individual love helps them survive.

Whether in characters or in situations, Betts often employs the grotesque. In the settings of her stories, generally the small-town South, the imagery is vivid and economical, and her narrative often produces striking turns of phrase.

In *Beasts of the Southern Wild and Other Stories* (1973), Violet Karl, of "The Ugliest Pilgrim," transcends discouraging circumstances with a combination of faith and action that leads unexpectedly to love. As she travels from the North Carolina mountains to Oklahoma in the hope that a faith healer can remove the ax scar from her face, she meets two soldiers on the bus, and her rejection of self-pity engages them and the reader. Her determination and comic perspective make her suffering redemptive, full of unassuming nobility. In Tulsa, she mentions the many mirrors and reflecting windows where her face "is waiting in ambush" for her. When she cries with disappointment after being sent away by the healer's assistant, she explains that, because of the scar on her cheek, she "cries crooked." One of the soldiers, who claims to love her, has promised to meet her at a bus station on her way back, but since she still has the scar, she doesn't want to see him. To her surprise, he catches her when she runs from him. After their own fashion, it appears that they will live happily ever after.

The title story also presents redemption from loneliness, but without the warmth and humor that pervade "The Ugliest Pilgrim"; the world of this story is much darker and colder. "Beasts" begins with third-person narration of the story of Carol Walsh, wife, mother, and teacher, and changes to Carol's first-person viewpoint in the interwoven story of the black revolution. Apparently, the revolution provides Carol with a fantasy, including outright violence and finally concubinage. The fantasy is a relief from the dull, subjugated propriety in which she lives, and appears to be her only satisfaction. In Doris Betts's stories, characters resort to extreme behavior in their need for love.

• • •

Ray Bradbury (1920—   ) displays such skill with words and humor as to rank his stories among the best in the field of science fiction. *I Sing the Body Electric* (1969) uses standard science-fiction devices such as the time-machine truck of "The Kilimanjaro Device" and the mechanical grandmother of the title story. Both tales circumvent the limits of death: the first provides the narrator a chance to travel back in time and offer Ernest Hemingway a more fitting place in which to die, while the second supplies a substitute to children whose mother has died. The book also contains some standard "space stories."

Like its predecessors, *Long After Midnight* (1976) has its Martian stories, but the emphasis of this volume is on the characters' destructive urges. In "The Blue Bottle," a description of a decayed Martian city shows what Bradbury does best: "Sometimes towers as beautiful as a symphony would fall at a spoken word. It was like watching a Bach cantata disintegrate before your eyes." "Forever and the Earth" is a story reminiscent of "The Kilimanjaro Device"; this time Thomas Wolfe is retrieved from death. One of the best stories in the volume is "Have I Got a Chocolate Bar for You!" It is funny and true to human nature, and uses not one extreme device, making it exceptional among Bradbury's stories. A priest becomes the confessor of an obese chocolate addict, who is incidentally a Jew. Each man, in his way, helps the other in this story that is written with considerable warmth and amusement.

· · ·

The stories of Herbert Gold (1929—   ) in *The Magic Will* (1971) are usually first-person narratives with little or no distinction between the storyteller's viewpoint and the author's: both usually speak their discoveries in one voice. Thus the immediacy of the works is strong.

Since there is so little difference between Gold and his characters, their lives, like his, are set in the bohemian communities of New York, San Francisco, Paris, or Haiti. He reflects on the aging of his generation and on the effects of war, career, the artist's life, divorce, love affairs, and changes in values. The recurring problem for Gold's characters is that nothing lasts—not love, family, or consolation before death. His style is simple and straightforward, and he includes a steady flow of humor in his observations.

Perhaps because of the autobiographical quality of his work, the structure is more casual than deliberate, and Gold's stories achieve their effect from mood, interesting dialogue, and detail instead of from tight, pointed structure.

Two stories that best reflect range in time and subject matter are "A Selfish Story" and "Song of the First and Last Beatnik." The former is a recollection by Herbert, the narrator, of his discovery of death; first with a classmate in a freshman literature class, while the professor spoke and they saw each other grasping what he had said; and later when the friend was killed in the war and Herbert felt his own mortality in the death of the young womanizer and fighter pilot. The nostalgia is genuine and forceful. The latter begins in San Francisco in 1957 and tells of Howard, the bohemian artist personified, a black man who began his nonconformity with the beatniks and endured through the hippies. Howard is a compulsive and flamboyant talker, but he makes sense. At the beginning he says to the narrator, "Howdya do. I got the water if you got the bucket." In his prime, he sometimes says he had the bucket *and* the water. As the story ends years later, Howard, broken by time and his society, says, "I ain't got the water." Gold ponders time and chance, which take their toll on everybody.

· · ·

The characters of Shirley Ann Grau (1929—   ) in *The Wind Shifting West* (1974) are lonely and trying to adjust to unexpected change, whether they are in the yachting set of the title story or in the primitive family of "The Last Gas Station."

In the former, the sudden change in the wind and its effect on Caroline's husband, who is out sailing, parallels the change in Caroline herself, who responds to the unexpected sexual advances of her brother-in-law. The brief adventure is an act of vengeance against her husband's insistence on sailing, which she dislikes, and against his family's pressure on her to say and do the right things. Her unfaithfulness is as much an act of rebellion against her role as it is a sexual act.

The boy who is the first-person narrator of "The Last Gas Station" is a more substantial character who effectively establishes his rural innocence and his ability to handle major shocks. His oldest brother leaves home; soon afterward the father dies, then the second brother nearly kills the third in an argument and flees. When the wounded brother recovers, he too decides to leave. Finally, the narrator, who is the youngest, realizes that he will have to make his own way quite alone. He needs human contact but knows its dangers and is caught between fear and loneliness. The boy's character is well developed, and this story is representative of Grau's most powerful tales of alienation.

· · ·

In his introduction to his portion of the anthology of short fiction *Fifteen by Three* (1957), James B. Hall (1918—   ) explains that, like Joyce, he is more concerned with diction and metaphor than narrative. Hall's claim for his work places the burden of proof on his use of language and imagery.

In this collection Hall's language is not especially startling, but his metaphors sometimes are, especially in the disjointed "Action Time in Twilight," where he uses five different sources of information to substitute for a narrative. In this self-consciously experimental piece, he tells his story in three first-person narratives, a doctor's reports, and letters. The result is interesting, but there is no coherent narrative to suggest what the reader should make of the decline and suicide of a madman. He refers to this story as a "studied reaction against the Laws of James," specifically, those requiring a unified narrative point of view; however, he perhaps loses as much as he gains by discarding this tradition. "In the Time of Demonstrations," a more effective story, achieves energy and insight through a church janitor's viewpoint. His understanding of a retarded man in the congregation, who, like the janitor, has suffered a life of losses, shows a brotherhood of man that is healthier outside of the church than inside.

Although the chilling alienation of his protagonists permeates Hall's stories, *Us He Devours* (1964) puts this motif to its best use. Cold, flatly written stories about a spinster bank teller ("Us He Devours"), an adolescent boy afraid of sex ("A View of the Beach"), and a compulsive gambler ("The Gambler: A Portrait of the Writer") foreshadow Raymond Carver's more barren style of the 1970s. Also like Carver, Hall occasionally relieves the bleak outlook of his work with grotesque humor, as in "The Claims Artist," in which a writer systematically dismembers himself so that he may draw workmen's compensation and be able to write full time. The price of art becomes metaphorically corporeal as the writer sees "the implication of what it was to be a writer, a really independent, nonkept, nonacademic, non-Hollywood writer." *The Short Hall* (1980) resembles the earlier collections in style. At his best, Hall writes with distinctive narration and informing irony, although he is sometimes obscure or predictable.

• • •

For sheer volume, Joyce Carol Oates (1938—   ) has no rivals. Her stories have been published in everything from the most obscure literary quarterlies to the most sophisticated commercial magazines.

She is skillful with dialogue, perhaps her greatest strength. She sets her stories convincingly in a variety of places—the campus, city, small town, farm—and uses different organizing principles.

The world view expressed in her fiction reflects the protest and disillusionment of its era. Her characters are generally alienated and obsessed, with the result that the stories often erupt into violence and dissolve into chaos. Her fiction raises problems that it seldom probes or clarifies.

One of her most frequently mentioned stories, "Pastoral Blood" from *By the North Gate* (1963), serves as a good representative of the body of her work to date. Grace is prototypical of most of Oates's women, trapped and frustrated—

in this case, in the rigid cast of the pretty girl. Even though she is pretty, popular, and about to marry, she is alienated from her society by the role she must play. She sees impending marriage, the logical completion of this role, as the end of her life; thus she plans to commit suicide in final rebellion against the mold that restricts her. As if to kill her image before killing herself, she buys gaudy clothes, picks up a seedy-looking older man, yields to him indifferently, picks up more hitch-hikers, wrecks her new car, and finally awakens at home in bed. Realizing that she has failed to fulfill her urge for death she resolves, "All the time in the world, and next time there will be no failure. . . . Experience is the best teacher." After her decision early in the story to kill herself, nothing develops or changes significantly. There is only the superficial twist of the above quotation: rather than finding life precious after courting death, she regards it as a trap that she will escape next time. The sheer coldness of the conclusion is arresting.

Upon the Sweeping Flood (1966) continues the emphasis on alienation. In "The Survival of Childhood," Carl, an insensitive college professor, struggles to escape "blood bondage" to his rural family. He is distant in all of his relationships, including those with his wife and students. Oates skillfully sums up his attitude in the treatment of a boy in his class: "The rebuff landed on the student's face, spread itself out visibly in all directions, slumping his shoulders." He goes back to visit his family "so that he might be finally free." He also refuses the closeness his ne'er-do-well brother antagonistically calls for. During Carl's visit, the brother commits suicide, but Carl is doomed by his insensitivity to live on.

Another hopelessly self-centered character is Klein of "Archways," whose consolation is the prolonged planning of suicide. The graduate student's shame (the collective cause of which is unspecified) is so great that he enjoys making his students suffer with him, being sure that they are "educated now into knowing their unworth." His contemplation of suicide is interrupted by an affair with a student, who makes him feel "worthy of love," but love proves only a temporary, if pleasant, distraction, and he turns inward more resolutely than before, hoping for "some random incidental death."

"Upon the Sweeping Flood" takes place in Oates's often-used setting of Eden County. Walter Stuart, returning from the funeral of his father, risks his life to save two farm children from rising floodwaters. Stuart believes in the order of the world, and as a child, had "shifted his faith" from God "to the things of this world." In saving the children, he realizes that he is trying to save himself by establishing order and purpose ("they had saved him as much as he had saved them"). Then for no apparent reason, Stuart kills the boy, tries to rape the teenage girl, and acts relieved when he sights a rescue party coming in a boat. He shouts, "Save me!" as he leaves the girl, apparently wanting to be saved from himself. These protagonists are alienated, seek release, and find no comfort; they are so cold as to be unreal.

In her third collection, *The Wheel of Love and Other Stories* (1970), Oates continues along the same lines. "In the Region of Ice," an O. Henry Award winner in 1967, is one of her best stories, and the theme of alienation is apparent from the title. The central irony is that Sister Irene, who fears involvement of any sort, gets involved with Allen Weinstein. The nun and the brilliant, unstable student are outsiders who find a common ground in literature. The difference between them is that he takes literature quite seriously, wanting to reconcile thought and action, while she does not. He comes to see her after his release from a mental hospital, and says, "Give me your hand or something, touch me, help me—please." She withdraws and he soon kills himself. Her character is almost developed to fullness, though his is not, despite the potential. They are more masks for ideas than people living out the inevitable.

In "Where Are You Going? Where Have You Been?," Connie is a pretty girl who likes the power that sexual appeal gives her; the power, however, is reversed on her. In the advances of a hoodlum, complete with mirror-lens sunglasses and greasy hair, she faces the force of sex as a collective obsession. He does not have to rape her, since he can badger and lure her into submission. The irony of the situation is interesting, but the story, which is narrated mostly in dialogue, becomes repetitive, and this undercuts the tension on which it depends for its effect. Alienation persists throughout Oates's works. Repeatedly, the main character, whether man or woman, is beset by loneliness and tries to escape the agony of isolated self-awareness by means of sex, violence, or suicide. Her characters become obsessive in their attempts to escape the emptiness of their lives.

Crossing the Border (1976), *The Seduction and Other Stories* (1975), and *All the Good People I've Left Behind* (1979) continue in this vein, although the rest of Oates's collections benefit from distinct unifying concepts. In *Marriages and Infidelities* (1972), the stories are responses to classics such as Kafka's "The Metamorphosis" and Joyce's "The Dead." The stories in *The Hungry Ghosts: Seven Allusive Comedies* (1974) satirize the desperate inadequacies of academic characters. *The Goddess and Other Women* (1974) presents stories only from a feminine point of view and is largely concerned with the suppressed evil within women. Tales in *Night-Side* (1977) deal with the dark side of personality and emphasize the mystery of evil. By far the best of Oates's collections based on a theme is *The Poisoned Kiss and Other Stories from the Portuguese* (1975).

At the beginning of the book, she disclaims authorship, insisting that she received these stories from Fernandes, a Portuguese writer who, she admits, is fictitious, but whose influence she claims was vital. Obsession being her element, she uses surreal motifs to a good effect. The stories are more abstract than her usual work, and she substitutes intensity of feeling for details of surface. "The Poisoned Kiss" and "The Son of God and His Sorrow" are the best of the collection.

Joyce Carol Oates employs virtually all of the conventions for structuring fiction: internal monologue, self-conscious and unself-conscious narrators, diaries, letters, time-marked notations, "notes on contributors," even stories by a fabricated author. She also demonstrates skill in assembling her reactions to classic pieces of literature. Some critics have compared her work to Flannery O'Connor's. Although O'Connor, too, shows strange people and often writes of violence, she does so with clearly different effects. She is just as critical of the world as Oates, but the difference is that she suggests how things *should* be. O'Connor suggests what is wrong by means of narrative distance, irony, and humor. Oates does not offer a clear distinction between what her characters see and what their creator sees, leading the critical reader to recall O'Connor's warning that "Competence by itself is deadly. What is needed is the vision to go with it."

• • •

As "The Girls in their Summer Dresses" and "The Eighty-Yard Run" attest, the stories of Irwin Shaw (1913—   ) are among the finest in recent fiction; however, much of his later work is entertaining but insubstantial. *God Was Here But He Left Early* (1973) provides a good sampling in the rambling "Whispers in Bedlam" and the well-crafted "When All Things Wise and Fair Descend."

The first plays with the fanciful notion of a professional football player who changes from ordinary to brilliant because he can suddenly hear the other team's plays being called. He reaches great success, pays a heavy price, and finally asks the doctor to limit his hearing to the way it was before. The second is a conventional initiation story, complete with vivid characters, rich images and turns of phrase, and a skillfully rendered epiphany. The story first presents Steve, absolutely the all-American boy, who is well described by the comment, "No wonder he woke up feeling good." In one day, however, Steve confronts death and begins to learn compassion. The story ends aptly: "But he wasn't going to wake up, feeling automatically good, ever again."

• • •

The setting for Guy Davenport's (1927—   ) stories in *Da Vinci's Bicycle* (1979) is history itself. His works range in time from the days of Herakleitos to those of

Da Vinci, Fourier, Tatlin, and Richard Nixon. Davenport's stories seem to be primarily vehicles for ideas rather than people; they are lapidarian—cold and hard—regardless of how wisely and well they are told. By trying to make time and place universal, he often denies his reader the continuity of details that allows one to identify a place and sympathize with the characters.

One of the most accessible narratives, complete with physical details, is "John Charles Tapner." The story is also a tour de force of style; for example, the first paragraph is written with heavy alliteration and the fourth displays several invented words that call to mind James Joyce. At the remote extreme are stories like "Au Tombeau de Charles Fourier" and "A Field of Snow on a Slope of the Rosenberg." Both are disjointed and deny the reader a consistent vantage point from which to see the action.

A story from each of his two collections illustrates Davenport's style and major theme. Tatlin, in the story and volume of the same name (1974), is a Russian designer, inventor, and artist whose career begins before the Revolution and changes with it. He is Davenport's metaphor for the artist. Tatlin tries to go backward into history with his invention of the glider, to recapture childlike simplicity, both of design and spirit. Of course the state values him only for his practical skills such as designing a one-piece work suit and teaching engineering. Tatlin realizes, "It would be a disaster of the spirit were man to become mechanized in his movement."

In "The Richard Nixon Freischutz Rag" (*Da Vinci's Bicycle*), the artist is similarly misused. The story is told in parallel narratives of Nixon talking to Mao and of Da Vinci sketching his bicycle. War is the undercurrent of the story: Nixon and Mao carry on a subtly hostile conversation, while Da Vinci's bicycle is being absurdly discussed as an alternative to the horse in a cavalry charge. On a third level the narrator discusses art and history, implying that history is shaped by the bellicose and short-sighted, not the creative. With considerable skill, Davenport turns history to his purposes.

• • •

In a subtly philosophic style, Russell Banks (1940—   ) writes stories that range in setting from the West Coast to New England to the Caribbean, and in subject matter from a spoiled rich girl trying to establish her identity through sexual adventure to Simon Bolivar approaching his death. Throughout his work, memory and imagination are the consolation of his characters: memory gives them a past and a sense of order, imagination allows them to shape the formless present and future.

"Searching for Survivors (I)" the title story from his first collection (1975), begins "Poor Henry Hudson, I miss him," which states a serious theme of

Banks's work in an amusing manner. Reed, the narrator, makes broad associations between the historical figure, who surely died at sea when cast adrift by mutineers, and the dazzling Hudson car owned by his friend's father. Reed tries to preserve Hudson by believing that the explorer reached shore safely, and tries to preserve his own youth in the vision of the man with a beautifully kept car. Neither Hudson nor the father is quite what Reed makes them become by means of willful forging of memory and imagination.

The alienation of "Searching for Survivors (II)" from the same collection is much more severe. Reed, having searched the wreckage of a train and found evidence of his brother's death, cannot tell his family members, who live scattered around the country, separated by divorce and divergent adult interests. Thus the memorial service becomes a symbolic funeral for the whole family. Ironically, Reed searches for survivors but refuses to accept the dead he finds in both parts I and II of the story. "The Defenseman"—a recollection of learning to ice skate and a musing on how "the act of remembering is an act of the body"—is another story of the power of memory.

While these stories were written as acts of memory, "The New World," the title story of Banks's second collection (1978), with its self-conscious third-person narrator, explicitly addresses the importance of the creative imagination. The parallel stories of a goldsmith and a prelate in sixteenth-century Jamaica show how each man shapes his destiny and justifies his existence by the exercise of will and imagination. The prelate reiterates, "We choose our destinies," by which he excuses his constant refusal to accept a deterministic view of life even though he fails to achieve his ambitions. He, through a second-rate epic poem, and the goldsmith, through a tale he tells, justify themselves with imaginative accomplishment. The New World of the story represents the emotional wilderness in which one must live self-sustained and "must have fantasies." The Puritan mentioned by the narrator is a metaphor for the stern rationalist who rejects the consolation of imagination. Banks shows that imaginative expression enables human beings to see purpose in their efforts, redemption in their suffering.

•   •   •

Much of the fiction of Paul Bowles (1911—   ) is set in Morocco (where Bowles has spent most of his writing years), some in Mexico or the Caribbean area; even those that take place in the United States have a cold, other-worldly quality. His characters always have to contend with spiritual, and usually physical, isolation. They fit into three categories: foreigners in an alien society, outcasts in their native society, or people going through a transfer of identity. His stories most often take the form of folk tales or of narratives of social conflict. The stylized texture of his writing reflects a bleak world of limitless conflict and loneliness.

Bowles first attracted attention around 1950 because of his surrealistic style, which he said resulted from "abandoning conscious control and writing whatever came from the pen." Exemplifying surrealism, "The Scorpion" tells of an old woman who lives in a cave, barely surviving. She likes her independence, but there is a man who lives in the world ouside whose attention she wants; this parallels her attitude toward society. The climactic event is her dream of swallowing a scorpion, apparently a dream of sex or death or both. "Allal" tells of an abandoned boy who trades spirits with a snake; the outcast child becomes an outcast animal, kills, and is killed.

Although Bowles has written many stark but imaginative folk tales such as these, his reputation has been largely built on stories of brutality and perversion. In "A Distant Episode," a professor studying dialects is captured by the cruelest of Bedouin tribes who rob him, cut out his tongue, and keep him as their slave and clown. He is finally sold but escapes, evidently insane. "The Delicate Prey," also set in Morocco, tells of the mutilation, rape, and killing of a boy by a member of a hostile tribe.

"Pages from Cold Point," which the narrator is self-consciously writing to the reader, created another sensation because of the implied seduction of the narrator by his son. "The Time of Friendship" is a conventional story, thus unusual in the body of Bowles's work. It is a prolonged account of the friendship of a Swiss woman and a Moroccan boy who are separated when she must leave the country and he prepares to go to war against France.

One of Bowles's best stories, "The Garden," tells of the joy a man gets from his garden, and of how his wife, then his neighbors, resent his satisfaction and turn on him. The story is an effective parable of society's intolerance of those who are self-sufficient. Even though they are simplistic, the actions have meaning.

• • •

H. E. Francis (1924—   ) has many stories that are quite traditional, some that are experimental, and others that are mixed in style. They range in setting from Long Island to Alabama to Argentina. The foreign stories tend toward sordid details and brutal action, while those in American settings have a less oppressive atmosphere, but still favor the seamy. The principal feature of his stories, whatever their style or setting, is obsession. Many protagonists are cut off from their parents by choice, circumstance, temperament, or physical distance. They are also alienated from their surroundings. Francis's characters often try to transcend their limits through seeking or suffering, both of which become obsessions. Whether they eradicate themselves by turning outward for fulfillment or inward in intense suffering, they try to escape the middle ground of normal human behavior. They look for peace in extremes, and suicide is a logical and frequent result.

The stories can be grouped according to the protagonists' obsessions. Inward-turning, which usually expresses itself as silent suffering, appears in "The Woman from Jujuy," "Trial," and "Two Lives" (the life of St. John of the Cross). Outward-turning is described in "Two Lives" (the life of an astronaut), "A Chronicle of Love," "Running," and "The Itinerary of Beggars," from the collection of that title (1973). The similarity of these apparently opposite preoccupations is pointedly shown in the parallel narratives of "Two Lives," each man being utterly absorbed in his pursuit and freed from self. Francis's command of tone distinguishes his stories, as their many voices demonstrate.

• • •

Paul Theroux (1941—   ), an expatriate American who spent considerable time in Singapore, among other places, sets most of his stories outside the United States, although his viewpoint character is usually American or British. In such places as San Juan, Bombay, and Singapore, characters confront the natives, and cultural differences are revealing. Sometimes a foreigner reacts to American culture, as in "The Love Knot." A comic story along similar lines is "Yard Sale," which concerns a Peace Corps volunteer returning to Cape Cod after two years in Samoa. He has become holier-than-thou, and criticizes all things American. Although cultural conflicts are usually severe and irreconcilable in the stories of Paul Bowles, they are generally enlightening in Theroux's work. He plays on amusing differences, and the greater the clash, the greater the humor tends to be.

Pointed satire operates in "A Political Romance," in which the main character has married a Czech woman almost as part of his doctoral program. As he loses interest in political developments in Czechoslovakia, his wife loses appeal; but when political events turn, and his specialty is back in demand, his ardor revives. The irony of an intellectual being so obtuse works well. Irony is equally strong in "Sinning with Annie." The narrator, eighty-three, an Indian, and a recent Christian convert, tells of marrying too young to be sexually capable, learning sex with his young wife, and now being resigned to celibacy for religious and physical reasons. Clearly the passion between him and his wife was a high communion and triumph. Despite having given up sex in his old age in word and deed, wholesome desire still burns in his heart.

In a very serious vein, "The Imperial Icehouse" is a parable of colonialism, a fictional analogue to Orwell's "Shooting an Elephant." A newcomer on a

Caribbean island is determined to carry ice to his plantation. He gives his workers beer in town but expects them to travel back home with him. By the end of the story, the laborers have stayed in the bar drinking for so long that the ice has melted and one of them has killed the newcomer. In "The Greenest Island," the characters are a young expatriate and the girl whom he has impregnated. Neither of them wants to marry, so finally facing a decision, they flee to San Juan, decide to return to America and put the child up for adoption, and start over separately. Like many of Theroux's characters, they have tried to escape themselves, but have matured instead.

• • •

The stories of Louis Auchincloss (1917—   ) are comfortable because they are evenly crafted, consistently realistic, and seldom surprising or disturbing. Often, as they deal with legal or social conflict, the characters tend to represent ideas or work out theories about society. The stories take place in New York City or New England.

Typical works in *Second Chance* (1970) are "Second Chance" and "The Sacrifice." The first is told through the point of view of a lawyer representing his sister-in-law in a divorce and observing the resentment of the family toward her husband. In the second, an aging judge, overwhelmed by the violence of his society, develops a nihilistic view of the world. When his grandson is murdered, the judge's despair deepens. In a twist of plot, his wife suffers a mental breakdown, leaving him independent and allowing some recovery from his despair.

Typical of Auchincloss's stories is the conflict between weak men and domineering women, a device that appears often in *The Winthrop Covenant* (1974). The Winthrop family of New England is portrayed as its members embrace and later reject the Puritan ethic. "The Covenant" is so full of exposition and religious debate that the characters are sometimes reduced to vehicles for ideas. Anne Hutchinson fulfills her "compulsion to martyrdom" and is banished. Auchincloss suggests here and elsewhere that people who live by their principles become martyrs to them, while those with weaker conviction live on in complacent hypocrisy. Either way, religion takes its toll. "The Penultimate Puritan" shows that the old order of Puritan New England is utterly gone, as demonstrated by the disintegrated family, divorce, and desertion. Although the modern descendants of the Winthrops have replaced faith in God with self-seeking ("my faith is me"), they still feel some pressure to conform and uphold the false fronts of a weakened society. The recurrent theme is that society has no place for the person of conviction.

• • •

James Alan McPherson (1943—   ) examines alienation of various sorts. The most obvious type is that of the black in white society, but he offers several variations on the problem. His black characters are misfits more because of their specific personality traits than because of their race. On this point, McPherson commendably avoids stereotype.

In *Hue and Cry* (1969), "A Matter of Vocabulary" portrays a boy learning hypocrisy first from black deacons who pocket collection money, then from whites who ignore him and will not speak to him. By the end of the story, the boy is disillusioned with both races. The problem of racial prejudice is pointedly expressed in "On Trains," in which one white woman complains about a black porter sleeping in her Pullman car, while another welcomes the black bartender into her bed. "Gold Coast" and "Of Cabbages and Kings" tell of the struggle of black intellectuals. The narrator in the first story, plagued by his own ambition and the insensitivity of the whites around him, begins to realize that he uses people as much as anyone else does.

The second story depicts the more vivid conflict of a black man trying to maintain his integrity against pressure from other blacks. Claude reverses his envy of whites and starts to speak the cant of black power, full of paranoia and hatred of established white society. Claude's friend Howard sees through the jargon but finally yields to the blind energy of Claude's views. Intellect succumbs to passion. The complexity of Howard's confusion and acquiescence is convincingly drawn. "The Faithful," from *Elbow Room* (1977), also shows a black man caught in social changes he cannot cope with. John Butler, preacher and barber, suffers the shock of having both his preaching and his barbering rejected and he refuses to adapt.

• • •

Because he shares their New York setting and their sense of comic absurdity, Leonard Michaels (1933—   ) can be compared to Grace Paley and Donald Barthelme. Beyond these surface similarities, however, the differences are great. Michaels' stories are usually built around characters and situations that begin in the realm of the believable and proceed to the outrageous, sometimes the surreal. Although not all of his stories are comic, his most distinctive and memorable ones are. The context is often New York, usually the city's Jews whose problems often stem from sexual desire. The style is marked by abrupt, short sentences that hang together with a vitality and logical progression that save his style from being choppy. In fact, they are not unlike the routine of a stand-up comedian, full of related one-liners.

"City Boy," from *Going Places* (1969), illustrates the point. This is one of the most profoundly funny stories in recent years, mainly because every bit of absurdity has believable origins. Beginning with the obvious comic potential of a father discovering his daughter and her boyfriend entangled on the floor at 3:00 a.m., Michaels never relents. First the father stumbles in the dark and steps on the boy's bare buttocks. The boy runs from the apartment nude, panicked, but somewhat encouraged by the thought that this was a real breakthrough with the father, who spoke to him for the first time during the misadventure. He decides to walk down the street on his hands, as if the only response to the situation is absurd bravado. What the boy says and thinks is ridiculous, but no more so than so-called reasonable behavior would be in his desperate circumstances. Several other stories in this volume treat the problems of sex and guilt; some are in the nearly traditional style of "City Boy" ("Crossbones" and "Sticks and Stones"), and others, less effectively, are attempts at surrealism ("Making Changes" and "Mildred").

I Would Have Saved Them If I Could (1975) follows the linear plot form of *Going Places* and the stories present far more believable actions ("Murderers," "Mackerel," and "Reflections of a Wild Kid," for example). The departure from the norm in this collection is not in incident, but in structure. "Eating Out" is a series of very short sketches that deal ironically with ambition, sexual needs, and failure of communication. Similarly, "I Would Have Saved Them If I Could" is a set of sketches that shows examples of suffering and loss. It has the effect of ritual acceptance of death and grief, but the self-mocking tone prevents the story from concluding in a whine. Irony, as used in "Reflections of a Wild Kid," allows characters to focus on the grim without yielding to despair. Michaels uses pity and humor to offer insight.

• • •

Even though his style is simple and his presentation is realistic, Hugh Nissenson (1933—   ) does not become ordinary or dull, because his characters confront interesting moral conflicts, both internal and vis-a-vis each other. Most of the stories of *In the Reign of Peace* (1972) are set in Israel from 1946 to 1970, and good illustrations of his work are "The Throne of Good" and the title story.

In the first, a doctor must choose between protecting a young Zionist who is on an assassination mission, and turning him over to the authorities before he dies of pneumonia. Although he sympathizes with the cause, he objects to both the mission and the official disregard for the boy's life. When the doctor finally decides to turn him in, the boy has fled. The doctor, who is also the narrator, asks, "Can any good come of it?" Free or captured, the boy will inevitably kill or be killed. Death begets death, endlessly.

The turmoil of the second story is religious rather than political. Chaim, a Moroccan laborer, has a strong religious faith, while few members of the Israeli kibbutz on which he works believe in anything and cannot understand why Chaim does. Chaim calls the narrator to see a trapped mouse being eaten alive by ants; to him, this illustrates the agonies that he expects will be alleviated by the coming of the Messiah. Chaim, with his simple but genuine faith that there is ultimate order and justice, serves as a rebuke to the rest who appear to have a purpose but feel no consolation. The contest of divided loyalties and a mixture of hope and despair enrich this collection.

• • •

Only eight of *The Complete Stories* (1971) of Flannery O'Connor (1925—1964) did not appear earlier in her two collections or, in an altered form, within her two novels. Of these eight, "The Partridge Festival" was written and published much later, and "Why Do the Heathen Rage?" was the beginning of a novel, even though it was published as a story. O'Connor clearly did not intend to have the latter appear except as part of the novel; she withdrew the former after submitting it as part of *Everything That Rises Must Converge* (1965), and she made no effort to get the others published in a volume. Therefore one cannot expect her usual compression and brilliance in these works. Still, the character of Old Dudley of "The Geranium" shows signs of what O'Connor was to achieve later, and "The Partridge Festival" contains pleasing, if heavy-handed, irony. Even O'Connor's weaker stories have substance.

• • •

Look How the Fish Live (1975), is a collection of stories about family life and Catholic priests, the traditional subjects of J. F. Powers (1917—   ). Control of narrative distance and incisive use of humor are the consistent strengths of his work. The theme of his stories is conflict, usually over everyday matters, that represent the characters' attitudes toward deeper things. Stories dealing with priests are intensified rather than trivialized by the restrictions of clerical life.

Two stories illustrate how irony is sharpened when it is applied to ethical context. "Bill" details the frustration of a mediocre pastor who drinks too much, spends his time thinking about new furniture, and looks forward to obtaining a curacy. The curate himself is cold and independent, and only exacerbates the pastor's loneliness and sense of failure. "One of Them" reverses the situation; this story is told from the viewpoint of the curate, a convert, who strains to be accepted by his aloof pastor. Although concerned with the church, "Pharisees" is an unusual story for Powers because it is nonrealistic in its use of characters and dialogue. The characters who confront each other in a diner are types who are given the roles of Pharisee, ex-Pharisee, and so on. The ex-Pharisee, a resigned priest-turned-secular humanist, pontificates more ineffectually than the Pharisees of Christ's day. Thus the most dangerous hypocrites are those who claim to have escaped hypocrisy by rejecting the church, but still don't minister to the needs of people.

In general, stories of family life are weaker than the church stories, but "Look How the Fish Live" is a notable exception. In dealing with a fallen baby dove that his children bring him, the father complains of the lack of order in nature, but finally faces his deeper complaint—that death is part of the order of nature. The design that he calls faulty is complete and relentless.

Powers is skillful in raising significant moral questions from small problems and handling his material with such control that it remains fresh and interesting.

• • •

Modesty is a distinguishing feature in the stories of Isaac Bashevis Singer (1909—   ). His stories, written in Yiddish and then translated, seem to treat simple subjects, but they are, in fact, profound. With his unassuming style, he sharpens the edges of the moral conflicts faced by characters trying to be true to themselves and loyal to their community.

Singer frequently writes about struggling writers and about young people wrestling with religious faith and ethnic loyalty. In *A Friend of Kafka and Other Stories* (1970), the title story and "Schloimele" depict the problems of unsuccessful men in Warsaw and New York, respectively. In the first, Jacques Kohn says that he is suffering the same crippling hypersensitivity that his friend Kafka did: "No defect can be hidden from me. That is impotence." Kohn sees fate as his opponent in a long, slow game to the death, but by telling a friend of his past, he preserves his identity. The narrator of the second story, apparently Kohn's friend, now older and in America, hopes to have one of his stories produced as a play by the grand-talking Schloimele. Schloimele, however, only makes promises and disappears, and the narrator realizes, "Schloimele symbolized for me wasted time, my own failure." After many years they do get together, and the narrator sees how old and broken Schloimele has become—until he smiles and talks of his latest hopes. In both of these stories, men save themselves from despair by sheer determination.

"The Crown of Feathers" and "Grandfather and Grandson" illustrate the second type of story in *The Crown of Feathers and Other Stories* (1973). In the first, the favored granddaughter of a wealthy man renounces Judaism and returns to it, but suffers greatly because of her uncertainty. She needs her search, however, even more than the answers she longs for. The story concludes, "Because if there is such a thing as truth, it is as intricate and hidden as a crown of feathers." The second story, set in Warsaw, shows the conflict between a grandfather's spiritual view of the world (Judaism) and his grandson's atheistic approach (Bolshevism). Each is sincere and argues cogently, and neither yields. The boy is killed by the Russians, thus demonstrating that his cause has only temporary remedies for permanent problems. Faith in the eternal and in ultimate justice sustains the grandfather in his grief. The weight of the past and the necessity of choice pervade Singer's stories.

•   •   •

Cynthia Ozick (1928—   ), in *The Pagan Rabbi and Other Stories,* (1971) and *Bloodshed and Three Novellas,* (1976), writes with particular strength about Jews facing religious and social conflicts. In this regard her stories resemble those of Singer. Ozick's style is not so deliberately simple, but her concern with Jews who cannot wholly accept the faith (the "pagan rabbi" who hangs himself) or wholly reject it (the skeptic in "Bloodshed" who visits a remote Hasidic community) reminds the reader of Singer. In "Envy," part of her first collection, she even has a Singer-like character, who writes in Yiddish and has had great success with translations of his work. The viewpoint character, full of valid objections to and blind envy of the successful writer, is an artful mixture of frustrated failure and truth-teller. The story comments on the fragility of worthy literature and the mindless fads that exalt the ordinary and subdue the excellent. All of Ozick's stories have a ponderous tone—a virtually unrelieved seriousness—as she presents grim and convincing accounts of people suffering the trials of faith, doubt, and art.

•   •   •

The three volumes of Frederick Busch (1941—   ) display progressive development in compression of narrative, effectiveness of characterization, and resonance of theme. An acute fear of death pervades the stories. Anxiety comes from facing death itself or from facing the next thing to it—hopeless isolation. The family, both an emotional and biological means of combatting death, figures prominently, with characters' hopes directly related to their families, or how to manage without one.

The title story of *Breathing Trouble* (1973), although uneven, is the best of the volume. A man who is obese, divorced, and anxiety-ridden has "breathing trouble," the story's metaphor. His illness, plus that of an orphaned asthmatic boy, represents (and largely stems from) his fear of loneliness and death. The boy is more a symbol than a character, and the narrative is needlessly obscure. Other stories in the collection depict more characters isolated by divorce and death.

Domestic Particulars (1976) follows the life of one family from 1919 to 1976, with Claire Miller and her son Harry as focal characters. The author's clear purpose is to show the pain of alienation within the family. In "The Goal of Life Is Death," Harry Miller recovers from a heart attack and subsequently muses on the meaning of his life. He speaks of himself as the "child who fled because families are—write it down, it's a definition—what you finally have to leave." He has left his parents so that he can start a family of his own. Harry recalls holding his own infant son and laments the passing of his child's youth just as his parents lamented the passing of his. He encounters the cycle of life and death from its very center, the family.

In dealing with a community instead of one family, *Hardwater Country* (1979) also regards death, but on a broader scale. The stories tell of families or of characters without families. In "Widow Water," a plumber, the man who can handle the mysterious life force of water, shows how people face helplessness, whether it is the result of well problems or deeper fears. The death image in "What You Might As Well Call Love" is not in the failure of wells, but in ceaseless rain. The specific threat of a flooded basement represents those forces people cannot control, such as death itself. Through the use of mundane images, this collection presents a vivid panorama of people resisting death.

• • •

In recent years, writers rejecting the middle way of traditional fiction have chosen obscurity, taking the risk of baffling the reader in the hope that they can surprise and delight. Raymond Carver (1938—   ), however, has elected instead to use utter simplicity. Typical are "They're Not Your Husband," "The Fling," and "Will You Please Be Quiet, Please?," the title story from his first collection (1976). Like most of Carver's fiction, they tell of a contest with loneliness. In "Will You Please Be Quiet, Please?," the husband, finally getting up his nerve, asks his wife if she had committed adultery two years before. She confesses; he hits her and leaves. When he returns home the next morning, she tries to talk, but he refuses to listen. She offers her body instead of words, and in spite of himself, he responds. The story seems to say that the physical man can overpower, and sometimes reconcile, the rational man, but it has too little detail and the dialogue is unrevealing.

Carver can round out his stories, as seen in "Bicycles, Muscles, Cigarettes" and "Distance." The first is sketchy but still vivid in such details as the smell of nicotine, which carries the hint of mortality for the protagonist. The narrative persona of "Distance" gives perspective on events, as a father tells his grown daughter about a day before he and her mother were divorced. In the particulars of the young couple's argument and reconciliation, the sweetness of that time is revived: "They danced, and then they held to each other as if there would always be that morning."

• • •

Daniel Curley (1918—   ) is a good example of the writer who is both traditional and experimental. Stories in Curley's first two volumes are traditional, while in the third book there is a mixture. The benchmark of his work is a sense of loss, whether it is disillusionment, aging, or death. Although some of his stories are thoroughly bleak, most have a steady current of humor that makes grave losses bearable and trivial ones interesting.

"Saccovanzetti," from *That Marriage Bed of Procrustes* (1957), uses a boys' game as a means to contemplate death. Mickey is repeatedly made to play the victim. Feeling the injustice of this, he knows that if he is ever to be one of the game's survivors, he will have to "outwit and outshoot those who could not be outwitted and outshot." Sacco and Vanzetti will be executed that night, and Mickey, the story's metaphor for mortal man, must accept the role he has been assigned. (He does avenge himself on his brother by talking of throwing the switch on the electric chair, then flushing the toilet on which his brother sits).

Characters face death in more serious terms in "The Night of the Two Wakes." Students working in a restaurant go first to a wake for the dishwasher's mother and then to one for a fellow worker who drowned. At both they try to show appropriate respect; still there is a limit to how well they can either fathom death or sustain adult behavior. "That Marriage Bed of Procrustes" tells of the pain of maturity besetting George and Alice Fuller. They agree that their life together is "no use," and George says, referring to the loss of innocence, "I have never since entered a mystery that didn't disappoint me."

The losses faced in middle age are the focus of "Where You Wouldn't Want to Walk" from *In the Hands of Our Enemies* (1970). While walking in the woods with a young woman, the narrator falls and suffers a slipped disc, which is symbolic of physical as well as imaginative limits. The story ends with the narrator frustrated and isolated. In terms explicitly reminiscent of Dostoyevsky, "A Story of Love, Etc." shows life as an inevitable compromise. A mixture of first-person and third-person narration describes a woman who prostitutes herself, with the knowledge of her husband, as a means of surviving the Depression. The narrator links compromise and redemption when he compares the woman to Sonia Marmeladov of *Crime and Punishment,* who "is also Jesus Christ crucified and saving the world."

Most of the stories in *Love in the Winter* (1976) are experimental, the later ones especially difficult to understand because of disjointed narrative. "What Rough Beast?" is an exception, since the vague description of the beast heightens the suspense and underlines the main character's need to be able to see and identify mortal danger.

"Who, What, When, Where—Why?" is pure metafiction. It is a writer telling a story about telling a story, and it exhibits a vividness and narrative drive that most metafiction lacks. The narrator is irresistibly candid and funny, and he establishes an effective fictional world despite his claim that it is real. Even though this account of a drunken night in Birmingham, Alabama, has an inconclusive ending, the story is effective as a device for seeking the truth of experience. The title story, also written with vivid and amusing turns of phrase, tells of a middle-aged college professor who finds himself unable to commit adultery as he set out to do. The story ends with him grieving over his lost nerve and lost youth. Curley writes with humor and variety on the subject of loss.

• • •

The stories of Andre Dubus (1936—   ), both in *Separate Flights* (1975) and in *Adultery and Other Choices* (1977), tend to deal with marital conflicts or youthful initiation experiences. Although Dubus has written good stories on other subjects, his most characteristic stories are in these two areas. The title story of each collection is a detailed treatment of an atrophied marriage from the viewpoint of the frustrated wife; in the first, she yields to futility, while in the second, she grows beyond her self-centered husband and decides to divorce him. In both, Dubus deftly portrays mixed feelings and divided loyalties.

The initiation stories dwell on the fears, guilt, and ambition of Paul Clement, a Catholic boy who goes to parochial school in Louisiana. He suffers with sexual desires and a test of his faith ("If They Knew Yvonne"); faces conflict with his father and gains a deepened understanding of him to the point that he defends his father's right to upbraid his foolishness ("Contrition"); and endures Marine Corps boot camp to win his own respect as well as his father's ("Cadence").

• • •

Many of the stories of Philip F. O'Connor (1932—   ) deal with insanity or pathologic despair, such as "Donovan, the Cat Man" and "Mastodon's Box" in *Old Morals, Small Continents, Darker Times* (1971), and "The Escape Artist" and "The Pony Track" in *A Season for Unnatural Causes* (1975)). The alienated characters in these stories tend to identify themselves in terms of the society as a whole. The reader sees much of what is wrong with these people but sees little of the people themselves: the author describes the disorders, not their victims.

O'Connor's best work is in a familial or ethnic context. His stories of family conflict have the vividness of intimate struggle; those of extreme alienation have flat language, drab settings, and predictably bleak endings. Both achieve memorable characterization. From the first collection, "The Gift Bearer" and "My Imaginary Father" are about the fights in an Irish family between a drinking father and a harsh mother, as seen by their son. "Story Hour" is told from the viewpoint of a similarly vulnerable boy who indirectly witnesses the suicide of a priest who had been a chaplain in the war and supposedly a wounded hero. The wound was psychological, and the faith the priest has exemplified is not strong enough to save him. The tension in such stories gives substance to character and theme.

The stories in the second collection tell predominantly of utter alienation. A notable and strong exception is "The Disciple," in which a Catholic boy struggles with the temptations of the flesh within a well-drawn religious framework. Others, such as "Other Lives" and "The Thumb," focus on alienation more than on an alienated human being. The stories are experimental in their use of disjointed narrative.

• • •

Grace Paley (1922—   ) had a reputation for manipulating language and structure for effect well before 1960. Thus the experimental surface of the stories in *Enormous Changes at the Last Minute* (1974) was nothing new to her readers. The style is terse, establishing a rhythm suitable to the New York City setting of her stories. The language combines humor and tension, especially in "Wants," "Debts," and "Enormous Changes at the Last Minute," in which principal characters are alienated from their families.

Paley relies on word play and tone to create atmosphere, and largely ignores physical details. In "Wants," the first-person narrator feels dislocated and lost in time as she realizes that her hopes have not matured along with the trees of the city. She complains, ". . . I don't understand how time passes," and does not know where her life has gone. Paley places more faith in the power of tropes than in realistic details. The narrator describes her former husband, not by physical features, but by an image: "He had had a habit throughout the twenty-seven years of making a narrow remark which, like a plumber's snake, could work its way through the ear down the throat halfway to my heart."

Repeatedly, time brings losses, and only language gives time's victims a means to clarify and preserve experience. The narrator of "Debts," a writer, says of her subjects that she wants "to tell their stories . . . to save a few lives." By telling a story within her story and distorting reality to her purposes, she implies that every story is worth telling, regardless of how many facts may have to be made up. The result is a theoretical comment about fiction rather than vivid characterization.

Alexandra, of "Enormous Changes at the Last Minute," is caught between the past and present. The opposing poles are represented by her father (old sense: speaking from his hospital bed, telling her that she is killing him) and by Dennis (new frenzy: hippie, rock musician, free-lover). She sees the folly of Dennis and his notion that his generation is revolutionary beyond all others, but she also understands the worth of his energy, humor, and vitality. The story runs the risk of being a trite tale of the liberated woman, and the song motif, which is contrived, emphasizes its weakness.

· · ·

In his fiction, Richard Stern (1928—   ) uses humor to strip human experience to the bare bones of despair, then fleshes out the figure again. His insight arrests, enlightens, and grudgingly consoles. His narrators and characters often say what many people have felt but could not say, because the perception to grasp difficult problems and the courage to describe them seldom come at the same time. The combination of keen sight and candid telling creates epiphanies that burst forth in short declarative sentences.

One story from each collection will illustrate Stern's technique. As the title suggests, *1968* (1970) examines American society by telling the stories of various people during the turbulent year. In many ways, Holleb of "Ins and Outs" is Stern's representative man, whose accomplishment never matches his vision. This vision is a handicap because it reduces him to Prufrock's despair, seeing but not acting. The story begins with an exceptionally funny scene devoted to Holleb's respiratory problems, which symbolize his overwhelming petty concerns. He summarizes his life: "Marriage: over. Son: miserable. Apartment: in bad shape. Work: third-rate. Books: unwritten. Victimizer: uncaught." His despair deepens when a black man beats him solely because he is white. He finally sympathizes with the frustration of his attacker, but decides to press charges in court if the man is caught, because seeing things through is necessary in a life that is already compromising. Thus, having experienced both personal and impersonal grief and still survived, he presses on.

Turning from society in general to the family in particular, the title story from *Packages* (1980) treats death with determined irreverence. In this story, as well as the others in the collection, Stern's characters are cut off from each other. The narrator of "Packages" spares no one: the undertaker—"Campbell's is a wonderful funeral factory"; his deceased mother—"My mother was not my type." A mixture of grief and bitterness churns through the story, implying that if the narrator did admit how much he loved his mother, he could not face the sorrow. He carries around a package containing his mother's ashes and tries to escape her by throwing it into a garbage truck. But he cannot shed his grief, and his inability to numb himself is the hope with which the story ends. Stern razes and rebuilds, starting stories in confusion, ending them in clarity.

· · ·

Like most recent serious writers, Barry Targan (1932—   ) has written at length of death and alienation; but unlike most, he offers redemption. In a world that presumably knows better than to hope for heroes, Targan writes stories with subtle, vivid heroes. His people fight—each other sometimes, but more often their own fears and limitations. Sometimes they only win their self-respect. More often, however, they jar and invigorate others with their battles.

Not all of Targan's stories have heroes, and some that do sink into sentimentality. In *Harry Belton and the Mendelssohn Violin Concerto* (1975), the stories without heroes tend to be flat and forgettable, like "Leaving" and "Leave My Mother Alone." In "The Clay Wars" and "And Their Fathers Who Begat Them," the concluding heroism is pure and pronounced, rather like that found in children's tales. These lapses, however, do not negate the force that is usually under control in his work: determination to sketch scenes of discovery for people who matter to the reader.

The art of Targan's stories is his controlled treatment of sentimental material, a risk few contemporary writers are willing to take. The main character of "Harry Belton and the Mendelssohn Violin Concerto" is a mediocre amateur violinist determined to perform in a concert hall. Considering the expense, hard work, and probable embarrassment, everyone discourages him; but he performs, makes mistakes, recovers admirably, and even plays an encore. Even though it is a clear, conventional narrative like the rest of Targan's stories, "Elizabeth Lanier" develops one of the strangest and most intriguing plots in recent fiction. The narrator finds himself about to be seduced by the beautiful Elizabeth Lanier, then beaten by her brother as his friends have been. Surely there is no more clearly defined approach-avoidance situation in any psychology book. He accepts Elizabeth's offer, then faces her brother and beats him. Simple enough, but the boy tells truths that are seldom spoken these days: "Dread is the worst of punishments," and at the end of the story, "Only this I know, there *is* victory and defeat. . . . For to have once won enormously and well is searing, a hot kindling of light, an illumination ever after as though you have no choice any more to ever lose or lie dark again."

Targan also creates heroes who do not win, but they still have their reward. "In Excelsis Deo" and "Kingdoms," from *Surviving Adverse Seasons* (1979), both have main characters who discover the cruelty of death and become obsessed with it. The stories present a bleak view of the human condition, but Targan never yields to the glib cynicism that often marks Beattie and Barthelme. Instead, the two men who are eager for answers, no matter what the price, learn to live with disillusionment and acceptance of pain. A widowed father tells his son, "The gods are not just. But they are *right*."

• • •

Like all of the stories of Peter Taylor (1917—   ) those in *In the Miro District and Other Stories* (1977) are rich in nuance. He depicts his world in a clear narrative voice and with revealing details, so that every statement and gesture carries more than surface meaning.

Four of these stories are in verse, particularly appropriate in "The Instruction of a Mistress," which consists of journal entries by a poet and a letter by the woman he discarded. The stories are most often set in Nashville, some quite vividly in the period from 1900 to the Depression; their milieu is one in which decorum is not a petty matter but a worthy concern of self-disciplined people. The importance of familial relations and social responsibility is especially pronounced.

In "The Captain's Son," the title character tries to expiate the failure of his father, only to fall prey, as if by biblical prophecy, to the same weaknesses. "The Hand of Emmagene," another verse story, tells of a country girl in the city who misinterprets the demands of her hostess and destroys herself. On the simplest level, "In the Miro District" is the story of a generation gap; deeper, it shows how a rift between a grandson and grandfather makes the old Civil War veteran see his own emptiness, despair of maintaining integrity, and yield to the superficial role his society wants him to play. With elegant language, Taylor's stories dwell on the difficulty of balancing inner needs and outer duties.

• • •

With the exceptions of *Bech: A Book* (1970), and *Museums and Women and Other Stories* (1972), the post-1969 collections of John Updike (1932—   ) focus primarily on married life and the related affairs, separations, and divorces that often attend marriage in modern America. In isolation, older stories such as "Pigeon Feathers," "A. & P.," and "In Football Season" are impressive, but as a body of work, his Maples stories and the many others dealing with varying stages of romantic harmony and discord are especially fine. Updike details the agony, humor, and regret of people trying to disengage unreasoning links of love and resentment, showing emotional turmoil so vividly that the worth of his characters magnifies as their confusion grows. With exact description and dialogue, he subjects his characters to pain and then makes it tolerable with humor and eloquence.

The main character of *Bech: A Book* is Henry Bech, a novelist who succeeded with his first novel, wrote quite poorly thereafter, and finally is faced with growing fame (belated, and now undeserved) and a writer's block. *Bech* and *Too Far to Go* (1979) have been called novels, and with some cause, but the stories in both stand alone well. The former, which has been widely and justly applauded, looks more at the relationship of the artist to society than at broader human experience.

Aside from the essays and experimental pieces in *Museums and Women,* most of the stories anticipate the style Updike uses in later collections. Early in "Museums and Women" the first-person narrator says of the mother—and, by extension, of all women—"Who she was was a mystery so deep it never formed into a question." And so the story continues: for all that they can be perceived and sensed, museums and women raise more questions than they answer. "When Everyone Was Pregnant" centers on the ripeness of young parenthood and on the excesses of guiltless youth in the 1950s. The first-person narrator explains that people then "Viewed the world through two lenses since discarded: fear and gratitude." Both bespeak a humility lost in the America of the 1970s. Trying to decide why that era, when all of their friends and he and his wife were having their children, is so precious in his memory, the narrator reflects on Shakespeare's "Ripeness is all" and decides that it means, "Ripeness is God." Finally he faces the lessons of youth, mutability, and death that have passed before him: "The decades slide seaward, taking us along. I am still afraid. Still grateful."

As the above passages suggest, John Updike is a master of the elegant phrase in contemporary American short fiction. He is also considerably more: a master of the substance of short stories who can employ imagery, humor, and dialogue to rivet and delight his reader. Perhaps the most vivid illustration of this appears in "Domestic Life in America" from *Problems and Other Stories* (1979). Symbolizing his failed efforts to sustain his recently dissolved marriage, the main character visits the house that used to be his and replaces "several of the stones of the little retaining wall he had built here in hopes of giving an amorphous area order." His marriage was his retaining wall. Humor mixes with grief as he recalls how his dog wagged her tail while he measured her for a grave before putting her to sleep. Self-mockery holds back sentimentalism as he recalls the dog's burial: "It appeared to him through his absurd, excessive tears that he was burying a dozen golden summers, his children's childhood and his own blameless prime." Updike's dialogue sharpens the rough edges smoothed by humor when his daughter accuses, "If you want to be so useful why don't you live with us?" Updike's dialogue sometimes overwhelms the reader with abruptly stated truths. "Problems" deals further with the complications of divorce, but in the format of mathematical word problems: "During the night, A, though sleeping with B, dreams of C," and later, "A's psychiatrist thinks he is experiencing growth. . . . However, by Tristan's Law appealingness is inversely proportional to attainability." The tone achieved is a blend of humor and

frustration. With inventive wit, Updike states qualitative problems in quantitative terms to show that reason is useless in matters of the heart.

As a whole piece, *Too Far to Go* (1979) is Updike's finest collection, and if one
values thought and feeling in literature, it must be one of the best since World
War II.

"Wife-wooing" displays bursts of poetic language, such as, "Seven years
since I wed wide warm woman, white-thighed. Wooed and wed. Wife. A knife
of a word that for all its final bite did not end the wooing. To my wonderment."
Of course, the alliteration here is heavy, even a parody; but beneath the arch
surface, the words are expressive. Trying to talk himself out of his enduring love
for his wife, the narrator later watches morning light as it "drains the goodness
from your thickness. . . . I feast with the coffee on your drabness," a blunt
counterpoint to the earlier passage. To his surprise and joy, a day of fault-finding
is undone that night "with a kiss of toothpaste to me moist and girlish and
quick; the momentous moral of this story being, An unexpected gift is not
worth giving." Intervening stories describe passionate married love and infidelities, as Richard and Joan Maples pull reluctantly apart and uncertainly back
together. "Gesturing" follows the separation of the couple, and the focal image
of the story is a movement of Joan's as she "tentatively, soundlessly, tapped the
fingers of one hand into the palm of the other, a gesture between a child's clap of
glee and an adult's signal for attention, 'I've decided to kick you out.'" The end
of the story reveals what living separately and having other lovers has taught
them: "that these lovers, however we love them, are not us, are not sacred as
reality is sacred. We are reality. We have made children. We gave each other our
young bodies. We promised to grow old together." In the stories of John
Updike great eloquence kindles simple warmth.

• • •

As America in the 1960s and 1970s changed faster and with less unity of purpose
than in the previous decades, so did the short story. The experimental theorists,
questioning the adequacy of old forms to describe a radically new world, jarred
traditional writers into a more self-conscious pursuit of their art. Conversely,
the traditional writers questioned the worth of what experimentalists had
produced when their declarations of theory were finished. The conflict
stimulated the members of both camps; and finally, most writers, finding their
own way and working out their own ideas and styles, took whatever suited
them from both approaches. By 1980, the tug of war in short fiction had
reached somewhat of an equipoise in which neither radicalism nor conser-

vatism was the crucial feature of a story. Regardless of how a writer achieved it, resonance of thought and feeling was still paramount.

James C. Robison

Belmont College

Selected Bibliography of American
Short Story Collections:
1945—1980

Abel, Robert. *Skin and Bones.* Fort Collins: Colorado State University Press, 1979.

Abish, Walter. *Minds Meet.* New York: New Directions, 1975.

Adams, Alice. *Beautiful Girl.* New York: Knopf, 1978.

Adler, Warren. *The Sunset Gang.* New York: Viking, 1977.

Algren, Nelson. *The Last Carousel.* New York: Putnam, 1973.

————. *Neon Wilderness.* Garden City, N.Y.: Doubleday, 1947.

Allen, Woody. *Side Effects.* New York: Random House, 1980.

Apple, Max. *The Oranging of America and Other Stories.* New York: Viking, 1976.

Auchincloss, Louis, *The Injustice Collectors.* Boston: Houghton Mifflin, 1950.

————. *The Partners.* Boston: Houghton Mifflin, 1974.

————. *Powers of Attorney.* Boston: Houghton Mifflin, 1963.

————. *The Romantic Egoists: A Reflection in Eight Minutes.* Boston: Houghton Mifflin, 1954.

————. *Second Chance: Tales of Two Generations.* Boston: Houghton Mifflin, 1970.

————. *Tales of Manhattan.* Boston: Houghton Mifflin, 1967.

————. *The Winthrop Covenant.* Boston: Houghton Mifflin, 1976.

Baker, Carlos. *The Talismans and Other Stories.* New York: Scribner's, 1976.

Baldwin, James. *Going to Meet the Man.* New York: Dial, 1965.

Ballard, James. *Rolling All the Time.* Urbana: University of Illinois Press, 1976.

Bambara, Toni Cade. *The Sea Birds Are Still Alive: Collected Stories.* New York: Random House, 1977.

Banks, Russell. *The New World.* Urbana: University of Illinois Press, 1978.

————. *Searching for Survivors.* Brooklyn, N.Y.: Fiction Collective, 1975.

Barth, John. *Lost In the Funhouse: Fiction for Print, Tape, Live Voice.* Garden City, N.Y.: Doubleday, 1968.

Barthelme, Donald. *Amateurs.* New York: Farrar, Straus & Giroux, 1976.

————. *City Life.* New York: Farrar, Straus & Giroux, 1970.

————. *Come Back, Dr. Caligari.* Boston: Little, Brown, 1964.

————. *Great Days.* New York: Farrar, Straus & Giroux, 1979.

————. *Guilty Pleasures.* New York: Farrar, Straus & Giroux, 1974.

————. *Sadness.* New York: Farrar, Straus & Giroux, 1972.

————. *Unspeakable Practices, Unnatural Acts.* New York: Farrar, Straus & Giroux, 1968.

Baumbach, Jonathan. *The Return of Service.* Urbana: University of Illinois Press, 1979.

Beck, Warren. *The Blue Sash, and Other Stories.* Yellow Springs, Ohio: Antioch Press, 1941.

————. *The Far Whistle, and Other Stories.* Yellow Springs, Ohio: Antioch Press, 1951.

————. *The First Fish, and Other Stories.* Yellow Springs, Ohio: Antioch Press, 1951.

————. *The Rest Is Silence, and Other Stories.* Denver: Swallow, 1963.

Bellow, Saul. *Mosby's Memoirs, and Other Stories.* New York: Viking, 1968.

————. *Seize The Day: With Three Short Stories and A One-Act Play.* New York: Viking, 1956.

Betts, Doris. *The Astronomer and Other Stories.* New York: Harper, 1965.

————. *Beasts of the Southern Wild and Other Stories.* New York: Harper, 1973.

————. *The Gentle Insurrection and Other Stories.* New York: Putnam, 1954.

Bingham, Sallie. *The Touching Hand and Six Short Stories.* Boston: Houghton Mifflin, 1967.

————. *The Way it Is Now: Stories.* New York: Viking, 1972.

Bovey, John. *Desirable Aliens.* Urbana: University of Illinois Press, 1980.

Bowles, Jane. *The Collected Works of Jane Bowles.* New York: Farrar, Straus & Giroux, 1966.

————. *My Sister's Hand in Mine.* New York: Ecco, 1978.

Bowles, Paul. *Collected Stories 1939—1976.* Santa Barbara: Black Sparrow, 1980.

————. *The Delicate Prey and Other Stories.* New York: Random House, 1950.

————. *A Hundred Camels in the Courtyard.* San Francisco: City Lights, 1962.

————. *Let it Come Down.* New York: Random House, 1952.

————. *Things Gone and Things Still Here.* Santa Barbara: Black Sparrow, 1977.

————. *Three Tales.* New York: F. Hallman, 1975.

————. *The Time of Friendship: A Volume of Short Stories.* New York: Holt, 1967.

Boyle, Kay. *The Crazy Hunter: Three Short Novels.* New York: Harcourt, 1940.

————. *Fifty Stories.* New York: Doubleday, 1980.

————. *The Smoking Mountain: Stories of Postwar Germany.* New York: McGraw-Hill, 1951.

————. *Thirty Stories.* New York: Simon & Schuster, 1946.

Boyle, T. Coraghessan. *Descent of Man.* Boston: Little, Brown, 1979.

Bradbury, Ray. *Dark Carnival.* Sauk City, Wis.: Arkham House, 1947.

————. *Fahrenheit 451.* New York: Simon & Schuster, 1967.

————. *The Golden Apples of the Sun.* Garden City, N.Y.: Doubleday, 1953.

————. *I Sing the Body Electric! Stories.* New York: Knopf, 1969.

————. *The Illustrated Man.* Garden City, N.Y.: Doubleday, 1951.

————. *Long after Midnight.* New York: Knopf, 1976.

————. *The Machineries of Joy: Short Stories.* New York: Simon & Schuster, 1964.

————. *The Martian Chronicles.* Garden City, N.Y.: Doubleday, 1958.

————. *A Medicine for Melancholy.* Garden City, N.Y.: Doubleday, 1959.

————. *The October Country.* New York: Ballantine, 1955.

————. *R Is for Rocket.* Garden City, N.Y.: Doubleday, 1962.

————. *S Is for Space.* Garden City, N.Y.: Doubleday, 1966.

————. *The Stories of Ray Bradbury.* New York: Knopf, 1980.

————. *Twice Twenty-Two; The Golden Apples of the Sun; A Medicine for Melancholy.* Garden City, N.Y.: Doubleday, 1966.

————. *The Vintage Bradbury: Ray Bradbury's Own Selection of His Best Stories.* New York: Vintage, 1965.

Brodkey, Harold. *First Love and Other Sorrows.* New York: Dial, 1958.

Bromell, Henry. *I Know Your Heart, Marco Polo.* New York: Knopf, 1979.

————. *The Slightest Distance.* Boston: Houghton Mifflin, 1974.

Brophy, Brigid. *The Adventures of God in His Search for the Black Girl.* Boston: Little, Brown, 1974.

Brown, Rosellen, *Street Games.* New York: Doubleday, 1974.

Buck, Pearl S. *The Woman Who Was Changed and Other Stories.* New York: Crowell, 1979.

Bullins, Ed. *The Hungered One.* New York: Morrow, 1971.

Busch, Frederick. *Breathing Trouble.* London: Calder & Boyers, 1973.

————. *Domestic Particulars: A Family Chronicle.* New York: New Directions, 1976.

————. *Hardwater Country.* New York: Knopf, 1979.

Calisher, Hortense. *The Collected Stories of Hortense Calisher.* New York: Arbor House, 1975.

————. *Extreme Magic: A Novella, and Other Stories.* Boston: Little, Brown, 1964.

————. *In the Absence of Angels: Stories.* Boston: Little, Brown, 1964.

————. *Tale for the Mirror: A Novella and Other Stories.* Boston: Little, Brown, 1962.

Canzoneri, Robert. *Barbed Wire and Other Stories.* New York: Dial, 1970.

Capote, Truman. *Breakfast at Tiffany's: A Short Novel and Three Stories* New York: Random House, 1958.

————. *Music for Chameleons.* New York: Random House, 1980.

————. *A Tree of Night and Other Stories.* New York: Random House, 1949.

Carr, Pat. *The Women in the Mirror.* Iowa City: University of Iowa Press, 1977.

Carver, Raymond. *Furious Seasons.* Santa Barbara: Capra Press, 1977.

————. *Will You Please Be Quiet, Please?.* New York: McGraw-Hill, 1976.

Cassill, R. V. *The Father and Other Stories.* New York: Simon & Schuster, 1965.

————. *The Happy Marriage and Other Stories.* West Lafayette, Ind.: Purdue University Press, 1956.

Cheever, John. *The Brigadier and the Golf Widow.* New York: Harper & Row, 1964.

————. *The Enormous Radio and Other Stories.* New York: Funk & Wagnalls, 1953.

————. *The Housebreaker of Shady Hill and Other Stories.* New York: Harper, 1958.

————. *Some People, Places, and Things that Will Not Appear in My Next Novel.* New York: Harper, 1961.

————. *The Stories of John Cheever.* New York: Knopf, 1978.

————. *The Way Some People Live: A Book of Stories.* New York: Random House, 1943.

————. *The World of Apples.* New York: Knopf, 1973.

Chesnutt, Charles W. *The Wife of His Youth and Other Stories.* Ann Arbor: University of Michigan Press, 1968.
Clark, Eleanor. *Dr. Heart: A Novella and Other Stories.* New York: Pantheon, 1974.
Clark, Walter Van Tilburg. *The Watchful Gods and Other Stories.* New York: Random House, 1950.
Clayton, John Bell. *The Strangers Were There: Selected Stories.* New York: Macmillan, 1957.
Clearman, Mary. *Lambing Out.* Columbia: University of Missouri Press, 1977.
Coates, Robert M. *All the Year Round.* New York: Harcourt Brace, 1943.
———. *Hour After Westerly and Other Stories.* New York: Harcourt Brace, 1957.
———. *The Man Just Ahead of You.* New York: Sloane, 1964.
Collier, John. *Fancies and Goodnights.* Garden City, N.Y.: Doubleday, 1951.
———. *The John Collier Reader.* New York: Knopf, 1972.
Colter, Cyrus. *The Beach Umbrella.* Iowa City: University of Iowa Press, 1970.
Colwin, Laurie. *Passion and Affect.* New York: Viking, 1974.
Connell, Evan S. *The Anatomy Lesson and Other Stories.* New York: Viking, 1957.
———. *At the Crossroads: Stories.* New York: Simon & Schuster, 1965.
———. *Saint Augustine's Pigeon.* Berkeley, Calif.: North Point Press, 1980.
Coover, Robert. *Pricksongs and Descants.* New York: Dutton, 1969.
Corrington, John William. *The Actes and Monuments.* Urbana: University of Illinois Press, 1978.
———. *The Lonesome Traveler.* New York: Putnam's, 1968.
Costello, Mark. *The Murphy Stories.* Urbana: University of Illinois Press, 1973.
Cullinan, Elizabeth. *The Time of Adam.* New York: Houghton Mifflin, 1971.
———. *Yellow Roses.* New York: Viking, 1977.
Curley, Daniel. *In the Hands of Our Enemies.* Urbana: University of Illinois Press, 1970.
———. *Love in the Winter.* Urbana: University of Illinois Press, 1976.
———. *That Marriage Bed of Procrustes.* Boston: Beacon, 1957.
Davenport, Guy. *Da Vinci's Bicycle: Ten Stories.* Baltimore: Johns Hopkins University Press, 1979.
———. *Tatlin! Six Stories.* New York: Scribner's, 1974.
Davis, Olivia. *The Scent of Apples.* Boston: Houghton Mifflin, 1972.
Dawkins, Cecil. *The Quiet Enemy.* New York: Atheneum, 1963.
Dawson, Fielding. *The Man Who Changed Overnight and Other Stories and Dreams.* Santa Barbara: Black Sparrow, 1976.
Dixon, Stephen. *14 Stories.* Baltimore: Johns Hopkins University Press, 1980.
Dubus, Andre. *Adultery and Other Choices.* Boston: Godine, 1977.
———. *Finding a Girl in America: Ten Stories and a Novella.* Boston: Godine, 1980.
———. *Separate Flights.* Boston: Godine, 1975.
Dumas, Henry. *Ark of Bones and Other Stories.* New York: Random House, 1974.
———. *Rope of Wind and Other Stories.* New York: Random House, 1979.
Dubek, Stuart. *Childhood and Other Neighborhoods.* New York: Viking, 1980.
Elkin, Stanley. *Criers and Kibitzers, Kibitzers and Criers.* New York: Random House, 1966.

————. *The Living End.* New York: Dutton, 1979.

————. *Searches and Seizures.* New York: Random House, 1973.

————. *Stanley Elkin's Greatest Hits.* New York: Dutton, 1980.

Elliott, George P. *Among the Dangs: Ten Short Stories.* New York: Holt, 1961.

————. *An Hour of Last Things and Other Stories.* New York: Harper & Row, 1968.

Enright, Elizabeth. *Borrowed Summer and Other Stories.* New York: Rinehart, 1946.

————. *Doublefields: Memories and Stories.* New York: Harcourt Brace, 1966.

————. *The Moment Before the Rain.* New York: Harcourt Brace, 1955.

————. *The Riddle of the Fly and Other Stories.* New York: Harcourt Brace, 1959.

Epstein, Leslie. *The Steinway Quintet Plus Four.* Boston: Little, Brown, 1976.

Epstein, Seymour. *A Penny for Charity.* Boston: Little, Brown, 1965.

Farrell, James T. *American Dream Girl.* New York: Vanguard, 1950.

————. *Childhood Is Not Forever.* Garden City, N.Y.: Doubleday, 1969.

————. *A Dangerous Woman and Other Stories.* New York: Vanguard, 1957.

————. *French Girls Are Vicious and Other Stories.* New York: Vanguard, 1955.

————. *Further Short Stories.* Garden City, N.Y.: Sun Dial, 1948.

————. *Judith and Other Stories.* Garden City, N.Y.: Doubleday, 1973.

————. *The Life Adventurous and Other Stories.* New York: Vanguard, 1947.

————. *Olive and Mary Anne.* New York: Stonehill, 1977.

————. *Omnibus of Short Stories.* New York: Vanguard, 1956.

————. *Short Stories.* New York: Vanguard, 1951.

Faulkner, William. *The Collected Stories of William Faulkner.* New York: Random House, 1950.

————. *Knight's Gambit.* New York: Random House, 1949.

————. *Uncollected Stories of William Faulkner.* New York: Random House, 1979.

Faust, Irvin. *Roar Lion Roar and Other Stories.* New York: Random House, 1964.

Fetler, Andrew. *To Byzantium.* Urbana: University of Illinois Press, 1976.

Fetler, James. *Impossible Appetites.* Iowa City: University of Iowa Press, 1980.

Fitzgerald, F. Scott. *The Price Was High: The Last Uncollected Stories of F. Scott Fitzgerald.* New York: Harcourt Brace Jovanovich, 1979.

Francis, H. E. *The Itinerary of Beggars.* Iowa City: University of Iowa Press, 1973.

————. *Naming Things.* Urbana: University of Illinois Press, 1980.

Friedman, Bruce Jay. *Black Angels: Stories.* New York: Simon & Schuster, 1966.

————. *Far from the City of Class and Other Stories.* New York: Frommer-Pasmantier, 1963.

Friedman, Paul. *And If Defeated Allege Fraud.* Urbana: University of Illinois Press, 1971.

Gaines, Ernest J. *Bloodlines.* New York: Dial, 1968.

Gallant, Mavis. *From the Fifteenth District.* New York: Random House, 1979.

Gardner, John. *The King's Indian: Stories and Tales.* New York: Knopf, 1974.

Garrett, George P. *Cold Ground Was My Bed Last Night.* Columbia: University of Missouri Press, 1964.

————. *In the Briar Patch: A Book of Stories.* Austin: University of Texas Press, 1961.

————. *King of the Mountain.* New York: Scribner's, 1957.

————. *The Magic Striptease.* Garden City, N.Y.: Doubleday, 1973.

Gass, William H. *In the Heart of the Heart of the Country and Other Stories.* New York: Harper & Row, 1968.

————. *Willie Masters' Lonesome Wife.* New York: Knopf, 1971.

Gellhorn, Martha. *The Honeyed Place: Stories.* Garden City, N. Y.: Doubleday, 1953.

————. *Pretty Tales for Tired People.* New York: Simon & Schuster, 1965.

————. *Two By Two.* New York: Simon & Schuster, 1958.

Gill, Brendan. *Ways Of Loving.* New York: Harcourt Brace Jovanovich, 1974.

Godwin, Gail. *Dream Children.* Knopf: New York, 1976.

Gold, Herbert. *Love and Like.* New York: Dial, 1960.

————. *The Magic Will: Stories and Essays of a Decade.* New York: Random House, 1971.

Goldberg, Gerald Jay. *A Hundred Twenty-Six Days of Continuous Sunshine.* New York: Dial, 1972.

Goldberg, Lester. *One More River.* Urbana: University of Illinois Press, 1977.

Gordon, Caroline. *The Forest of the South.* New York: Scribner's, 1945.

————. *Old Red and Other Stories.* New York: Scribner's, 1963.

Goyen, William. *The Collected Stories of William Goyen.* Garden City, N.Y.: Doubleday, 1975.

————. *The Faces of Blood Kindred: A Novella and Ten Stories.* New York: Random House, 1960.

————. *Ghost and Flesh: Stories and Tales.* New York: Random House, 1952.

————. *Selected Writings of William Goyen: Eight Favorites by a Master American Storyteller.* New York: Random House, 1974.

Grau, Shirley Ann. *The Black Prince and Other Stories.* New York: Knopf, 1954.

————. *The Wind Shifting West.* New York: Knopf, 1973.

Greenberg, Alvin. *The Discovery of America and Other Tales of Terror and Self-Exploration.* Baton Rouge: Louisiana State University Press, 1980.

Greenberg, Joanne. *High Crimes and Misdemeanors.* New York: Holt, Rinehart & Winston, 1980.

————. *Rites of Passage.* New York: Holt, Rinehart & Winston, 1972.

Hale, Nancy. *Between the Dark and the Daylight.* New York: Scribner's, 1943.

————. *The Empress's Ring.* New York: Scribner's, 1955.

————. *The Pattern of Perfection: Thirteen Stories.* Boston: Little, Brown, 1960.

Hall, James B. *Fifteen by Three.* New York: New Directions, 1957.

————. *The Short Hall: New and Selected Stories.* Denver: Stonehenge Books, 1980.

————. *Us He Devours.* New York: New Directions, 1964.

Hannah, Barry. *Airships.* New York: Knopf, 1978.

Harnack, Curtis. *Under My Wings Everything Prospers.* New York: Doubleday, 1977.

Harrison, William. *Roller Ball Murder.* New York: Morrow, 1974.

Hawkes, John. *Lunar Landscapes.* New York: New Directions, 1969.

Hedin, Mary. *Fly Away Home.* Iowa City: University of Iowa Press, 1979.

Helprin, Mark. *A Dove of the East and Other Stories.* New York: Knopf, 1975.

Hemenway, Robert. *The Girl Who Sang With the Beatles.* New York: Knopf, 1970.

Henson, Robert. *Transports and Disgraces.* Urbana: University of Illinois Press, 1980.

Hermann, John. *An Agreement Between Us.* Columbia: University of Missouri Press, 1972.

Himes, Chester. *Black on Black: Baby Sister and Selected Writings.* New York: Doubleday, 1973.

Hoffman, William. *Virginia Reels.* Urbana: University of Illinois Press, 1978.

Huddle, David. *A Dream With No Stump Roots in It.* Columbia: University of Missouri Press, 1975.

Hughes, Langston. *The Best of Simple.* New York: Hill & Wang, 1961.

―――. *The Langston Hughes Reader.* New York: Braziller, 1965.

―――. *Laughing to Keep from Crying.* New York: Holt, Rinehart, 1952.

―――. *Simple's Uncle Sam.* New York: Hill & Wang, 1965.

―――. *Something in Common and Other Stories.* New York: Hill & Wang, 1963.

Hughes, Mary Gray. *The Calling.* Urbana: University of Illinois Press, 1980.

Humphrey, William. *The Last Husband and Other Stories.* New York: Morrow, 1953.

―――. *A Time and a Place: Stories of the Red River Country.* New York: Knopf, 1968.

Jackson, Charles. *Earthly Creatures: Ten Stories.* New York: Farrar, Straus, 1953.

―――. *The Sunnier Side: Twelve Arcadian Tales.* New York: Farrar, Straus, 1950.

Jackson, Shirley. *Come Along With Me: Part of a Novel, Sixteen Stories and Three Lectures.* New York: Viking, 1968.

―――. *The Lottery: or, The Adventures of James Harris.* New York: Farrar, Straus, 1949.

―――. *The Magic of Shirley Jackson.* New York: Farrar, Straus & Giroux, 1966.

Jacobsen, Josephine. *A Walk with Raschid and Other Stories.* Winston-Salem, N.C.: Jackpine Press, 1978.

Johnson, Josephine. *The Sorcerer's Son and Other Stories.* New York: Simon & Schuster, 1965.

Jones, Ann. *Hope Should Always.* Columbia: University of Missouri Press, 1973.

Jones, Gayl. *White Rat.* New York: Random House, 1977.

Just, Ward. *The Congressman Who Loved Flaubert and Other Washington Stories.* Boston: Little, Brown, 1973.

―――. *Honor, Power, Riches, Fame, and the Love of Women.* New York: Dutton, 1979.

Kavaler, Rebecca. *The Further Adventures of Brunhild.* Columbia: University of Missouri Press, 1978.

Kentfield, Calvin. *The Angel and the Sailor: A Novella and Nine Stories.* New York: McGraw-Hill, 1957.

―――. *The Great Wandering Goony Bird: Ten Short Stories.* New York: Random House, 1963.

Kim, Yong Ik. *Love in Winter.* New York: Doubleday, 1969.

Knowles, John. *Phineas: Six Stories.* New York: Random House, 1968.

Kranes, David. *Hunters in the Snow.* Salt Lake City: University of Utah Press, 1979.

LaFarge, Oliver. *All the Young Men.* Boston: Houghton Mifflin, 1949.

―――. *The Door in the Wall: Stories.* Boston: Houghton Mifflin, 1965.

―――. *Pause in the Desert: A Collection of Short Stories.* Boston: Houghton Mifflin, 1957.

LaSalle, Peter. *The Graves of Famous Writers and Other Stories.* Columbia: University of Missouri Press, 1980.

Lowry, Robert. *Happy New Year, Kamerades!* Garden City, N.Y.: Doubleday, 1954.
————. *The Last Party: A Memorable Collection of Short Stories.* New York: Popular Library, 1965.
————. *New York Call Girl.* Garden City, N.Y.: Doubleday, 1958.
————. *Party of Dreamers.* New York: Fleet, 1962.
————. *The Wolf that Fed Us.* Garden City, N.Y.: Doubleday, 1949.
MacMillan, Ian. *Light and Power.* Columbia. University of Missouri Press, 1980.
Madden, David. *The Shadow Knows.* Baton Rouge: Louisiana State University Press, 1970.
Malamud, Bernard. *Idiots First.* New York: Farrar, Straus, 1963.
————. *The Magic Barrel.* New York: Farrar, Straus, 1958.
————. *A Malamud Reader.* New York: Farrar, Straus & Giroux, 1967.
————. *Rembrandt's Hat.* New York: Farrar, Straus & Giroux, 1973.
Marsh, Willard. *Beachhead in Bohemia.* Baton Rouge: Louisiana State University Press, 1970.
Matthews, Jack. *Bitter Knowledge.* New York: Scribner's, 1964.
————. *Dubious Persuasions.* Baltimore: Johns Hopkins University Press, 1980.
McCarthy, Mary. *Cast a Cold Eye.* New York: Harcourt Brace, 1950.
McCullers, Carson. *The Ballad of the Sad Cafe: The Novels and Stories of Carson McCullers.* Boston: Houghton Mifflin, 1951.
————. *The Mortgaged Heart.* Boston: Houghton Mifflin, 1971.
McNulty, John. *A Man Gets Around.* Boston: Little, Brown, 1951.
————. *Third Avenue, New York.* Boston: Little, Brown, 1946.
————. *The World of John McNulty.* Garden City, N.Y.: Doubleday, 1957.
McPherson, James Alan. *Elbow Room.* Boston: Little, Brown, 1977.
————. *Hue and Cry.* Boston: Little, Brown, 1969.
Michaels, Leonard. *Going Places.* New York: Farrar, Straus & Giroux, 1969.
————. *I Would Have Saved Them If I Could.* New York: Farrar, Straus & Giroux, 1975.
Michener, James A. *Return to Paradise.* New York: Random House, 1951.
————. *Tales of the South Pacific.* New York: Macmillan, 1950.
Mills, William. *I Know a Place.* Baton Rouge: Press of the Nightowl, 1976.
Minot, Stephen. *Crossings.* Urbana: University of Illinois Press, 1975.
Morgan, Berry. *The Mystic Adventures of Roxy Stoner.* Boston: Houghton Mifflin, 1974.
Morgan, Speer. *Frog Gig and Other Stories.* Columbia: University of Missouri Press, 1976.
Morris, Mary. *Vanishing Animals and Other Stories.* Boston: Godine, 1979.
Morris, Wright. *Green Grass, Blue Sky, White House.* Los Angeles: Black Sparrow, 1970.
————. *Here Is Einbaum.* Los Angeles: Black Sparrow, 1973.
————. *Real Losses, Imaginary Gains.* New York: Harper & Row, 1976.
Munro, Alice. *The Beggar Mind.* New York: Knopf, 1979.
————. *Something I've Been Meaning to Tell You.* New York: McGraw-Hill, 1974.
Nabokov, Vladimir. *Details of a Sunset and Other Stories.* New York: McGraw-Hill, 1976.
————. *Nabokov's Congeries.* New York: Viking, 1968.

————. *Nabokov's Dozen: A Collection of Thirteen Stories.* Garden City, N.Y.: Doubleday, 1958.

————. *Nabokov's Quartet.* New York: Phaedra, 1966.

————. *Nine Stories.* New York: New Directions, 1947.

————. *A Russian Beauty and Other Stories.* New York: McGraw-Hill, 1973.

————. *Tyrants Destroyed and Other Stories.* New York: McGraw-Hill, 1975.

Nelson, Kent. *The Tennis Player.* Urbana: University of Illinois Press, 1977.

Nelson, Richard K. *Shadow of the Hunter.* Chicago: University of Chicago Press, 1980.

Nemerov, Howard. *A Commodity of Dreams and Other Stories.* New York: Simon & Schuster, 1959.

————. *Stories, Fables and Other Diversions.* Boston: Godine, 1971.

Neugeboren, Jay. *Corky's Brother.* New York: Farrar, Straus & Giroux, 1969.

Newhouse, Edward. *Anything Can Happen.* New York: Harcourt Brace, 1941.

————. *The Iron Chain.* New York: Harcourt Brace, 1946.

————. *Many Are Called: Forty-Two Short Stories.* New York: Sloane, 1951.

Nissenson, Hugh. *In the Reign of Peace.* New York: Farrar, Straus & Giroux, 1972.

————. *A Pile of Stones: Short Stories.* New York: Scribner's, 1965.

Oates, Joyce Carol. *All the Good People I've Left Behind.* Santa Barabara: Black Sparrow, 1979.

————. *By the North Gate.* New York: Vanguard, 1963.

————. *Crossing the Border: Fifteen Tales.* New York: Vanguard, 1976.

————. *The Goddess and Other Women.* New York: Vanguard, 1974.

————. *The Hungry Ghosts: Seven Allusive Comedies.* Santa Barbara: Black Sparrow, 1974.

————. *Marriages and Infidelities: Short Stories.* New York: Vanguard, 1972.

————. *Night-Side: Eighteen Tales.* New York: Vanguard, 1977.

Oates, Joyce Carol, and Fernandes. *The Poisoned Kiss, and Other Stories from the Portuguese.* New York: Vanguard, 1975.

Oates, Joyce Carol. *The Seduction, and Other Stories.* Santa Barbara: Black Sparrow, 1975.

————. *Upon the Sweeping Flood and Other Stories.* New York: Vanguard, 1966.

————. *The Wheel of Love and Other Stories.* New York: Vanguard, 1970.

————. *Where Are You Going, Where Have You Been? Stories of Young America.* New York: Fawcett, 1974.

O'Connor, Flannery. *The Complete Stories.* New York: Farrar, Straus & Giroux, 1971.

————. *Everything That Rises Must Converge.* New York: Farrar, Straus & Giroux, 1965.

————. *A Good Man is Hard to Find and Other Stories.* New York: Harcourt Brace, 1955.

O'Connor, Philip F. *Old Morals, Small Continents, Darker Times.* Iowa City: University of Iowa Press, 1971.

————. *A Season for Unnatural Causes.* Urbana: University of Illinois Press, 1975.

O'Hara, John. *And Other Stories.* New York: Random House, 1968.

————. *Assembly.* New York: Random House, 1961.

————. *The Cape Cod Lighter.* New York: Random House, 1962.

————. *49 Stories.* New York: Modern Library, 1963.

————. *The Good Samaritan and Other Stories.* New York: Random House, 1974.

————. *The Hat on the Bed*. New York: Random House, 1963.

————. *Hellbox*. New York: Random House, 1947.

————. *Here's O'Hara: Three Novels and Twenty Short Stories*. New York: Duell, Sloan, and Pearce, 1946.

————. *The Horse Knows the Way*. New York: Random House, 1964.

————. *The O'Hara Generation*. New York: Random House, 1969.

————. *Pipe Night*. New York: Duell, Sloan, and Pearce, 1945.

————. *Selected Short Stories*. New York: Modern Library, 1956.

————. *The Time Element and Other Stories*. New York: Random House, 1972.

————. *Waiting for Winter*. New York: Random House, 1966.

Olsen, Tillie. *Tell Me a Riddle: A Collection*. Philadelphia: Lippincott, 1961.

Osborn, Carolyn. *A Horse of Another Color*. Urbana: University of Illinois Press, 1977.

Otto, Lon. *A Nest of Hooks*. Iowa City: University of Iowa Press, 1978.

Ozick, Cynthia. *Bloodshed and Three Novellas*. New York: Knopf, 1976.

————. *The Pagan Rabbi and Other Stories*. New York: Knopf, 1971.

Paley, Grace. *Enormous Changes at the Last Minute: Stories*. New York: Farrar, Straus & Giroux, 1974.

————. *The Little Disturbances of Man*. Garden City, N.Y.: Doubleday, 1959.

Peden, William Harwood. *Night in Funland and Other Stories*. Baton Rouge: Louisiana State University Press, 1968.

Peterkin, Julia. *Collected Short Stories of Julia Peterkin*. Columbia: University of South Carolina Press, 1970.

Petesch, Natalie L. M. *After the First Death, There Is No Other*. Iowa City: University of Iowa Press, 1974.

Petrakis, Harry Mark. *Pericles on 31st Street*. Chicago: Quadrangle, 1965.

————. *The Waves of Night*. New York: McKay, 1969.

Petry, Ann. *Miss Muriel and Other Stories*. Boston: Houghton Mifflin, 1971.

Phillips, Jayne Ann. *Black Tickets*. New York: Delacorte, 1979.

Phillips, Robert. *The Land of Lost Content*. New York: Vanguard, 1970.

Poverman, C. E. *The Black Velvet Girl*. Iowa City: University of Iowa Press, 1976.

Powers, J. F. *Look How the Fish Live*. New York: Knopf, 1975.

————. *The Presence of Grace*. Garden City, N.Y.: Doubleday, 1956.

————. *Prince of Darkness and Other Stories*. Garden City, N.Y.: Doubleday, 1947.

Price, Reynolds. *The Names and Faces of Heroes*. New York: Atheneum, 1963.

————. *Permanent Errors*. New York: Atheneum, 1970.

Purdy, James. *Children Is All*. New York: New Directions, 1962.

————. *Color of Darkness: Eleven Stories and a Novella*. New York: New Directions, 1957.

Ritcher, Conrad. *The Rawhide Knot and Other Stories*. New York: Knopf, 1978.

Rogin, Gilbert. *The Fencing Master and Other Stories*. New York: Random House, 1965.

Rooke, Leon. *Last One Home Sleeps in the Yellow Bed*. Baton Rouge: Louisiana State University Press, 1968.

Rosten, Leo. *The Many Worlds of L*e*o R*o*s*t*e*n*. New York: Harper & Row, 1964.

————. *The Return of H*y*m*a*n K*a*p*l*a*n*. New York: Harper & Row, 1959.

Roth, Philip. *Goodbye, Columbus and Five Short Stories*. Boston: Houghton Mifflin, 1959.

————. *My Life As a Man.* New York: Holt, 1974.

Salinger, J. D. *Franny and Zooey.* Boston: Little, Brown, 1961.

————. *Nine Stories.* Boston: Little, Brown, 1953.

————. *Raise High the Roof Beam, Carpenters, and Seymour: An Introduction.* Boston: Little, Brown, 1963.

Saroyan, William. *The Assyrian and Other Stories.* New York: Harcourt Brace, 1950.

————. *Love.* New York: Lion, 1955.

————. *The Man with His Heart in the Highlands and Other Stories.* New York: Dell, 1968.

————. *A Saroyan Special: Selected Short Stories.* New York: Harcourt Brace, 1948.

————. *The William Saroyan Reader.* New York: Braziller, 1958.

————. *The Whole Voyald and Other Stories.* Boston: Little, Brown, 1956.

Schaeffer, Susan Fromberg. *The Queen of Egypt.* New York: Dutton, 1980.

Sayles, John. *The Anarchists' Convention.* Boston: Little, Brown, 1979.

Schorer, Mark, and August Derleth. *Colonel Markesan and Less Pleasant People.* Sauk City, Wis.: Arkham House, 1966.

Schorer, Mark. *Pieces of Life.* New York: Farrar, Straus & Giroux, 1977.

————. *The State of Mind.* Boston: Houghton Mifflin, 1947.

Schott, Max. *Up Where I Used to Live.* Urbana: University of Illinois Press, 1978.

Schwartz, Delmore. *In Dreams Begin Responsibilities and Other Stories.* New York: New Directions, 1978.

————. *The World Is a Wedding.* New York: New Directions, 1948.

Shaw, Irwin. *Act of Faith and Other Stories.* New York: Random House, 1946.

————. *God Was Here But He Left Early: Short Fiction.* New York: Arbor House, 1973.

————. *Love on a Dark Street and Other Stories.* New York: Delacorte, 1965.

————. *Selected Short Stories of Irwin Shaw.* New York: Modern Library, 1961.

————. *Short Stories: Five Decades.* New York: Delacorte, 1978.

————. *Tip On a Dead Jockey and Other Stories.* New York: Random House, 1957.

Schelnutt, Eve. *The Love Child.* Santa Barbara: Black Sparrow, 1979.

Sherwin, Judith Johnson. *The Life of Riot.* New York: Atheneum, 1970.

Singer, Isaac Bashevis. *A Crown of Feathers and Other Stories.* New York: Farrar, Straus & Giroux, 1973.

————. *A Day of Pleasures.* New York: Farrar, Straus & Giroux, 1969.

————. *A Friend of Kafka and Other Stories.* New York: Farrar, Straus & Giroux, 1970.

————. *Gimpel the Fool and Other Stories.* New York: Noonday, 1957.

————. *An Isaac Bashevis Singer Reader.* New York: Farrar, Straus & Giroux, 1971.

————. *Old Love.* New York: Farrar, Straus & Giroux, 1979.

————. *Passions and Other Stories.* New York: Farrar, Straus & Giroux, 1975.

————. *The Seance and Other Stories.* New York: Farrar, Straus & Giroux, 1975.

————. *Selected Short Stories of Isaac Bashevis Singer.* New York: Modern Library, 1966.

————. *Short Friday and Other Stories.* New York: Farrar, Straus, 1964.

————. *The Spinoza of Market Street.* New York: Farrar, Straus, 1961.

————. *When Schlemiel Went to Warsaw and Other Stories.* New York: Farrar, Straus & Giroux, 1968.

————. *Zlateh the Goat and Other Stories.* New York: Harper & Row, 1966.

Sontag, Susan. *I, Etcetera*. New York: Farrar, Straus & Giroux, 1978.
Southern, Terry. *Red Dirt Marijuana and Other Tastes*. New York: New American Library, 1967.
Spencer, Elizabeth. *Ship Island and Other Stories*. New York: McGraw-Hill, 1968.
Stafford, Jean. *Bad Characters*. New York: Farrar, Straus, 1964.
————. *Children Are Bored on Sunday*. New York: Harcourt Brace, 1953.
————. *The Collected Stories of Jean Stafford*. New York: Farrar, Straus & Giroux, 1969.
Steele, Max. *When She Brushed Her Hair and Other Stories*. New York: Harper & Row, 1968.
Stegner, Wallace. *The City of the Living and Other Stories*. Boston: Houghton Mifflin, 1956.
————. *The Women On the Wall*. Boston: Houghton Mifflin, 1950.
Stern, Richard. *1968*. New York: Holt, Rinehart & Winston, 1970.
————. *Packages*. New York: Coward, McCann & Geoghegan, 1980.
Stewart, John. *Curving Road*. Urbana: University of Illinois Press, 1975.
Stuart, Jesse. *Clearing the Sky and Other Stories*. New York: McGraw-Hill, 1950.
————. *Come Back to the Farm*. New York: McGraw-Hill, 1971.
————. *Come Gentle Spring*. New York: McGraw-Hill, 1969.
————. *Dawn of Remembered Spring*. New York: McGraw-Hill, 1972
————. *A Jesse Stuart Harvest*. New York: Dell, 1965.
————. *A Jesse Stuart Reader*. New York: McGraw-Hill, 1963.
————. *My Land Has a Voice*. New York: McGraw-Hill, 1966.
————. *Plowshare in Heaven: Stories*. New York: McGraw-Hill, 1958.
————. *Save Every Lamb*. New York: McGraw-Hill, 1964.
————. *Tales from the Plum Grove Hills*. New York: Dutton, 1946.
————. *32 Votes Before Breakfast: Politics at the Grass Roots as Seen in Short Stories*. New York: McGraw-Hill, 1974.
Styron, William. *The Long March*. New York: Random House, 1956.
Sukenick, Ronald. *The Death of the Novel and Other Stories*. New York: Dial, 1969.
Summers, Hollis. *How They Chose the Dead*. Baton Rouge: Louisiana State University Press, 1973.
Swan, Gladys. *On the Edge of the Desert*. Urbana: University of Illinois Press, 1979.
Targan, Barry. *Harry Belten and the Mendelssohn Violin Concerto*. Iowa City: University of Iowa Press, 1975.
————. *Surviving Adverse Seasons*. Urbana: University of Illinois Press, 1979.
Taylor, Harry H. *The Man Who Tried Out for Tarzan*. Baton Rouge: Louisiana State University Press, 1973.
Taylor, Peter. *The Collected Stories of Peter Taylor*. New York: Farrar, Straus & Giroux, 1969.
————. *Happy Families Are All Alike: A Collection of Stories*. New York: McDowell, Obolensky, 1959.
————. *In the Miro District and Other Stories*. New York: Knopf, 1977.
————. *A Long Fourth and Other Stories*. New York: Harcourt Brace, 1948.

―――. *Miss Leonara When Last Seen and Fifteen Other Stories.* New York: Obolensky, 1963.

―――. *The Widows of Thornton.* New York: Harcourt Brace, 1954.

Theroux, Paul. *Sinning With Annie and Other Stories.* Boston: Houghton Mifflin, 1972.

―――. *World's End and Other Stories.* Boston: Houghton Mifflin, 1980.

Thompson, Jean. *The Gasoline Wars.* Urbana: University of Illinois Press, 1979.

Traven, B. *The Kidnapped Saint and Other Stories.* New York: Lawrence Hill, 1975.

―――. *The Night Visitor and Other Stories.* New York: Hill & Wang, 1966.

Updike, John. *Bech: A Book.* New York: Knopf, 1970.

―――. *Museums and Women and Other Stories.* New York: Knopf, 1972.

―――. *The Music School: Short Stories.* New York: Knopf, 1966.

―――. *Olinger Stories: A Selection.* New York: Vintage, 1964.

―――. *Pigeon Feathers, and Other Stories.* New York: Knopf, 1962.

―――. *Problems, and Other Stories.* New York: Knopf, 1979.

―――. *The Same Door: Short Stories.* New York: Knopf, 1959.

―――. *Too Far To Go: The Maples Stories.* New York: Fawcett, 1979.

Van Doren, Mark. *Collected Stories.* New York: Hill & Wang, 1962.

―――. *Collected Stories.* Vols. II & III. New York: Hill & Wang, 1965.

―――. *Home With Hazel and Other Stories.* New York: Harcourt Brace, 1957.

―――. *Nobody Said a Word and Other Stories.* New York: Holt, 1953.

―――. *Short Stories.* New York: Abelard-Schumann, 1950.

Vonnegut, Kurt, Jr. *Welcome To The Monkey House.* New York: Delacorte, 1968.

Walker, Alice. *In Love and Trouble: Stories of Black Women.* New York: Harcourt Brace Jovanovich, 1973.

Warren, Robert Penn. *The Circus in the Attic and Other Stories.* New York: Harcourt Brace, 1948.

Weaver, Gordon. *The Entombed Man of Thule.* Baton Rouge: Louisiana State University Press, 1972.

―――. *Getting Serious.* Baton Rouge: Louisiana State University Press, 1980.

―――. *Such Waltzing Was Not Easy.* Urbana: University of Illinois Press, 1975.

Weidman, Jerome. *The Captain's Tiger.* New York: Reynal, 1947.

―――. *The Death of Dickie Draper and Nine Other Stories.* New York: Random House, 1965.

―――. *My Father Sits in the Dark and Other Selected Stories.* New York: Random House, 1961.

Welty, Eudora. *The Bride of the Innisfallen and Other Stories.* New York: Harcourt Brace, 1955.

―――. *The Collected Stories of Eudora Welty.* New York: Harcourt Brace Jovanovich, 1980.

―――. *Curtain of Green.* Garden City, N.Y.: Doubleday, 1941.

―――. *The Golden Apples.* New York: Harcourt Brace, 1949.

―――. *The Ponder Heart.* New York: Harcourt Brace, 1954.

―――. *Selected Stories.* New York: Modern Library, 1954.

————. *The Wide Net and Other Stories*. New York: Harcourt Brace, 1953.

West, Jessamyn. *Crimson Ramblers of the World, Farewell*. New York: Harcourt Brace Jovanovich, 1970.

————. *Except for Me and Thee: A Companion to the Friendly Persuasion*. New York: Harcourt Brace, 1969.

————. *The Friendly Persuasion*. New York: Harcourt Brace, 1945.

————. *Love, Death, and the Ladies' Drill Team*. New York: Harcourt Brace, 1955.

Wier, Allen. *Things About to Disappear*. Baton Rouge: Louisiana State University Press, 1978.

Williams, Tennessee. *Eight Mortal Ladies Possessed: A Book of Stories*. New York: New Directions, 1974.

————. *Hard Candy: A Book of Stories*. New York: New Directions, 1954.

————. *The Knightly Quest: A Novella and Four Short Stories*. New York: New Directions, 1967.

————. *One Arm and Other Stories*. New York: New Directions, 1954.

Wilson, Robley, Jr. *The Pleasures of Manhood*. Urbana: University of Illinois Press, 1977.

Windham, Donald. *Emblems of Conduct*. New York: Scribner's, 1963.

————. *The Warm Country*. New York: Scribner's, 1962.

Yates, Richard. *Eleven Kinds of Loneliness: Short Stories*. Boston: Little, Brown, 1962.

Wright, Richard. *Eight Men*. Cleveland: World, 1961.

Zacharias, Lee. *Helping Muriel Make It Through the Night*. Baton Rouge: Louisiana State University Press, 1975.

Zelver, Patricia. *The Man of Middle Age and Other Stories*. New York: Holt Rinehart & Winston, 1980.

Selected Bibliography of
Articles of General Interest

Baldeshwiler, Eileen. "The Lyric Short Story: The Sketch of a History." *Studies in Short Fiction* 6, no. 4 (1969): 443—53. Traces its evolution from Turgenev through Welty and Updike.

Fitz Gerald, Gregory. "The Satiric Short Story: A Definition." *Studies in Short Fiction* 5, no. 4 (1968): 349—54. Includes well-chosen examples to illustrate the author's rather precise assertions.

Friedman, Melvin J. "Dislocations of Setting and Word: Notes on American Fiction Since 1950." *Studies in American Fiction* 5, no. 1 (1977): 79—98. Covers most authors in this book, viewing their relationships to contemporary aesthetics.

Friedman, Norman. "What Makes a Short Story Short?" *Modern Fiction Studies* 4, no. 2 (1958): 103—117. Uses object and manner for its criteria.

Galloway, David D. "Clown and Saint: The Hero in Current American Fiction." *Critique* 7, no. 3 (1965): 46—64. Includes discussion of Bellow, Elkin, and Updike.

Gibaldi, Joseph. "Towards a Definition of the Novella." *Studies in Short Fiction* 12, no. 2 (1975): 91—98. Uses mostly Renaissance examples to define this genre.

Gullason, Thomas A. "Revelation and Evolution: A Neglected Dimension of the Short Story." *Studies in Short Fiction* 10, no. 4 (1973): 347—56. Takes issue with Mark Schorer's idea of the short story as "moral revelation."

―――. "The Short Story: An Underrated Art." *Studies in Short Fiction* 2, no. 1 (1964): 13—31. Another attempt to define the short story.

Hansen, Arlen J. "The Celebration of Solipsism: A New Trend in American Fiction." *Modern Fiction Studies* 14, no. 1 (1973): 5—16. Includes discussion of Vonnegut, Barthelme, and Gass.

May, Charles E. "The Unique Effect of the Short Story: A Reconsideration and an Example." *Studies in Short Fiction* 13, no. 3 (1976): 289—98. The short story is "primarily a literary mode that embodies and recapitulates mythic perception itself."

Olderman, Raymond M. "American Fiction 1974—1976: The People Who Fell to Earth." *Contemporary Literature* 19, no. 4 (1978): 497—527. A conveniently categorized, wide-ranging summary of the state of fiction in the mid-1970s.

Spilka, Mark. "The Necessary Stylist: A New Critical Revision." *Modern Fiction Studies* 6, no. 4 (1960—61): 283—97. Discusses the relationship between objectivity and style.

Selected Bibliography of
Books of General Interest

Aldridge, John W. *In Search of Heresy: American Literature in an Age of Conformity.* New York: McGraw-Hill, 1956. A collection of essays concerning affirmation and rejection of traditional moral values in contemporary fiction.

Balakian, Nona, and Simmons, Charles, eds. *The Creative Present: Notes on Contemporary American Fiction.* Garden City, N.Y.: Doubleday, 1963. Contains essays on Baldwin, Nabokov, Salinger, Bellow, Updike, Welty, Malamud, McCullers, and others.

Bates, H. E. *The Modern Short Story: A Critical Survey.* Boston: The Writer, 1972. Using mostly European examples, this volume is a historical survey beginning with Gogol and Poe.

Bruck, Peter. *The Black American Short Story in the 20th Century.* Amsterdam: B. R. Gruner, 1977. Essays on Hughes, Gaines, Baldwin, and others.

Core, George, ed. *Southern Fiction Today: Renascence and Beyond.* Athens: University of Georgia Press, 1969. Five essays on contemporary Southern fiction.

Current-Garcia, Eugene, and Patrick, Walton R. *What Is the Short Story?* Chicago: Scott, Foresman, 1961.

Finkelstein, Sidney. *Existentialism and Alienation in American Literature.* New York: International Publishers, 1965. Discusses the origins of existentialism and its relationship to Styron, Salinger, Updike, Mailer, Bellow, and Baldwin.

Gardner, John. *On Moral Fiction.* New York: Basic Books, 1978.

Gass, William H. *Fiction and the Figures of Life.* New York: Knopf, 1970. Includes discussion of Nabokov, Barthelme, Singer, and Updike, and an excellent section entitled "The Concept of Character in Fiction."

Graff, Gerald. *Literature Against Itself: Literary Ideas in Modern Society.* Chicago: University of Chicago Press, 1979.

Harper, Howard M., Jr. *Desperate Faith: A Study of Bellow, Salinger, Mailer, Baldwin, and Updike.* Chapel Hill: University of North Carolina Press, 1968. Finds parallels among these authors' view of the human condition.

Hendin, Josephine. *Vulnerable People: A View of American Fiction Since 1945.* New York: Oxford University Press, 1978. Contains interesting discussions of Barth, Bellow, Capote, Oates, O'Connor, Updike, and others, emphasizing real-world application of these writers' views.

Klinkowitz, Jerome. *The Practice of Fiction in America. Writers from Hawthorne to the Present.* Ames: Iowa State University Press, 1980.

Kumar, Shiv K, and McKean, Keith, eds. *Critical Approaches to Fiction.* New York: McGraw-Hill, 1968. Twenty-six diverse essays on the components of fiction and critical approaches—includes Bellow, Mary McCarthy, Welty, Mark Schorer, Philip Rahv, Wayne C. Booth, George P. Elliott, and more.

Lesser, Simon O. *Fiction and the Unconscious.* Boston: Beacon, 1957. Surveys the relationship between literature and psychology.

May, Charles E., ed. *Short Story Theories.* Athens: Ohio University Press, 1976. Twenty-four diverse selections and a valuable bibliography.

O'Connor, Frank. *The Lonely Voice: A Study of the Short Story.* Cleveland: World, 1963.

Peden, William. *The American Short Story: Continuity and Change, 1940—1975.* 2nd ed. Boston: Houghton Mifflin, 1975. A thorough survey of many genres and subgenres of short fiction.

Podhoretz, Norman. *Doings and Undoings: The Fifties and After in American Writing.* New York: Farrar, Straus, 1964. Includes discussion of O'Hara, McCarthy, Bellow, Baldwin, and Updike.

Ross, Danforth. *The American Short Story.* Minneapolis: University of Minnesota Pamphlets on American Literature, 1961.

Rubin, Louis D., and Jacobs, Robert D. *South: Modern Southern Literature in its Cultural Setting.* Garden City, N.Y.: Doubleday, 1961. Includes discussion of R. P. Warren, Welty, and McCullers.

Rupp, Richard H. *Celebration in Postwar American Fiction: 1945—1967.* Coral Gables: University of Miami Press, 1970. Includes discussion of Cheever, Updike, Welty, O'Connor, Salinger, Malamud, and Bellow.

Simonini, Rinaldo C., Jr., ed. *Southern Writers: Appraisals In Our Time.* Charlottesville: University Press of Virginia, 1964. A collection of essays from a cultural-historical perspective.

Tanner, Tony. *City of Words: American Fiction, 1950—1970.* New York: Harper & Row, 1971. Includes discussions of Nabokov, Bellow, Purdy, Vonnegut, Barth, Updike, Roth, and Malamud. Although devoted to their novels, the book contains much that is relevant to these authors' stories.

Thurston, Jarvis et al. *Short Fiction Criticism: A Checklist of Interpretations Since 1925 of Stories and Novelettes (American, British, Continental), 1800—1958.* Denver: Swallow Press, 1960.

Voss, Arthur. *The American Short Story: A Critical Survey.* Norman: University of Oklahoma Press, 1973. A historical survey and synthesis.

Walker, Warren S. *Twentieth-Century Short Fiction Explication: Interpretations, 1900—1975, of Short Fiction Since 1800,* 3rd ed. Hamden, Conn. Shoe String Press, 1977.

West, Ray B., Jr. *The Short Story in America, 1900—1950.* Chicago: Regnery, 1952.

Articles and Books Devoted
to Specific Authors

Louis Auchincloss

Kane, Patricia. "Lawyers at the Top: The Fiction of Louis Auchincloss." *Critique* 7, no. 2 (1964—65): 36—46. Surveys Auchincloss's fictional world and the standards of his characters.

John Barth

Bienstock, Beverly Gray. "Lingering on the Autognostic Verge: John Barth's *Lost in the Funhouse.*" *Modern Fiction Studies* 19, no. 1 (1973): 69—78. Finds the book's unity in the self's search for identity.

Gillespie, Gerald. "Barth's *Lost in the Funhouse:* Short Story Text in its Cyclic Context." *Studies in Short Fiction* 12, no. 3 (1975): 223—30.

Kyle, Carol A. "The Unity of Anatomy: The Structure of Barth's *Lost in the Funhouse.*" *Critique* 13, no. 3 (1972): 31—43. Uses Frye's concept of anatomy to explain unity "in its inherent multiplicity."

Morrell, David. *John Barth: An Introduction.* University Park: Pennsylvania State University Press, 1976. Traces the creative process for each of Barth's works.

Tharpe, Jac. *John Barth: The Comic Sublimity of Paradox.* Carbondale: Southern Illinois University Press, 1974. Surveys the major works and their underlying philosophy.

Weixlmann, Joe, and Weixlmann, Sher. "Barth and Barthelme Recycle the Perseus Myth: A Study in Literary Ecology." *Modern Fiction Studies* 25, no. 2 (1979): 191—208. Works using the Perseus figure by both authors are cited to show their differences.

Saul Bellow

Clayton, John Jacob. *Saul Bellow: In Defense of Man.* Bloomington: Indiana University Press, 1968. Bellow is seen as a psychological novelist of affirmation who rejects the impersonality of his contemporaries' work.

Cohen, Sarah Blacher. *Saul Bellow's Enigmatic Laughter.* Chicago: University of Illinois Press, 1974. Emphasizes Bellow's use of comedy as a retaliation against despair.

Critique 3, no. 3 (1960). An all-Bellow/Styron issue with six essays and a bibliography.

Demarest, David, P., Jr. "The Theme of Discontinuity in Saul Bellow's Fiction: 'Looking for Mr. Green' and 'A Father-To-Be.'" *Studies in Short Fiction* 6, no. 2 (1969): 175—86. These stories are viewed as introductions to the theme of inconsistency in Bellow's overall vision.

Donoghue, Denis. "Bellow in Short." *Art International* 12 (1969): 59—60, 64. Contrasts *Mosby's Memoirs* with *Herzog*.

Epstein, Joseph. "Saul Bellow of Chicago." *New York Times Book Review*, May 9, 1971, pp. 4—16. Contains many thoughtful comments from Bellow on his work and literary position.

Fuchs, Daniel. "Saul Bellow and the Modern Tradition." *Contemporary Literature* 15, no. 1 (1974): 67—89. Provides a new definition of modernism, with Bellow as its major exponent.

Lippit, Noriko M. "A Perennial Survivor: Saul Bellow's Heroine in the Desert." *Studies in Short Fiction* 12, no. 3 (1975): 281—83. Surveys an atypical story from Bellow's canon.

Malin, Irving, ed. *Saul Bellow and the Critics*. New York: New York University Press, 1967. Thirteen essays, most tracing various themes through the canon.

————. *Saul Bellow's Fiction*. Carbondale: Southern Illinois University Press, 1969. An easy-to-read book, divided into sections ("The Themes," "The Images," and so on).

Modern Fiction Studies 25, no. 1 (1979). An all-Bellow issue with eleven articles and a bibliography.

Opdahl, Keith Michael. *The Novels of Saul Bellow: An Introduction*. University Park: Pennsylvania State University Press, 1967. Treats psychological and social issues raised by Bellow.

Pinsker, Sanford. "Saul Bellow in the Classroom." *College English* 34 (1973): 975—82. Coverage of a Bellow lecture, contains analyses by Bellow.

Porter, M. Gilbert. *Whence the Power? The Artistry and Humanity of Saul Bellow*. Columbia: University of Missouri Press, 1974. Surveys the novels through *Mr. Sammler's Planet*.

Rovit, Earl, ed. *Saul Bellow: A Collection of Critical Essays*. Englewood Cliffs, N.J.: Prentice-Hall, 1975. Twelve essays, some literary biography, some treatments of individual works, others tracing ideas through multiple works.

Paul Bowles

Stewart, Lawrence Delbert. *Paul Bowles: The Illumination of North Africa*. Carbondale: Southern Illinois University Press, 1974.

Stanley Elkin

LeClair, Thomas. "The Obsessional Fiction of Stanley Elkin." *Contemporary Literature* 16, no. 2 (1975): 145—62. Includes discussion of his two volumes of short fiction.

Sanders, Scott. "An Interview with Stanley Elkin." *Contemporary Literature* 16, no. 2 (1975): 131—45. Elkin discusses his work, his penchant for extremes, and his debt to Faulkner and Gass.

George Garrett

Broughton, Irv, ed. "In Appreciation of George Garrett." Seattle: *Mill Mountain Review*, 1971. Articles, essays, and personal reminiscences.

William H. Gass

Bassoff, Bruce. "The Sacrificial World of William Gass: *In the Heart of the Heart of the Country.*" *Critique* 18, no. 1 (1976): 36—58. Surveys the book's thematic and symbolic unities.

Kane, Patricia. "The Sun Burned on the Snow: Gass's 'The Pedersen Kid.'" *Critique* 14, no. 2 (1972): 89—97. Discusses how the story is a unique variation on the initiation theme.

Caroline Gordon

Critique 1, no. 1 (1956). Issue devoted exclusively to Gordon contains six essays and a bibliography.

Rubin, Larry. "Christian Allegory in Caroline Gordon's 'The Captive.'" *Studies in Short Fiction* 5, no. 3 (1968): 283—89. Examines Calvinist elements in one of Gordon's early stories.

Stuckey, W. J. *Caroline Gordon.* New York: Twayne, 1972.

Shirley Ann Grau

Berland, Alwyn. "The Fiction of Shirley Ann Grau." *Critique* 6, no. 1 (1963): 78—84. Surveys three collections of stories.

Pearson, Ann. "Shirley Ann Grau: Nature Is the Vision." *Critique* 17, no. 2 (1975): 47—58. Discusses the influences of a natural setting on thematic purpose.

William Goyen

Phillips, Robert. *William Goyen.* Boston: Twayne, 1979. Contains chapters on *Ghost and Flesh, The Faces of Blood Kindred,* and *The Collected Stories.*

Langston Hughes

Emmanuel, James A. *Langston Hughes.* New York: Twayne, 1967.

Shirley Jackson

Friedman, Lenejmaja. *Shirley Jackson.* Boston: Twayne, 1975.

Bernard Malamud

Astro, Richard, and Benson, Jackson J., *The Fiction of Bernard Malamud.* Corvallis: Oregon State University Press, 1977. Seven essays and a bibliography, includes Ihab Hassan and Leslie Fiedler.

Avery, Evelyn Gross. *Rebels and Victims: The Fiction of Richard Wright and Bernard Malamud.* Port Washington, N.Y.: Kennikat Press, 1979. Covers the overlapping and contrasting attitudes toward suffering of black and Jewish characters.

Bellman, Samuel Irving. "Women, Children, and Idiots First: The Transformation Psychology of Bernard Malamud." *Critique* 7, no. 2 (1964—65): 123—38. Discusses what Bellman calls "Malamud's partial Judaization of society."

Ducharme, Robert. *Art and Ideas in the Novels of Bernard Malamud.* The Hague: Mouton, 1974. Divided into thematic subdivisions: myth, irony, suffering, family, and history.

Field, Leslie A., and Field, Joyce W., eds. *Bernard Malamud: A Collection of Critical Essays.* Englewood Cliffs, N.J.: Prentice-Hall, 1975. Eleven varied essays.

————. *Bernard Malamud and the Critics.* New York: New York University Press, 1970. Contains twenty-one essays in four areas: "In the Jewish Tradition?"; "Myth, Ritual, Folklore"; "Varied Approaches"; and "Specific Novels and Stories."

Goldman, Mark. "Bernard Malamud's Comic Vision and the Theme of Identity." *Critique* 7, no. 2 (1964—65): 92—109. Disagrees with Rovit; discusses affirmation and the search for identity.

Perrine, Lawrence. "Malamud's 'Take Pity.'" *Studies in Short Fiction* 2, no. 1 (1964): 84—86. Establishes the story's ambiguous setting from textual references.

Richman, Sidney. *Bernard Malamud.* New York: Twayne, 1966. Contains a chapter on the stories.

Rovit, Earl. "Bernard Malamud and the Jewish Literary Tradition." *Critique* 3, no. 2 (1959): 3—10. Discusses Malamud's self-conscious relation to the tradition.

James A. Michener

Day, A. Grove. *James Michener.* Boston: Twayne, 1977.

Vladimir Nabokov

Appel, Alfred, Jr. "An Interview with Vladimir Nabokov." *Wisconsin Studies in Contemporary Literature* 8, no. 2(1967):127—52. A wide-ranging interview in which Nabokov discusses criticism, Joyce, and details in his own work.

Fowler, Douglas. *Reading Nabokov.* New York: Cornell University Press, 1974. Limited, but useful as an introduction.

Lee, L. L. "Duplexity in V. Nabokov's Short Stories." *Studies in Short Fiction* 2, no. 4(1965):307—15. Discusses Nabokov's use of doubles, mirror imagery, and multiple levels of meaning.

————. *Vladimir Nabokov.* Boston: Twayne, 1976. Chapters two, eight, and nine are relevant to Nabokov's short works.

Modern Fiction Studies 25, no. 3 (1979). An all-Nabokov issue, including eight articles, three reviews, and a bibliography.

Rowe, William Woodin. *Nabokov's Deceptive World.* New York: New York University Press, 1971. Although devoted to the novels, this book contains much worthwhile discussion of Nabokov's linguistic technique, explicating many passages.

Stegner, Page. *Escape into Aesthetics: The Art of Vladimir Nabokov.* New York: Dial, 1966. Part One (chapters one, two, and three) is an overview of his career and works and is thus relevant to the short stories.

Williams, Carol T. "Nabokov's Dozen Short Stories: His World in Microcosm." *Studies in Short Fiction* 12, no. 3(1975):213—22. Nabokov's short fiction is about the "quest to unify the two worlds of the mundane and the ecstatic."

Joyce Carol Oates

Barza, Steven. "Joyce Carol Oates: Naturalism and the Aberrant Response." *Studies in American Fiction* 7, no. 2(1979):141—53. In the relationship between stimulus and response, Oates creates a contemporary naturalism.

Creighton, Joanne V. *Joyce Carol Oates*. Boston: Twayne, 1979. Chapter six deals exclusively with the short stories.

Friedman, Ellen G. *Joyce Carol Oates*. New York: Frederick Ungar, 1980. Treats the short stories only in passing.

Grant, Mary Kathryn. *The Tragic Vision of Joyce Carol Oates*. Durham, N.C.: Duke University Press, 1978. A survey of Oates's work from 1963 to 1973. Discusses her vision of violence and her theory of art.

Park, Sue Simpson. "A Study in Counterpoint: Joyce Carol Oates' 'How I Contemplated the World from the Detroit House of Correction and Began My Life Over Again.'" *Modern Fiction Studies* 22, no. 2(1976):213—24. Shows how the story's structure attempts to recreate the experiencing mind.

Pinsker, Sanford. "Joyce Carol Oates in the New Naturalism." *Southern Review* 15, no. 1(1979):52—63. Surveys affinities between naturalism (Pizar's definition) and Oates.

Wagner, Linda W., ed. *Critical Essays on Joyce Carol Oates*. Boston: Hall, 1979.

Walker, Carolyn. "Fear, Love, and Art in Oates' 'Plot.'" *Critique* 15, no. 1(1973):59—70. Discusses how fear contributes to the story's structure.

Waller, G. F. *Dreaming America: Obsession and Transcendence in the Fiction of Joyce Carol Oates*. Baton Rouge: Louisiana State University Press, 1979. Devoted mainly to the novels but includes discussion of themes relevant to the short stories.

Flannery O'Connor

Asals, Frederick. "The Mythic Dimensions of Flannery O'Connor's 'Greenleaf.'" *Studies in Short Fiction* 5, no. 4(1968):317—330. Discusses a symbology "of divine harmony."

Browning, Preston M., Jr. "Flannery O'Connor and the Demonic." *Modern Fiction Studies* 11, no. 1(1973):29—42. "Miss O'Connor seems to say that, in a time so well adjusted to itself that reflection becomes superfluous, the only way to the Holy is through the Demonic."

———. "'Parker's Back': Flannery O'Connor's Iconography of Salvation by Profanity." *Studies in Short Fiction* 6, no. 5(1969):525—35. Discusses O'Connor's treatment of fate and free will.

Coles, Robert. "Flannery O'Connor: A Southern Intellectual." *Southern Review* 16, no. 1(1980):46—64. Discusses pride and intellectualism in her work and life.

Doxey, William S. "A Dissenting Opinion of Flannery O'Connor's 'A Good Man is Hard to Find.'" *Studies in Short Fiction* 10, no. 2(1973):199—204. Doxey believes that this story is flawed by a superfluous shift in point of view.

Drake, Robert. "The Paradigm of Flannery O'Connor's True Country." *Studies in Short Fiction* 6, no. 4(1969):433—42. Views O'Connor's settings as microcosms in the tradition of Faulkner's Yoknapatawpha county and Hardy's Wessex.

Driskell, Leon V., and Brittain, Joan T. *The Eternal Crossroads: The Art of Flannery O'Connor*. Lexington: University Press of Kentucky, 1971. Chapters five and six are devoted to the short stories.

Edenstein, Mark G. "Flannery O'Connor and the Problem of Modern Satire." *Studies in Short Fiction* 12, no. 2(1975):139—44. Views O'Connor as a satirist.

Eggenschwiler, David. *The Christian Humanism of Flannery O'Connor*. Detroit: Wayne State University Press, 1972. The author argues that O'Connor "consistently wrote from the point of view of a Christian humanist."

Friedman, Melvin J., and Lawson, Lewis A. *The Added Dimension: The Art and Mind of Flannery O'Connor*. New York: Fordham University Press, 1977. Includes eleven diverse essays and a bibliography.

Kane, Patricia. "Flannery O'Connor's 'Everything that Rises must Converge.'" *Critique* 8 no. 1(1965):85—91. This review provides an excellent overview of the volume.

Maida, Patricia Dinneen. "Convergence in Flannery O'Connor's 'Everything that Rises must Converge.'" *Studies in Short Fiction* 7, no. 4(1970):549—55. Discusses the function of the book's title.

———. "Light and Enlightenment in Flannery O'Connor's Fiction." *Studies in Short Fiction* 13, no. 1(1976):31—36.

Marks, W. S., III. "Advertisements for Grace: Flannery O'Connor's 'A Good Man Is Hard to Find.'" *Studies in Short Fiction* 4, no. 1(1966):19—27. An allegorical approach that views her in the Hawthorne tradition.

Martin, Carter W. *The True Country: Themes in the Fiction of Flannery O'Connor*. Nashville: Vanderbilt University Press, 1969. A study of Christian themes and the "thematic significance of her use of symbolism, the grotesque, humor, and irony."

Milder, Robert. "The Protestantism of Flannery O'Connor." *Southern Review* 11, no. 4(1975):802—19. Milder's thesis is that "this most aggressively Catholic of American writers" produced works "uncompromisingly Protestant in substance."

Montgomery, Marion. "Flannery O'Connor and the Jansenist Problem in Fiction." *Southern Review* 14, no. 3(1978):438—48. Discusses determinism in O'Connor's works.

———. "On Flannery O'Connor's 'Everything that Rises must Converge.'" *Critique* 13, no. 2(1971):15—29. Discusses character of Julian in this story.

Orvell, Miles. *Invisible Parade: The Fiction of Flannery O'Connor*. Philadelphia: Temple University Press, 1972. Chapter four deals exclusively with the short stories.

Shinn, Thelma J. "Flannery O'Connor and the Violence of Grace." *Contemporary Literature* 9, no. 1(1968):58—73. Discusses how violence is used as a vehicle for redemption.

Shloss, Carol. *Flannery O'Connor's Dark Comedies: The Limits of Influence.* Baton Rouge: Louisiana State University Press, 1980. Discusses rhetorical devices and their significance.

Tate, J. C. "Flannery O'Connor's Counterplot." *Southern Review* 16, no. 4(1980):869—78. An interesting comparison of O'Connor's relationship with evil with Milton's relationship with Satan in *Paradise Lost.*

John O'Hara

Carson, Edward Russell. *The Fiction of John O'Hara.* Pittsburgh: University of Pittsburgh Press, 1961. Chapter three deals exclusively with the short stories.

Grebstein, Sheldon Norman. *John O'Hara.* New York: Twayne, 1966. Chapter five deals exclusively with the short stories.

O'Hara, John. *An Artist Is His Own Fault: John O'Hara on Writers and Writing.* Matthew J. Bruccoli, ed. Carbondale: Southern Illinois University Press, 1977. Forty-one lectures, essays, reviews, and interviews by O'Hara.

James Purdy

Schwarzschild, Bettina. *The Not-Right House: Essays on James Purdy.* Columbia: University of Missouri Press, 1968.

J. D. Salinger

French, Warren. *J. D. Salinger.* Boston: Twayne, 1976.

Goldstein, Bernice, and Goldstein, Sanford. "'Seymour: An Introduction'—Writing as Discovery." *Studies in Short Fiction* 7, no. 2(1970):248—256. Treats Salinger's focus on the process of creation through the character Buddy.

Modern Fiction Studies 12, no. 3(1966). An all-Salinger issue, including seven essays and a bibliography.

Perrine, Lawrence. "Teddy? Booper? or Blooper?" *Studies in Short Fiction* 4, no. 3(1967):217—224. A suggested interpretation of Salinger's ambiguous ending to this story.

William Saroyan

Floan, Howard R. *William Saroyan.* New York: Twayne, 1966.

Isaac Bashevis Singer

Alexander, Edward. *Isaac Bashevis Singer.* Boston: Twayne, 1980.

Allentuck, Marcie, ed. *The Achievement of Isaac Bashevis Singer.* Carbondale. Southern Illinois University Press, 1969.

Anderson, David M. "Isaac Bashevis Singer: Conversations in California." *Modern Fiction Studies* 16, no. 4(1970—71):423—40. A very articulate and informative interview with Singer.

Bezanker, Abraham. "I. B. Singer's Crises of Identity." *Critique* 14, no. 2(1972):71—88. Uses Erik Erikson's theories to explain problems in Singer.

Buchen, Irving H. "Isaac Bashevis Singer and the Eternal Past." *Critique* 8, no. 3(1966):5—18. Emphasizes the universality of Singer and the Yiddish tradition.

———. *Isaac Bashevis Singer and the Eternal Past.* New York: New York University Press, 1968. Emphasizes the universality of Singer and the Yiddish tradition.

Kresh, Paul. *Isaac Bashevis Singer: The Magician of West 86th Street.* New York: Dial, 1979.

Malin, Irving, ed. *Critical Views of Isaac Bashevis Singer.* New York: New York University Press, 1969.

Pinsker, Sanford. "The Fictive Worlds of Isaac Bashevis Singer." *Critique* 11, no. 2(1968):26—39. Discusses *Gimpel the Fool.*

———. "Isaac Bashevis Singer: An Interview." *Critique* 11, no. 2(1968):16—25. Singer discusses his goals and the process of translation.

Pondrom, Cyrena N. "Isaac Bashevis Singer: An Interview and a Biographical Sketch." *Contemporary Literature* 10, no. 1(1969):1—38. A broad, open interview and a chronology of his works.

———. "Isaac Bashevis Singer: An Interview, Part II." *Contemporary Literature* 10, no. 3(1969):331—51. Discusses stories in *Short Friday.*

Siegel, Ben. "Sacred and Profane: Isaac Bashevis Singer's Embattled Spirits." *Critique* 6, no. 1(1963):24—47. Discusses characters, themes, and the tradition, including *Gimpel the Fool.*

Zatlin, Linda G. "The Themes of Isaac Bashevis Singer's Short Fiction." *Critique* 11, no. 2(1968):40—48. Discusses Singer's theology.

Wallace Stegner

Robinson, Forrest G., and Robinson, Margaret G. *Wallace Stegner.* Boston: Twayne, 1977.

Jesse Stuart

Blair, Everetta Love. *Jesse Stuart: His Life and Works.* Columbia: University of South Carolina Press, 1967. Chapter three is devoted to the short stories.

Foster, Ruel E. *Jesse Stuart.* New York: Twayne, 1968. Chapter three is devoted to the short stories.

John Updike

Burehard, Rachael C. *John Updike: Yea Sayings.* Carbondale: Southern Illinois University Press, 1971.

Detweiler, Robert. *John Updike.* New York: Twayne, 1972.

Gado, Frank, ed. *First Person: Conversations on Writers & Writing.* Schenectady, N.Y.: Union College Press, 1973. Contains an informative 1970 interview with Updike.

Hunt, George W. *John Updike and the Three Great Secret Things: Sex, Religion, and Art.* Grand Rapids, Mich.: Eerdmans, 1980. Covers the religious and philosophical foundations of Updike's work.

Markle, Joyce B. *Fighters and Lovers: Themes in the Novels of John Updike.* New York: New York University Press, 1973.

Modern Fiction Studies 20, no. 1(1974). An all-Updike issue, including eight essays, three reviews, and a bibliography.

Oates, Joyce Carol. "Updike's American Comedies." *Modern Fiction Studies* 21, no. 3(1975):459—72. Discusses Updike's use of comedy, character types, and love.

Taylor, Larry E. *Pastoral and Anti-Pastoral Patterns in John Updike's Fiction.* Carbondale: Southern Illinois University Press, 1971.

Thornburn, David, and Eiland, Howard. *John Updike: A Collection of Critical Essays.* Englewood Cliffs, N.J.: Prentice-Hall, 1979. Contains articles on *The Same Door, Pigeon Feathers, The Music School, Bech: A Book,* and *Museums and Women.*

Robert Penn Warren

Bohner, Charles H. *Robert Penn Warren.* New York: Twayne, 1965.

Eudora Welty

Appel, Alfred, Jr. *A Season of Dreams: The Fiction of Eudora Welty.* Baton Rouge: Louisiana State University Press, 1965. Close readings of many stories.

Curley, Daniel. "Eudora Welty and the Quandam Obstruction." *Studies in Short Fiction* 5, no. 3(1968):209—24. An interpretation of the story "A Still Moment."

Davis, Charles E. "The South in Eudora Welty's Fiction: A Changing World." *Studies in American Fiction* 3, no. 2(1975):199—210. Welty treats the transition between the old and new South by placing her emphasis on the individual.

Desmond, John F., ed. *A Still Moment: Essays on the Art of Eudora Welty.* Metuchen, N.J.: Scarecrow, 1978. Six of this book's ten selections are relevant to the short stories.

Dollarhide, Louis, and Abadie, Ann J., eds. *Eudora Welty: A Form of Thanks.* Jackson: University Press of Mississippi, 1979. Six of this book's seven selections are relevant to the short stories.

Howard, Zelma Turner. *The Rhetoric of Eudora Welty's Short Stories.* Jackson: University Press of Mississippi, 1973. Discusses narrative voice, semantics, rhetorical devices, and so on.

Jones, William M. "The Plot as Search." *Studies in Short Fiction* 5, no. 1(1967):37—43. Speculates as to Welty's creative method.

Kreyling, Michael. *Eudora Welty's Achievement of Order.* Baton Rouge: Louisiana State University Press, 1980. Contains separate chapters on the respective story volumes.

McDonald, W. U., Jr. "Eudora Welty's Revisions of 'A Piece of News.'" *Studies in Short Fiction* 7, no. 2(1970):232—47. An eye-opening study of the impact of minor revisions.

————. "Welty's 'Social Consciousness': Revisions of 'The Whistle.'" *Modern Fiction Studies* 16, no. 2(1970):193—97. Shows how revision between periodical and book publication heightens social consciousness.

Oppitz, Kurt. "Eudora Welty: The Order of a Captive Soul." *Critique* 7, no. 2(1964—65):79—91. Welty characters search for order through the soul.

Vande Kieft, Ruth M. *Eudora Welty.* New York: Twayne, 1962.

Welty, Eudora. "Words into Fiction." *Southern Review* 1, no. 3(1965):543—53. Discusses the writer's craft. Welty makes no specific references to any of her works.

Jessamyn West

Shivers, Alfred T. *Jessamyn West.* New York: Twayne, 1972.

Index

Pablo Picasso

by Linda Lowery
illustrations by Janice Lee Porter

 Carolrhoda Books, Inc./Minneapolis

For Judith Fisher—like Picasso, she has made her life a colorful expression of personal freedom.   *—L.L.*

For my dad—who showed me the artists, made art in his spare time, bought the art supplies, displayed the pictures, and sent me to art school—eternal love.   *—J.L.P.*

Text copyright © 1999 by Linda Lowery
Illustrations copyright © 1999 by Janice Lee Porter

Photographs courtesy of: © Corbis, pp. 30–31; Illustrated London News Picture Library, p. 46.

Publisher's note: The artwork in this book is inspired by the life and work of Pablo Picasso. Every effort was made to secure permission from the Picasso Administration to include reproductions of original Picasso paintings, but permission was denied.

This book is available in two editions:
Library binding by Carolrhoda Books, Inc.,
  a division of Lerner Publishing Group
Soft cover by First Avenue Editions,
  an imprint of Lerner Publishing Group
241 First Avenue North
Minneapolis, MN 55401 U.S.A.

Website address: www.lernerbooks.com

Library of Congress Cataloging-in-Publication Data

Lowery, Linda.
    Pablo Picasso / by Linda Lowery ; illustrations by Janice Lee Porter.
      p. cm. — (Carolrhoda on my own books)
    Summary: Tells the story of Pablo Picasso as he grows through his early days as an artist, his discovery of cubism, and his later years of sculpture and painting to become a famous artist.
    ISBN 1–57505–331–4 (lib. bdg. : alk. paper)
    ISBN 1–57505–370–5 (pbk. : alk. paper)
    1. Picasso, Pablo, 1881–1973—Juvenile literature. 2. Artists—France—Biography— Juvenile literature. [1. Picasso, Pablo, 1881–1973. 2. Artists.] I. Porter, Janice Lee, ill. II. Title. III. Series.
N6853.P5L78 1999
709'.2—dc21
[B]   99-21965

Manufactured in the United States of America
2 3 4 5 6 7 – JR – 05 04 03 02 01 00

Author's Note

When we look at a painting by Pablo Picasso, we each see it in a different way. I might see a beautiful woman, while you might see a jumble of puzzle pieces.

This is also true of the events that happened during Picasso's life. Everyone who knew him saw him in a different way. The stories they tell about him are all a little different. Pablo himself liked to brag and exaggerate. So we don't know exactly which facts about Picasso's life are entirely true.

We *do* know the facts about Picasso's art, however. And the art that Pablo Picasso created will always be the most exciting and most colorful part of his life.

Pablo Picasso stared at his math test.

He was confused.

Adding numbers made his mind go fuzzy.

It was 1891, and Pablo was nine.

When he looked at numbers,

all he saw were shapes and pictures.

"I'll show them what I can do!" he thought.

In his mind, he turned the numbers

into a beautiful pigeon.

The 0 looked like the pigeon's eye.

The 6 was its head and body.

The 3 fit perfectly under that,

making little bird feet.

The 2s became wings.

The line above the answer

looked just like a table

for the bird to perch its feet on!

And right under the pigeon's table

sat the answer: 13.

As a grown man, Pablo Picasso
told the pigeon story many times.
He loved to brag about his early days
as an artist.
The first word he ever said was *piz*,
which is short for "pencil" in Spanish.

His dark eyes flashed
when he told stories about his life
and his art.
Pablo was short, and his hands were small.
But his stories made him seem
gigantic and powerful.
So did his art.

As a young student, Pablo filled the margins
of his books with doodles.

He turned ink blobs into animals.

His teachers were not pleased.

They sent him to the "cells."
The cells were tiny rooms
of empty white walls
with nothing in them except a bench.
Most students hated to be all alone in a cell.
Not Pablo.
He took his pad of paper
and his pencil with him.
"I could have stayed there forever," he said,
"drawing, drawing, drawing."

Pablo's family lived in Spain.
Until he was 10, he lived
in the sunny south.
He drew what he saw around him:
people, pigeons, bullfights, and guitars.
When he went out to play,
he drew in the dirt with a stick.
At the seashore, he drew huge
dolphins in the sand.
At home, Pablo drew his little sister Lola.

Then Pablo's family moved to Corunna,
a rainy town on the Atlantic Ocean.
He made pictures of the lighthouse
and the foggy sea.
Pablo's father, Don José, was a painter.
He saw that his son was very talented.

When Pablo was 13,
his father asked him to finish a painting
he had started.
It was a picture of pigeons.

Pablo added the feet to his father's painting,
using his father's paints.

Pablo did such a wonderful job that
Don José gathered all his brushes and
paints and gave them to Pablo.

Pablo was excited.

He could finally work on real canvas
with real paints.

He painted beautiful portraits of people.

Pablo wanted to make money
from his paintings.

He carried his portraits to a junk shop
near his house.

The shopkeeper hung them
in the front window.

It was Pablo's first art show.

Two of his paintings were sold.

At 16, Pablo was too restless
to stay home.
He tried going to art school.
But it did not give him
the excitement he craved.
He moved to France.
Sometimes he went back to Spain
for long visits looking for adventure.
His art became adventurous, too.
Pablo had huge emotions—as big as
the stories he told about himself.
When he was mad, he was fiery.
When he was sad, he was stormy.
When he was happy, he was wildly joyful.
So why not put all those huge feelings
into his art?

When Pablo Picasso left home,

he had little money and often felt lonely.

He painted people who felt like he did:

homeless people and beggars and prisoners.

He did not paint them exactly

the way they looked in real life.

He made their faces and fingers

very long and droopy.

Mostly, he used blue paint,

even for the color of their skin.

This time is called Pablo Picasso's

"Blue Period."

Many of his Blue Period paintings

make people feel sad and lonely.

While making these sad paintings,
Pablo learned something about himself.
He needed people.
He liked to be alone to paint all day,
but he wanted to be with friends at night.
During his Blue Period, Pablo spent
some time in Barcelona, Spain.
But in 1904, he moved to Paris, France,
to a neighborhood called Montmartre.
It was full of artists.
Pablo met many friends there.
He also fell in love with a woman
named Fernande.
As he began to cheer up, he painted
some happier pictures.
He added pink and rosy colors
to his paintings.

This is called his "Rose Period."
But Pablo quickly got bored
with his happy paintings.

Pablo was like the weather—
changing all the time.
In 1907, he and his friend Georges
Braque tried out a new idea.
They painted things
that looked broken.
If they painted a cup, it looked
as if they had smashed the cup
against the wall.
Then they painted the broken pieces
all mixed up.
Some people had a hard time seeing
what was really in these paintings.
They could see only triangles,
squares, and cubes.
This new style was named "cubism."

Pablo was excited about cubism.

Every day, he worked and worked.

He made one cubist painting after the next.

Every night, Pablo and Georges

visited each other's studios.

"Each of us *had* to see what the other

had done during the day," Pablo said.

At first, most people thought
cubism was strange.
All over the world, people complained
about Picasso's new "broken" way
of painting.
Even Pablo's artist friends did not like
what he was doing.

The complaints did not bother Pablo one bit.
He even put numbers and letters
onto his paintings.
He glued on pieces of newspaper
and sheet music.
He made a guitar out of cardboard, paper,
a tin can, and some wire.
Pablo was having lots of fun.
He and Georges started to wear
matching overalls when they painted.

Pablo and Georges wanted to look
like inventors.
They did not want to be confused
with ordinary artists
who painted ordinary pictures.

As the years went on,

Pablo kept "drawing, drawing, drawing."

His art kept changing with his moods.

In 1936, war broke out in Spain.

Nazis from the German air force

flew warplanes over a Spanish town

called Guernica.

They destroyed the town with bombs

and killed 1,600 people.

Pablo got the news in Paris.

Rage tore through him.

Guernica was not far from Corunna,

where he had grown up.

How dare the Nazis destroy

the Spain he loved!

How dare they kill people

who had done nothing wrong!

What could he do?

Pablo Picasso fought back.

His weapons were not guns and bombs.

His weapons were pencils

and paintbrushes.

Pablo Picasso stretched a giant canvas.

It was 12 feet high and 26 feet long.

Only a huge space

would have room for his anger.

He painted horses and
people in flames.
He painted a child dead
in its mother's arms.
He painted women screaming,
with their heads thrown back
so heaven could hear their cries.
He painted their pain.
He painted his rage.
Pablo used no color in his picture—
no yellow, no red, no blue.
It was simply black and white and gray.

The painting was called *Guernica*,
after the town the Nazis had destroyed.
It gave Pablo some peace to know
he had told the terrible story of Guernica
through his painting.

Guernica *(1937)*
by Pablo Picasso

He could not change what
the Nazis had done.
But he had shown
everyone the truth.
Maybe that would help stop war from
happening in the world again.
In 1944, *Guernica* was put on display at the
World's Fair in Paris.
War was still going on in France then.

The Nazis hated *Guernica.*

One day, they came to see Pablo

in his studio.

They saw a photograph of *Guernica.*

"Did you do this?" one of them

asked Picasso.

Pablo's black eyes flashed.

He stood firm, his feet planted

on the floor of his studio.

"No," answered Pablo. "You did."

Pablo had not created the violence.

He had painted a picture that showed

how violent the Nazis were.

During the war, Pablo fell in love
with a woman named Françoise.
Pablo was 62, but he did not feel old.
He became the father of two children,
Claude and Paloma.
The family moved to southern France.

Pablo continued to create art—
even from trash!
Years before, he had found a seat
and handlebars from an old bike.
To him, they looked like a bull.
The seat was the head.
The handlebars were the horns.
He put them together and made a sculpture.

Every day, Pablo and Françoise
walked together to his studio.
As they walked, Pablo looked in trash cans
for treasures to take to his studio.
He turned a faucet and an old shovel
into a crane.
A wastebasket, tree branches,
and flowerpots became a goat.

He used two of Claude's toy cars
to make a baboon.
The cars made the head.
The ears were handles
from a broken pitcher.

Claude was not very happy.
But Pablo was delighted.
He also made pottery:
vases, cups, and bowls.
He painted bullfights on plates
that he had made himself.
He scratched pictures in metal.
These were called engravings.

Pablo had become very famous.
Crowds of people often gathered outside
Pablo's studio, wanting to meet him.
If he was in a bad mood, he would
lock his doors and stay in bed.
"I live like a prisoner," he complained
when he was cranky.
If he was in a good mood,
he would let people visit.
He would tell them lively stories
about himself.

Pablo was proud to live his life
in his own way.
Sometimes he painted in his boxer shorts.
Other times, he wore colorful costumes
such as clown noses and gorilla feet,
cowboy hats and witch masks.
At night, he stayed up late with friends.
He told stories, argued about art,
and laughed until tears ran down his face.

Pablo Picasso was not easy to live with.
He was stubborn and bossy.
He did whatever pleased him,
even if it hurt the people he loved.
Finally, Françoise and Claude
and Paloma left.
Pablo found new people to love.
In 1961, he got married again, this time
to a woman named Jacqueline.

They often went to bullfights in Spain.
There, Pablo was the center of attention.
People shouted to him, calling him
"the best painter in the world."
Police guarded him from crowds of fans.
Bullfighters gave him gifts.
Sometimes they tossed him
a bullfighter's hat.

When Pablo was 85 years old,

the city of Chicago asked him to make

a sculpture for a building there.

He decided to make the sculpture

out of steel.

He drew the design.

But it was too big for him to build

by himself.

It was larger than anything

he had ever made.

It took 20 workers one year to cut the steel

and put up the sculpture.

Crowds and marching bands gathered

when it was finished.

When the cover was pulled off,

people did not know what to think.

Some people loved it.

Others said it looked like a rusty old dog.

Pablo refused to explain his sculpture.
He wanted people to imagine
whatever they saw in it.

Pablo believed art was magical.

When he drew and painted,

he did not think.

He let his mind wander

and his feelings run free.

"Everyone wants to understand art,"

Pablo complained.

He said art was like the song of a bird.

Why try to understand it?

To think about it too much

spoils the magic of the art.

All his life, Pablo never knew
what would happen when
he picked up a pencil or a paintbrush.
Each new creation seemed to appear
magically on the canvas.
People never knew what he would do next.
They were always surprised
by what they saw.
So was Pablo Picasso.

Pablo Picasso works on a painting in 1945.

Afterword

Pablo Picasso kept "drawing, drawing, drawing" until he died at age 91. Almost every day, from the time he was 13, Picasso drew in his journal and painted in his studio. He even painted until dawn the night before he died. He left behind 78 years of artwork.

Many of Picasso's works are very famous. Others can be hard to recognize. He was always trying new styles and new techniques—more than any artist who ever lived. There are Picasso plates and sculptures, Picasso paintings and collages, and Picasso engravings and drawings.

His work changed as he did, so Pablo Picasso's art always stayed new and young. Even in his old age, people called him "the youngest artist in the world."

Important Dates

October 25, 1881—Pablo Picasso was born in
　　　Málaga, Spain.
1894—Showed his paintings for first time in a
　　　Corunna junk shop
1895—Family settled in Barcelona, and Picasso
　　　entered Fine Arts Academy
1901—Began his Blue Period
1904—Moved to Paris, met Fernande Olivier, and
　　　began his Rose Period
1907—Began cubism
1937—Town of Guernica, Spain, destroyed; Picasso
　　　painted *Guernica*
1943—Met Françoise Gilot in Paris
1947—Claude born
1948—Took first of many trips to World Peace Congress
　　　meetings
1949—Paloma born
1961—Married Jacqueline Roque
1967—Chicago Monument finished
April 8, 1973—Died at Mougins, France, at age 91

Contents

[*vii*]

CONTENTS

Illustrations

ILLUSTRATIONS

THE STORY OF
Davy Crockett

He shouted loudly: "David Crockett! Da-a-vy!"

CHAPTER ONE

To Bed with No Supper

M RS. CROCKETT set some corn pone on the table. She sniffed at the stew which bubbled in the big pot over the fire. She picked up the baby who was crawling on the hard dirt floor. Then she stepped to the door of the cabin.

"Supper's ready," she called loudly. "Come on, all you Crocketts, and get your supper."

Little Becky and tiny Jane were making a corncob house near the cabin door. They scrambled to their feet.

Joey, the youngest Crockett boy, climbed down from the maple tree at the edge of the

[*3*]

clearing. Ten-year-old Wilson came running from the river, beyond the clearing.

Bill, who was nearly twelve, dropped his hoe where he had been working in the corn patch. Jim and John, the oldest boys, finished milking the two cows and turned them loose to roam in the woods.

Mr. Crockett stopped sharpening his axe and put it in the shed. And everyone crowded into the cabin, laughing and talking at once.

Mr. Crockett lifted Becky and little Jane to one of the benches at the puncheon table.

"The rest of you sit down, now," he commanded. "And stop your gibble-gabble. You sound like a mess of wildcats."

"I'm hungry enough to eat a wildcat," Wilson declared, sliding into his place beside Joey.

His mother smiled. "Possum stew will taste a heap better," she said. She set a wooden trencher full of stew before him. Then she glanced around.

"Where's Davy?" she asked.

"I don't know," Wilson replied.

[4]

"Neither do I," Bill added, reaching for a piece of corn pone. "He didn't help me in the corn patch like Pa told him to. And I ain't seen him since dinner."

"I have," Joey piped up. "He took that play rifle that he made yesterday, Ma, and he went along the river into the woods."

Ma Crockett looked uneasy. "He promised he wouldn't go out of hollering distance," she said. "It seems strange he don't come. Do you reckon anything's happened to him, Pa?"

Pa Crockett shook his head. "Like as not he's sitting on a log, trying to make a noise like a wild turkey," he replied. "He'll come afore long."

He picked up his horn spoon and took a big helping of stew. Then he began to talk about the new mill he was building on the creek, a short distance from the cabin.

He and a man named Tom Galbreath had been working hard on the mill for a long time. They had put the big paddle wheel in place. But they had not yet set up the wooden trough which would carry the water to turn the wheel.

[5]

"The creek's still too high after that big rain we had yesterday," Pa Crockett said. "Soon as it goes down, we'll get the trough up. Then we'll start the mill a-working."

"And folks will come from all around to bring you their corn to grind," Joey added happily. "It sure will be nice to have folks coming to the cabin all the time, won't it, Ma?"

Ma Crockett nodded and sat down at the table. Now and then, as she ate her supper, she glanced anxiously at the cabin door.

"Davy's so tall, Pa, that you forget he's not nine years old yet," she said at last. "He shouldn't be out in the woods so late."

Pa sighed. "Anybody'd think the Indians roaming around here were still unfriendly!" he exclaimed.

But he was beginning to worry, too. So he pushed his stool back from the table and stood up.

"I'll holler at him this time," he said. And he crossed the cabin and opened the door.

The April sun had set. The Tennessee hills on the opposite side of the river were black against the sky. It was already dark in the little clearing around the cabin.

Pa did not see the figure which was stealing through the underbrush at the edge of the clearing. He did not hear a sound as that figure crept on its hands and knees toward the cabin. Making a trumpet of his hands, he shouted loudly.

"Davy! David Crockett! D-a-a-vy!"

"I'm here, Pa," a voice said. And the figure suddenly stood up so close to Pa Crockett that he jumped back in surprise.

"Drat you, Davy!" he exclaimed angrily. "What did you do that for?"

Davy grinned and tossed a lock of shaggy dark hair back from his face.

"I didn't aim to scare you," he declared with a little chuckle. "But I got all the way home like that, Pa, quiet as a fox sneaking up on a chicken. I tracked a big coon from the creek right to his tree, too. If I'd had a real rifle I could have shot him, easy. When can I learn to shoot?"

His father made no answer to this question. He was cross because Davy had startled him. And because Davy had worried his mother. And for other reasons.

"Didn't you hear your ma holler a while back?" he asked sternly.

"Yes," Davy replied quickly. "I heard her. And I came right away. Only it took a long time, coming like a fox. I—"

"Then next time don't come like a fox," his father broke in.

"Yes, Pa," Davy said soberly.

He started into the cabin. But his father blocked his way.

"What did you do with those squirrel skins

[8]

I gave you this morning?" he asked. "Did you scrape them and stretch them to dry like I told you?"

Davy shook his head.

"You didn't help Bill in the corn patch either, did you?" his father went on.

"No," Davy admitted. "I—"

"Did you fetch your share of creek water for your ma?"

Again Davy shook his head. "I meant to," he said in a low tone. "But I—I reckon I just forgot."

"Then I reckon you can forget about your supper, too," his father announced. "And since you ain't going to eat, you might as well go right to bed. Get on up to the loft now, quick as you can."

He stepped aside. Without a word, Davy marched into the cabin and started across the room.

His mother was so glad to have him safe at home that she smiled at him when he passed the table. So did little Becky. But Jim poked John with his elbow.

[9]

"Here comes the great hunter," he drawled in a teasing voice. "Look at him! He ain't even got a rabbit!"

Davy's eyes flashed. He whirled around.

"You couldn't shoot a rabbit, either, if you'd nothing but a stick for a rifle," he shouted angrily. "When I get a real rifle, I'll be the greatest hunter in all the world. Just you wait and see, you—"

He clenched his fist and started for Jim.

"Davy!" Pa's voice boomed behind him. "Do you want a good whipping?"

"No," Davy cried. And he scrambled up the ladder to the loft as fast as he could go.

He kicked off his moccasins and pulled off his homespun shirt and trousers. Then he crawled into one of the beds on the floor.

He was mad clear through. Mad at Jim for teasing him. Mad at Pa for sending him to bed without supper. Mad at himself because he had forgotten again to do his work around the cabin.

But Davy could never be angry about anything for very long. Humping his knees up

He scrambled up the ladder as fast as he could go

under the cover, he stared into the dark. And he began to plan what he would do the next day.

"I'll scrape those old squirrel skins the very first thing," he told himself. "And I'll stretch them on the cabin wall to dry.

"Then I'll fill Ma's water bucket fifteen times if she wants me to. And I'll hoe the rest of the corn for Bill, and I'll—"

He broke off and turned over restlessly on his pine-needle mattress. Shutting his eyes, he tried to forget how hungry he was.

As he drifted off to sleep a few minutes later, he did not know that next day there would be no squirrel skins for him to scrape. There would be no water bucket to be filled. There would be no corn patch to hoe.

He did not even hear the wind begin to sigh through the trees. Or the noise the raindrops made as they spattered down on the roof.

CHAPTER TWO

The Flood

ALL NIGHT long the rain fell. It knocked the blossoms from the swamp apple and the wild cherry trees. It drove the rabbits deeper into their burrows.

It soaked the fur of a big red fox, out hunting for food. It dripped from the feathers of an old gray owl, huddled on the branch of a pine tree.

Little streams of rain trickled down the hillsides and splashed into the creek and the river. Big drops of rain fell down the Crocketts' chimney and sizzled as they hit the glowing backlog in the fireplace.

Again and again Pa Crockett left his bed and opened the door to peer outside. As soon as it was light enough to see, he pulled on his clothes and went out to look at the mill.

Then Ma Crockett got up, too, and began to fry some cornmeal mush for breakfast.

Pa's face was grave when he came into the cabin again.

"This storm sure is a humdinger," he said, shaking the water from his coonskin cap. "I ain't never seen Cove Creek so wild. And the old Nolichucky River's getting higher every minute."

He took off his wet coat and hung it on a wall peg. As he turned around he saw Davy climbing down the ladder from the loft.

" 'Tain't hardly light yet, Davy," Pa said. "What got you up so early?"

"Rain," Davy replied, tightening the deerskin string which held his trousers up. "It leaked in on me and on Joey, too. Only Joey's not awake yet. Nor the other boys, either."

He walked quietly past the trundle bed where Becky and Jane were still asleep. And past the baby in her cradle. Then he spoke to his mother.

"Ma, I'm terrible hungry," he declared. "Can I have some of that mush now?"

His mother nodded. "Soon as you wash your face," she replied. "I reckon your pa's ready to eat, too."

She dished out the mush. Davy turned to the water bucket, which stood on a shelf in the corner. He washed his face quickly. Sitting down beside his father, he began his breakfast.

The rain was coming down harder now, beating against the cabin and spilling down the chimney. Wind howled around the house and whistled through the cracks between the logs.

Suddenly there was a great rush of wind. The heavy cabin door blew open with a bang. Rain slanted in. Torrents of rain!

Davy sprang to his feet. So did Pa. Together they pushed the door shut.

"It seems like all the water in the sky is coming down at once," Davy cried excitedly.

"Too much water!" Pa exclaimed. "I don't like the looks of it!"

He had to shout to make himself heard above the noise of the storm. The baby started to cry. The little girls climbed out of bed. Up in the loft, the boys were dressing quickly. Pa stood by the fire with his trencher in his hand and finished his mush in three bites.

"Going out to take a look at the mill," he yelled as he pulled on his coat.

"So am I," Davy declared. A moment later he and Pa were outside, running toward the mill.

The rain pelted down. Trees swayed and

[*16*]

tossed in the wind. The creek roared as it raced past the mill to join the river beyond.

The river roared, too. It was swollen, and yellow with mud. Angrily it rushed along, carrying small trees and broken branches with it.

Davy stared at it in amazement. "Look at

it!" he cried. "Pa! Look at the river! It's 'most out of its banks!"

Pa nodded. "Go tell your ma!" he shouted. "She may have to get out of the cabin quick as scat. Send John here! Jim, too! We'll get the grindstones and gear out of the mill and up to higher ground if we can. Hurry up, now!"

Davy turned without a word and ran toward the cabin. The ground was slippery with rain. He tripped and fell headlong over a tree root. But he picked himself up and ran again. He reached the cabin. He put his hand on the door. And at that very moment he heard Pa shout behind him.

"The river's out, Davy! She's over the bank!"

Davy looked around. The swift-flowing Nolichucky had suddenly grown wider. Yellow water was spreading out rapidly over the clearing. Already it had reached the edge of the corn patch. Davy pushed the door open.

"Ma!" he cried. "The river! It's coming right for us!"

Then everything began to happen at once. There was no time now to save anything in the mill. Pa was running toward the cabin. Ma snatched the baby from her cradle and began to give orders quickly.

"Wilson, grab the covers off the bed! Pick up that sack of cornmeal, Jim! The salt, too!

And the bag of bullets John made last night. Wrap them all in a quilt.

"Bill, gather up all the pots and kettles you can. Davy, you—oh, stop your crying, Becky and Jane! Here's your pa. He'll get you away afore the water hurts you."

"Come on," Pa said hastily. He picked Jane up under one arm and Becky under the other. "You, too, Joey! Hang on to my coat. I'll get these young 'uns to high ground, Ma, and be back as soon as I can."

With Joey hanging to his coat, he ran from the cabin and splashed across the clearing.

Water was coming into the cabin now. Ma pulled a deerskin hunting shirt from a wall peg. She wrapped it around the baby and set off through the rain after Pa.

"You boys get the rifle and the powder," she shouted over her shoulder. "Don't wait for your pa. There isn't time."

"We won't," John told her. He took two powder horns down from the wall and gave one to Davy. He looked around. The other boys had their arms full.

[*19*]

"Can you carry the rifle, too?" he asked Davy quickly. "I'm going to the shed to get some tools."

Davy nodded. He slung the powder horn over his shoulder and took the long, heavy rifle from John.

The swirling water was already up to his knees. The baby's cradle was almost afloat. A low stool bobbed up and down in the doorway.

Davy pushed past it. Holding the rifle tightly, he waded across the clearing. Bill and Wilson and Jim splashed along beside him. John followed a moment later with a small box of nails, the axe, the hoe, and his father's hammer. Slipping and sliding in the mud, the five boys scrambled up the hill.

Soon all the Crocketts stood together in the rain, looking down at their home.

The corn patch and Ma's fine truck garden had disappeared. The woodpile was floating away. So were two stools and a chair and the bucket from the shelf in the corner of the cabin.

A yellow sea of water swept over the clearing

and flowed into the creek. It rose higher and higher around the little log house. It swirled around the mill. Suddenly one corner of the mill sagged.

"Pa!" Joey shouted shrilly. "The mill's tumbling over! Look!"

Slowly the mill tipped to one side, as the water washed away the posts that held it up. With a terrible crackling sound it toppled and fell. Parts of it were swept away at once by the creek.

Pa groaned. "There it goes," he said grimly. "After six months of hard work! And I still owe money for the—"

He broke off suddenly and dragged his hand across his eyes. Davy looked up at him in surprise. He had never heard his father sound so mournful before. He had never seen him look so discouraged. He put his hand on Pa's arm.

"Pa, we can build us another mill," he said eagerly. "Soon as the water goes down, we can start. I'll help you every day, till it's done."

Pa shook his head. "Nope," he said. "We ain't going to build another mill, Davy. And

we ain't going back to that cabin. We had too
much bad luck there. We're going somewhere
else."

"Where?" Ma asked anxiously, as she tried
to shield the baby from the rain.

"Don't know yet," Pa replied. "We'll light
out for Tom Galbreath's cabin now. It ain't
more than four miles off. I got to tell him
what's happened to our mill. And we can wait

there till the storm's passed. Then we'll find us another place to live."

"What about the cows, Pa?" Bill asked. "Do

you want Davy and me to find them and drive them along with us, now?"

"You can fetch them tomorrow," Pa replied. "There won't be anything else left that's worth saving."

He reached for the long rifle, which Davy

was still holding. "Here, son, I'll tote that," he said. "It's a mite heavy for you to carry such a long way."

Davy drew back quickly. "No, it's not," he protested. "Honest, it's not. I could tote it clear to Rogersville and back."

He stood as straight and tall as he could. And he hugged the rifle so tightly that Pa couldn't help smiling, in spite of all his trouble.

"You just tote that rifle as far as Galbreath's without help," he said, "and I'll teach you how to shoot it."

He picked up Jane. Taking Becky by the hand, he started through the trees, and up the muddy trace which led over the hill.

The others followed him. Two hours later they were drying out their clothes before the fire in Tom Galbreath's cabin.

Davy's legs were tired and his arms ached clear to his shoulders. But he didn't care a bit. For he had carried the heavy rifle all the way.

CHAPTER THREE

"He Won't Amount to a Hill of Beans"

IT WAS a fine October afternoon. The sun shone brightly. A little wind rippled the waters of the Holston River. And a log canoe moved swiftly down the stream.

Davy kneeled in the bow of the boat. He was happy. So happy that he couldn't keep quiet. First he whistled and then he sang, as he and Bill pushed their paddles through the water.

"Met Mr. Catfish coming down the stream," Davy chanted,

"Says Mr. Catfish, 'What do you mean?'
"Caught Mr. Catfish by the snout—"
"And turned Mr. Catfish wrong side out,"

[25]

Bill joined in from the stern of the boat. "Here we are, Davy."

He swung the canoe to the left bank of the river. A moment later he and Davy had hauled it part way up on shore.

Bill hid the paddles in the bushes. Davy took a rifle from the canoe and propped it against a tree. He looked down at the five squirrels and the ring-tailed raccoon which lay in the bottom of the boat.

"I'll carry the coon," he announced proudly.

"You've a right to," Bill agreed. "You killed it! And for a ten-year-old that was a mighty fine shot."

Davy grinned. "I'm all through with hunting birds and little things, now I've shot a coon," he boasted. "Some day I aim to get me a bear."

He picked up the raccoon and looked it over. "Do you reckon it's big enough so's Ma can make me a cap out of the skin?" he asked.

"If you don't get a swelled head over shooting it," Bill replied.

"I'll carry the coon," Davy announced proudly

Gathering up the squirrels, he stuffed them inside his deerskin shirt. Then he glanced at the sun.

"Wow!" he exclaimed, reaching for the rifle. "It's 'most time for wagoners to be rolling up to our house."

"Pa will be mad as a hornet if we're not home to tend to the horses," Davy said quickly. "I'm going to hurry."

He pushed his way through the bushes and started up the path which led from the river to a log house.

It was a rough, two-story house, with a log barn just behind it. The yard around the house was bare and half full of stumps.

A winding road ran past the house. And a wooden sign over the doorway swung back and forth in the wind. It said: CROCKETT'S TAVERN.

Davy remembered the day that Pa had decided to open this tavern. It was soon after the flood. The family had stayed in Tom Galbreath's cabin while Pa looked around for a place to live. He had found some land near the Holston River, about fifteen miles to the west.

"The land's near a settlement, and it's close to a road," Pa had told Ma and the others, when he returned to the cabin. "I aim to build a good house there. And to open a tavern where folks can come to eat and spend the night."

"A tavern!" Ma had exclaimed in dismay. "You don't know how to run a tavern."

"I can learn," Pa said. And that's just what he had tried to do.

Everyone in the family except Baby Sally and little Jane had worked hard to help him. But Pa hadn't had much money to spend in starting this new business. And the tavern was a poor-looking place.

The road which ran past it was a busy one. It stretched from Abingdon in Virginia to the little town of Knoxville in Tennessee. From there it ran west through the wilderness as far as the settlement of Nashville.

Families used that road, going west in wagons and carts to settle new homes. Hunters and trappers used it, heading east with pack horses loaded with furs.

Drovers traveled over it, driving cattle to sell to farmers in Virginia and Kentucky. And wagoners rolled along it, in big covered wagons, carrying freight between the settlements in the West and the towns in the East.

Many of these travelers looked at Pa Crockett's tavern and passed it by. But sometimes a hunter or a trapper or a drover stopped to spend the night. And wagoners arrived nearly every day.

Often there were eight or ten huge white-topped wagons in the tavern yard by sundown. Then Pa talked to the men. Ma cooked the evening meal. And the boys unhitched the horses and carried water to the watering trough.

Davy liked the wagoners, for they were a jolly lot of men. But he didn't like caring for the horses, or lugging water.

"No wagoners here yet," he cried joyfully to Bill as the two boys drew near the tavern. "I'm going to show my coon to Ma."

Bill nodded and stopped to fasten his moccasins, which were both untied. Davy ran

[*30*]

ahead, across the yard and around to the front
of the house.

Jim was sitting on the log doorstep, scraping
out a cow's horn. A long-eared black-and-tan
dog lay at his feet. The hound got up to greet
Davy and to sniff at the raccoon.

Davy held it high, out of the dog's reach.

"Get down, Zip!" he commanded. He spoke to Jim. "Where's Ma?" he asked.

"Inside fixing supper," Jim replied. "Who gave you that squirrel? It's the biggest one I ever saw."

Davy's face turned scarlet. "It's not a squirrel!" he exclaimed hotly. "It's a—" Suddenly he stopped. Even Jim's teasing couldn't make him angry today.

"It's my first raccoon," he replied proudly. "Do you want to know how I got it?"

"Sure I do," Jim replied.

"Well," Davy said, with a twinkle in his eyes, "it was this way. Bill had the rifle and he was back a piece down the river bank. All at once I spied old Mr. Coon high up in a tree.

"Well, I couldn't shoot him without a gun. So I just grinned at him, hard as I could. Like a possum grins when it's getting ready for a fight. Mr. Coon got so scared he fell right out of the tree at my feet, dead as a door nail. And that's all there was to it!"

Jim laughed. And Davy heard a low chuckle just behind him. He looked around quickly.

There stood Pa and a wagoner named John Dunn. Pa didn't seem much pleased with Davy's story. But Mr. Dunn clapped the boy on the shoulder.

"That's a good yarn, young 'un," he declared. "A fellow who can grin a coon to death ought to make a first-rate hunter."

Davy flushed. "I didn't know anyone was around here but Jim," he said sheepishly. "Where's your wagon, Mr. Dunn?"

"Down the road," Mr. Dunn replied. "A piece of harness broke, so I left my boy, Tom, to fix it. And I walked ahead to have a talk with your pa. We've been sitting back of the shed, trying to figure out who's going to be the next President."

"What's the matter with George Washington?" Jim asked, getting to his feet. "Ain't he going to be President any more?"

Mr. Dunn shook his head. "He's been President for eight years, and figures that's long enough," he replied. "He says it's time we elected another man now. At least that's what I read in the Knoxville paper."

[*33*]

"It will be hard to find a man as good as Washington," Pa declared. He took the raccoon, which Davy was still holding, and looked it over.

"That ain't a bad coon," he remarked, handing it back. "You get it skinned in a hurry now, Davy. Then tend to that wood you forgot to chop afore you went hunting."

Davy nodded. "I'll show the coon to Ma first," he said. And, stepping around Zip, he went into the tavern.

Mr. Dunn watched him go. "That's a fine strong boy you've got there, Crockett!" he exclaimed.

Pa Crockett smiled. "Davy's strong enough," he agreed. "And he's getting to be a good shot with the rifle. But he's wild. Always telling crazy stories like that one about the coon. And off in the woods half the time when he ought to be working."

He shook his head. "I don't know what's going to become of the boy when he grows up," Pa went on. "I reckon he won't amount to a hill of beans."

But Pa Crockett was wrong.

CHAPTER FOUR

The Frolic

Davy grunted. He turned over in bed and opened one eye.

"Quit shaking me," he said to Wilson. "I'm awake."

"You'd better get up, then," Wilson told him, starting for the ladder. "Ma has hollered at you more times than a hen has feathers. And folks from the settlement have started coming here already."

"What folks?" Davy asked, still half asleep. Then suddenly he remembered.

He sprang out of bed. Grabbing his trousers, he pulled them on hastily. What a thickwit he was to sleep late on such a day!

It was Fourth of July! Independence Day! People from miles around were coming to celebrate with a frolic in the tavern yard. And he wasn't even dressed yet!

He slipped his arms into his brown linsey shirt and combed his hair with his fingers. In no time he was scrambling down the ladder.

In the room below, Ma Crockett and several other women were talking. None of them paid any attention to Davy. And he stopped just long enough to snatch a large piece of cornbread from the shelf, for his breakfast. Then he went outside. For a moment he stood on the log step, eating his cornbread and looking around.

It was a splendid day, with the sky as blue as Becky's shortgown. The sun said it wasn't nearly eight o'clock. And the yard was already filling up with people.

They came in wagons, on horseback, and on foot. There were girls and boys of all ages. There were women carrying babies. And other women carrying big baskets filled with good things to eat.

There were men with rifles, who planned to take part in the shooting match in the afternoon. And men with no rifles.

It seemed to Davy that there must be nearly fifty people in the clearing. All laughing and talking and getting ready to have a good time.

Before long, Jed Flint arrived with the drum he had carried in the Revolutionary War. Abe Tobin had his fife. And a man named Blake brought a big American flag, which he had bought in Philadelphia before he had come to Tennessee.

Davy ran to fetch an axe and chopped down a slim tree for a flagpole. When the tree was trimmed he helped Mr. Blake and another man set the pole in the ground.

Then he held the flag while Mr. Blake tied it to the rope, which he had slung from the top of the pole. Davy had never seen a flag before, and he counted the stars curiously. There were fifteen.

"They're real pretty, ain't they?" Davy said.

Mr. Blake nodded. "There's a star for each state in the Union except Tennessee," he told

They came in wagons, on horseback, and on foot

the boy as he tightened a knot in the rope. "This flag was made before Tennessee became a state, two years ago."

He took the flag from Davy. "Well, Jed, here she goes," he cried.

Jed Flint nodded his head and began to beat loudly on his drum. Abe Tobin played "Yankee Doodle" on his fife. The crowd became quiet. And up went the red, white, and blue flag to the top of the pole.

Then all the men with rifles fired them off with a great bang. And someone shouted, "Three cheers for the United States of America!"

"Hurray!" yelled the people. "Hurray! Hurray!"

"The good free United States!" another man shouted. "Let's hope she always stays free and never does anything wrong."

"Hurray!" the people cried again.

A little wind caught the flag and blew it out against the sky. Davy's heart fluttered.

He didn't know much about his country. He didn't know how big it was or what lay beyond it. But something about that flag made him feel good all over. And he knew suddenly that his country would never do anything wrong if *he* could help it.

"Hurray!" he shouted at the top of his lungs.

Once more the men shot off their rifles. As the smoke cleared away, the people began to laugh and talk again. Then it was time for the games to begin.

The wrestling matches came first and lasted a long time. For no man could throw Ned Hardman, the blacksmith. Next came the foot races. There was one for the men and one for the boys.

Davy ran like a deer in the boys' race and won it with no trouble at all. But in the knife-throwing contest, he threw his knife too far. And it stuck in the ground nearly a foot beyond the mark.

It was noon when this contest was over, and everyone was ready for dinner. So the women sat down on logs or tree stumps, and opened their baskets of food, and gathered their children around them. The men gave everybody juicy hunks of warm venison and bear meat which they had roasted over hot coals in a big pit.

Ma Crockett called her family together under the sycamore tree near the house. All except Pa and John and Jim and Bill. John and

Jim were away working on near-by farms. Pa
and Bill had stayed in the tavern to wait on
people who might want to buy food or drink.

Davy ate and ate and ate. Finally he wiped
his mouth on the back of his hand.

"I'm full," he announced happily. "When
does the shooting match start, Ma?"

"I don't know," his mother replied, rubbing some bear grease from Sally's chin. "That Mr. Blake, who's just settled here, has asked your pa if he can't have a meeting first. He aims to start a school for the settlement if folks want one bad enough."

Davy looked alarmed. "I don't want one," he declared hastily.

"Me neither," Wilson added. "I'm not going."

"You are if your pa tells you to," his mother said firmly. "Land sakes! Here you are, thirteen years old. Davy's near twelve. Joey's ten. And not one of you can even write your name, or read it, either. It's a—"

"But, Ma," Davy broke in, "I don't want to—"

"Hush!" his mother commanded. "Here's your pa now to tell about the meeting."

And there was Pa Crockett, standing on the tavern steps and banging on a pan to make folks listen to him. He told them all that the meeting was just for grownups. And he said that the children had better go off and play.

[*44*]

So the girls went off to the wood lot for a game of Blind Man's Buff. And the boys started for the Holston River.

They had such good fun swimming, and diving from the canoe, that they almost forgot about the shooting match. At the sound of the first shot, they started splashing out of the water. In a few minutes they were dressed and racing for the tavern.

The men had been shooting at a board which was nailed to a big oak tree at the end of the fenced-in pasture. Now they were trying to hit a horn button which had been fastened to the center of the board.

One after another they tried it. Some came close, but none succeeded. Then lanky Tim Taylor raised his rifle. He was the best hunter for miles around. Davy stood as near him as he could, watching him closely.

"Zing!" went Tim's bullet, straight to the mark. The button disappeared as it broke into tiny pieces. The crowd cheered. Several men pounded Tim on the back, and shook his hand. Davy looked up at him admiringly.

[45]

"I bet you could hit a mosquito right between the eyes if you wanted to," Davy said.
"I aim to shoot as good as you do some day."

Tim Taylor laughed. "You don't need to,
young 'un," he said, winking at the man who
stood next to him. "All you have to do is to
grin at a coon and he falls right down out of a
tree! At least that's what John Dunn told me
a while back."

Davy's face turned red. But he beamed
happily when Tim handed him his rifle.

"She's loaded, son," said Tim, eyeing the
boy with a kindly smile. "Want to try one shot
at the board?"

Davy was speechless. His eyes shone as he
carefully took the rifle. It was longer and heav-
ier than Pa's. But it balanced nicely as Davy
lifted it to his shoulder.

"She's got a good, strong kick," said Tim.
"Brace yourself. That's right."

"Whillikens! Davy's going to shoot Tim
Taylor's rifle!" shouted Wilson. Several men
turned to watch and Joey came running up.
Everybody was quiet while Davy aimed.

Bang! Wilson ran toward the board. "Davy hit it!" shouted Wilson. "He hit it on the side."

"And I was aiming right at the middle," said Davy, shaking his head as Tim Taylor took the rifle.

"Not bad, though," said Tim. Davy felt better. "You practice a lot and you might be a real good shot some day."

The shooting match was over now, and people were beginning to go home. Pa set Davy, Wilson, and Bill to cleaning up the yard.

When the work was finished, there wasn't a soul in the clearing but Bill and Davy. They were lying on the ground, tired out, and looking up at the evening sky.

"Before Ma calls us to supper, tell me one thing," Davy said anxiously. "Are they sure enough going to start that dratted school?"

"Sure as a catfish has got horns," replied Bill, slapping at a mosquito. "They're cutting logs for it next month. And, come frost, you'll be there, too. You see if you won't."

But when Mr. Blake opened his school that fall, Davy Crockett was many miles away.

CHAPTER FIVE

Davy Leaves Home

IT HAD been drizzling all day. Davy was soaked to the skin. He was tired of tramping along the rough muddy road, and he was tired of driving cattle. He waved his stick at a big black cow which was straying into the underbrush.

"Get over there, you bug-eyed bullfrog," he shouted. "Get over there, or I'll tie your stringy tail right to your horns."

Mr. Jacob Siler chuckled. "Getting mad at them don't do no good, Davy," he said, walking faster to catch up with the boy. "We stop when we get over this hill and make camp. Then you shoot some meat for supper, *ja?*"

Davy nodded soberly at the old Dutchman. "How much farther have we got to go afore we get to that there Natural Bridge?" he asked.

"Only three hundred miles," Mr. Siler replied cheerfully. "We walk a hundred miles in fifteen days already. Do you still feel bad sometimes that you come with me?"

"Yes," Davy replied honestly. And he pushed on, so that he would not have to talk any more.

There were times when he liked driving cattle for Mr. Siler. But there were other times when he longed to see Ma and Pa and the rest of his family. He wondered how they all were and what they were doing at home.

He had left home very suddenly. All because Pa Crockett needed money, and Mr. Siler wanted help in driving his cattle.

The old Dutchman and his herd of cows had arrived at the tavern one warm evening in September. John and Jim were away, working on farms near by. Bill and Wilson were busy unhitching horses. So Pa had called Davy to take Mr. Siler's cattle to the fenced-in pasture.

[*49*]

The boy had managed the cows well, and Mr. Siler was pleased. That night he told Pa that he would like to hire Davy to drive the cattle all the way to his farm near Natural Bridge, in Virginia.

Pa looked doubtful when he heard this, and Ma had shaken her head.

"He was only twelve last month!" she exclaimed. "He's too young to go so far. How will he ever get home again?"

Mr. Siler laughed. "Oh, I take care of that," he had promised. "I send him back with someone right away. And I pay you good money right now for his help. So you let him go, *ja?"*

He pulled his purse from his pocket and laid it on the table.

Pa Crockett eyed it thoughtfully. Times were hard and he was not doing very well with his tavern. He turned to his wife.

"You know, Ma," he said, "Davy ain't much use to me around here, 'cause he's always off in the woods with the rifle. Half the time he don't do his chores. Maybe a job like this would be good for him."

"Maybe it would," Ma agreed. "And if Mr. Siler will send him home quick, I—"

"*Ja! Ja!"* Mr. Siler broke in. "I take care of that."

And so the matter had been settled.

That night Davy had been puffed up with pride because he was going away on a long journey. But his heart sank the next morning when Ma handed him a knapsack full of clothing and kissed him good-by.

Yet he had done his best to smile when Pa clapped him on the back and told him to mind

[*51*]

Mr. Siler. And he had laughed at Becky when she cried and said she'd never see him again. Then he had set out, whistling loudly, so that no one would know how badly he felt about leaving home.

Ever since that morning, he and Mr. Siler had been traveling together. From dawn until late afternoon each day they had driven the cattle over the rough road which led northeast to Natural Bridge.

They had climbed high hills and splashed through creeks. They had passed through a large village and through several small settlements.

Once they had spent the night in a tavern. Twice they had slept in log farmhouses. But the rest of the time they had made camp by the roadside wherever Mr. Siler wanted to stop.

"I hope the old man can find us a good place tonight," Davy thought, as he poked a thin spotted cow with his long gad. "A nice dry place, where we can build us a fire."

He had reached the top of the hill by this

time. He looked about quickly. Suddenly he shouted for joy. Turning around, he called back to Mr. Siler, who was puffing up the hill some distance behind him.

"Hey, Mr. Siler!" he cried. "There's a cabin here, back from the road a piece. An old one that's kind of tumbling down. But there's no one living in it. I'll drive the critters into the clearing."

"*Ja!*" Mr. Siler called back.

Davy ran to the head of the herd and turned the cows back. As soon as they were feeding peacefully he looked over the cabin.

The door sagged open and the roof was partly gone. But the chimney was still standing. There was a pile of dry leaves in one corner of the cabin which someone had used as a bed. And there were a few sticks of partly burned wood in the fireplace.

Dropping his knapsack to the dirt floor, Davy opened it quickly. He rummaged around until he found the tinder box which Ma had packed with his extra shirt. By the time Mr. Siler arrived, the boy had a fire going.

[*53*]

The old Dutchman was delighted. "Davy, you get us a rabbit now like you did last night!" he said, handing Davy his rifle. "I have bread we bought in Blue Plum settlement this morning. So we eat good and sleep dry and tomorrow we feel fine. *Ja?*"

"*Ja!*" Davy agreed with a grin. He had forgotten already how homesick he had been just a short time before. Whistling gaily, he struck off for the woods behind the cabin. In less than an hour he was back with a fat rabbit.

Mr. Siler had watered the cows at a near-by stream and had found more wood for the fire.

It was damp and it smoked when he laid it on the flames. But it was soon burning brightly.

Davy skinned the rabbit and cut it up. Before long he and the Dutchman were feasting well, while rain dripped through the hole in the cabin roof, and the cows huddled together outside the sagging door. Then Mr. Siler wiped his greasy hands on his trousers and lighted his pipe.

"You feel good now, eh, Davy?" he asked.

Davy nodded. "Feel like I could whip my weight in wildcats," he declared, tossing a rabbit bone into the fire.

Mr. Siler chuckled. He liked this fine strong boy, with his shining black eyes and his quick smile. He liked the way he could handle a rifle. And the way he swung along the road after the cows, hour after hour, without complaining.

"He is a nice boy," he said to himself. "Maybe I don't send him back to his father after all. Maybe I just keep him in Virginia with me."

Puffing on his pipe, the old Dutchman sat

[55]

for a long time before the fire, wondering how he could manage this. But he did not speak of it next morning, when they set out again with the cows. Indeed, Mr. Siler did not mention it at all until they had reached his farm in Virginia several weeks later.

CHAPTER SIX

A Lucky Meeting

THE ROAD which ran southwest past Natural Bridge was winding and rough. But the three covered wagons had been rolling along steadily all the afternoon, under the gray December sky. Suddenly the driver of the first wagon pulled hard on his reins.

"Whoa, there!" John Dunn shouted to his rearing horses. "Whoa!"

The brake on the big wagon squealed. The wagon came to a quick stop. Both lead horses snorted and tossed their heads. Then they stood still. Mr. Dunn jumped to the ground, with his long black whip in his hand.

"Consarn you!" he cried angrily, shaking

the whip at the boy who stood by the roadside. "What are you up to, anyway? Scaring my poor critters half to death, running up that way! I've a good mind to—"

He stopped short. "Lord bless me! It's Davy Crockett!" he exclaimed. "What in blazes are you doing four hundred miles from home?"

"Working," Davy replied, panting for breath. "I mean—I'm not working right now. I—I was fooling around up the road—a bit, and I spotted your wagons. I—I just had to stop you!"

He drew a deep breath. Mr. Dunn started to speak. But Davy went on quickly. "I didn't aim to scare your horses. But I just had to talk to you, Mr. Dunn. How far are you going?"

"Clear to Knoxville in Tennessee," Mr. Dunn replied, wondering why the boy seemed so upset.

"Then you'll go right past our house!" Davy exclaimed joyfully. "Can I ride that far with you? I'll look after the horses and do anything you want me to do, if you'll just take me along. Will you?"

Mr. Dunn tossed his long black whip into the wagon. "It depends on why you want to go," he said slowly. "How in thunder did you get 'way over here in Virginia, anyway?"

"Pa sent me," Davy replied. "He hired me out to drive cattle for a man named Siler, who lives about half a mile from here. Mr. Siler promised he'd send me back home with someone right away. But now he won't do it."

"Why not?" Mr. Dunn asked, turning up his coat collar as a cold wind swept down from the north.

Davy shook his head. "I don't know," he said. "He just keeps telling me that I'm his boy now, and that I have to stay here. I'd run off but I can't get home alone, 'cause it's so far and I haven't enough money to buy food. I'll work like anything if you'll take me along with you."

Mr. Dunn rubbed his chin thoughtfully. "It sounds to me like your pa bound you out to this man, Davy, and didn't tell you about it," he said. "I'm liable to get into a peck of trouble if I help you run away."

[*59*]

"But Pa didn't bind me out," Davy protested. "Honest, he didn't. I've been working here for Mr. Siler for more than a month now. And I want to see my folks so bad, I—"

He ducked his head quickly, for tears had started to his eyes. Bending over, he pretended to fasten his shoe. When he straightened up, Mr. Dunn was looking at him soberly.

"Davy," he said, putting his hand on the boy's shoulder, "I ain't going to help you run away from Siler. But listen sharp, now.

"There's a tavern down the road about seven miles ahead. I aim to put in there tonight with my wagons. I've got some room in one of the wagons. And if you should happen to get to that tavern by daylight tomorrow—"

He stopped speaking and winked slowly.

Davy grinned from ear to ear. "I'll be there!" he exclaimed joyfully. "Don't you go without me!"

"Can't even remember that I said I'd take you," Mr. Dunn replied with a smile. He glanced at the sky. "Looks like snow," he went on. "We'd better get on our way."

"Davy," he said, "listen sharp, now."

He shouted to his two sons, who had stopped the other wagons by the roadside. "Let's roll!" he called, and, climbing up into his seat, he picked up his reins. The horses strained at the traces and the wheels began to turn.

Davy ran off at once toward the Silers' house, which was half a mile away. It was Sunday and Mr. and Mrs. Siler were visiting neighbors.

"But they'll be home soon," Davy thought, as he opened the door of the empty house. "I'll just have time to get my things together afore they come back. Then tonight I'll sneak off, when I'm sure they're asleep."

Climbing to the loft quickly, Davy gathered up his clothes. He stuffed them into his knapsack and thrust it under the head of his bed. Then he scrambled down the ladder just as he heard the Silers coming up the path. When they opened the door, Davy was busily mending the fire.

The boy found it hard to eat supper that night, for he was almost too excited to choke down his food. As soon as the meal was over, he went back to the loft again. Without taking his clothes off, he crawled between his blankets. And there he lay, turning and tossing uneasily, waiting for the Silers to go to bed.

At last, late in the evening, he heard Mr. Siler bar the door and bank the fire. Half an hour later the old Dutchman began to snore loudly. But a long time passed before the sound of Mrs. Siler's heavy breathing told Davy that she, too, was asleep.

Even then, Davy waited awhile before he crawled quietly out of bed. Shouldering his knapsack, he crept to the ladder.

He began climbing down, stopping on each rung to listen. Suddenly Mrs. Siler murmured in her sleep. Davy's heart pounded with excitement. He waited for a long minute. Nothing happened. At last he went on down the ladder. He tiptoed to the door.

He lifted the heavy bar without a sound. Stepping outside, he closed the door carefully behind him. Then he gasped in dismay.

It was snowing hard! So hard that Davy could see only a few feet ahead of him. Already the snow was deep. And the path which led to the main road had completely disappeared.

"I'll just have to guess which way to go," Davy thought. And he set off through the trees as fast as he could travel. Before long he had found the main road and was headed for the tavern, seven miles away!

An icy wind cut through Davy's clothes. Snow beat against his face and stuck to his eyelashes, nearly blinding him. But he couldn't help chuckling as he bent his head forward and fought his way against the storm.

"The snow's filling my tracks up so fast that old Siler will never know which way I went," he said, half aloud. "I'd just like to see his face when he finds I'm gone."

He stopped for a minute to pull his coon-skin cap down over his ears. Then on he plodded. And on, and on—all alone in a wet, cold, white world. Only the trees on either side of him told him where the road lay.

Soon the snow was nearly up to his knees, and his legs ached so that he longed to rest. He tried to whistle to keep up his courage. But the wind nearly choked him.

"Better save my breath," he thought. "I've got to keep going ahead. I've got to keep going ahead until I reach that tavern because when I get there I'm going to start for home! I've got to keep going ahead!"

And he did keep going ahead, stumbling and slipping in the snow. He was so tired now that he could hardly lift his feet. Still he pushed on bravely, as the sky grew lighter in the east. At last he rounded a bend in the road. And there was the tavern!

Several men were hitching horses to three wagons which stood in the yard. It was Tom

Dunn who first spied Davy, struggling through the snow.

"Hey, Pa!" he shouted. "Here's young Crockett!"

He left the horse he was harnessing and ran to meet Davy. So did Mr. Dunn.

"Lord love us!" he exclaimed, taking the boy by the arm. "You're most froze to death, lad. I never thought you'd try to make it in this storm."

"But I did try!" Davy exclaimed with a feeble grin. "And I got here!"

Mr. Dunn laughed. "Reckon you could wade right across the Mississippi River if you had to," he said. "Now into the tavern with you. Our wagons ain't going to turn a wheel till you're warmed up and so full of food you're ready to bust."

He led Davy into the tavern and sat him down before the fire. Then he shouted to the tavern keeper to bring hot hominy and eggs and cornbread and bacon.

Half an hour later Mr. Dunn's wagon train was on its way to Tennessee. In the first wagon

Davy Crockett lay curled up on a pile of furs, covered with a warm bearskin, and sound asleep.

It was many weeks before Davy finally reached home. And then what a joyful meeting there was! Again and again the boy had to tell of his trip to Virginia with Mr. Siler. And of his escape from the old Dutchman's house.

Ma Crockett smiled proudly when Davy told how he had fought his way through the blizzard. Pa vowed that he would make the fur fly, if Mr. Siler ever set foot in the tavern again. And before the evening was over, Wilson gave Davy a piece of good news.

Mr. Blake, the schoolmaster, had moved away. The school was closed up, tight as a drum.

"I reckon it won't open up ever again," Wilson said.

But the school was opened the following fall. And Davy Crockett was there on the very first day.

CHAPTER SEVEN

Davy Wins a Fight

IT WAS warm in the little log schoolhouse. So warm that Mr. Kitchen, the new school-master, told Joey Crockett to open the door wide and leave it open.

Davy winked at his brother when Joey came back and sat down beside him on the puncheon bench. Then he took a quick look over his shoulder to see what was going on outside.

The woods were red and gold in the bright October sunlight. It was just the kind of weather for hunting coons and possums. Or for paddling up the Holston River in search of wild grapes and hickory nuts. Yet here he was, spending his fourth day in school!

[68]

Davy sighed impatiently. Then he remembered how pleased Ma had been when he had promised to learn his letters. So he picked up his goose-quill pen and bent over his brown-paper copybook.

There was a name at the top of the page. It was his own name, which Mr. Kitchen had written out for him. Dipping his pen into his horn inkwell, Davy copied it, slowly and carefully, several times.

Big Matt Brown, who sat right behind him, watched him with a sly smile. Suddenly Matt's hand shot out. Quickly he tipped Davy's inkwell to one side, spilling ink all over the carefully written page. Davy was on his feet in an instant.

"You big buzzard!" he cried angrily, turning to the older boy. "I'm going to—" He drew back his fist.

At the sound of his voice all the other boys turned around and Mr. Kitchen jumped to his feet. He pounded on his desk.

"I'll have no fighting in this school!" he cried. "Sit down, David, or I'll thrash you."

"But he spoiled my copybook," Davy said hotly. "He—"

"Sit down!" thundered Mr. Kitchen, reaching for his long birch rod.

Davy sat down hastily, while the other boys snickered.

"Now get back to your lessons, all of you," ordered the schoolmaster. "And remember that I'll whip any boy in this school who starts a fight." Still frowning, Mr. Kitchen took his seat and began whittling a pen from a gray goose feather.

Every boy went back to work at once. For Mr. Kitchen was a strong man and he used his stinging birch rod frequently.

Davy mopped up the ink on his copybook with his shirtsleeve.

"You just wait till I get you outside," he muttered to Matt. "I'll fix you."

Matt smiled. He was the biggest boy in the school. He bullied the younger boys whenever he wanted to. And no one had yet been brave enough to fight him.

"You little runt—you wouldn't dare touch me!" he whispered to Davy. And then he promptly forgot Davy's threat.

But Davy didn't forget it. That afternoon Mr. Kitchen dismissed Davy and the younger boys as usual. But he kept the older boys so that they could finish their spelling.

The minute Davy was outside of the school-house, he raced off toward the side road where Matt Brown lived. Joey followed close at his heels.

"Where are you going?" Joey panted. "What are you going to do?"

"Lay for Matt Brown! That's what!" Davy explained rapidly. "I'm going to ambush him, Joey, and scratch his face all to a flitterjig. All by myself, too. Don't you mess into it."

He dived into the bushes at the roadside, pulling Joey in after him. For several minutes the two boys crouched there, waiting for Matt. At last he came along, swaggering down the road.

"Remember what I told you," Davy whispered to Joey, who was looking a little scared. "Leave him to me. I can handle him."

It was risky to fight such a big boy as Matt, and Davy knew it. But he was so angry that he didn't care.

His heart pounded as Matt came closer to the bushes. He drew a deep breath. Suddenly he sprang from his hiding place, yelling like a wildcat.

Like a wildcat, he made a long leap at big Matt's face and scratched it for all he was worth. Matt was taken off guard. He shouted in fear and fell back. Davy came at him with all his strength, and butted him so hard that Matt nearly went down.

Joey jumped up and down in excitement.

"Give it to him!" he yelled. "Give him salt and vinegar, Davy! Knock him into a cocked hat!"

Davy punched and pounded and kicked. Matt swung out wildly and tried to grab him. But Davy was too quick. Soon Matt was turning his head away to escape Davy's blows. Like most bullies, he was no good in a real fight.

" 'Nuff," he whimpered. " 'Nuff! I've had enough!" And he blubbered like a little boy.

Davy stood back and looked up at him.

"Now, are you ever going to plague me again?" he demanded. "Answer me quick or I'll give you some more."

"No," Matt wailed miserably. "No, I ain't —never!" He turned suddenly and ran down the road without looking back.

Davy laughed a shaky little laugh and wiped his hot face with his sleeve. He looked around at Wilson and two other boys who had come up just as the fight ended.

"I sure—fixed—him!" he panted.

"You sure did," Nick Duncan exclaimed, slapping Davy on the back. "We won't any of us ever be scared of Matt again."

Davy grinned proudly, but Wilson looked at him soberly.

"You're in bad trouble now, Davy," he said. "Matt will tell on you, and old Kitchen will give you a terrible thrashing because you started this fight."

Davy shrugged his shoulders. However, as he walked home later with Joey and Wilson, he thought about what Wilson had said.

"I reckon I won't go back to school for a few days," he announced as they drew near the tavern. "Not till old Kitchen's had time to forget about this. I'll just start off when you do in

[75]

the morning, so's Pa won't know about it, and hide out in the woods all day and—"

"And come back with us at night," Joey added quickly. "That idea's a humdinger!"

"It will work, too, if neither of you tell on me," Davy declared.

"We won't," both boys promised together. And they kept their promise.

For several days Davy carried out his plan. He wasn't very happy about it, though. For he didn't have much fun alone in the woods all day, without a rifle.

He felt a little ashamed of himself, too. Especially when Ma asked him hopefully how he was getting on with his lessons. Yet he could not muster up enough courage to go back and face Mr. Kitchen.

Then one morning, just as he was getting ready to start out with Wilson and Joey, there was a knock at the door. Pa answered it, and came back with a note in his hands. He read it through slowly and turned to Davy.

"This note's from Mr. Kitchen," he said, looking puzzled. "He wants to know why you ain't in school. You've been going every day, Davy, haven't you?"

"No," Davy confessed unhappily. "You see, I had a fight, and Mr. Kitchen's going to whip me for it if I go back, so—"

Pa interrupted him. "You mean you ain't going to school 'cause you're afeard of a whipping!" he exclaimed angrily. "Look here, boy, I've paid Mr. Kitchen a whole pile of coonskins and a bushel of corn to teach you your lessons. Now you march yourself off to that school in double-quick time."

Davy shook his head. "Mr. Kitchen will cook me up to a crackling if I go, Pa," he protested. "And—"

"I'll cook you up to a worse crackling if you don't do what you're told," Pa interrupted angrily, and he picked up a hickory stick which stood in the corner of the room.

There were few things that ever frightened Davy Crockett. One of them was a whipping. Without a word, he ran from the tavern and raced across the clearing. Pa ran after him with his stick in his hand.

[77]

Up the road Davy sped, with Pa behind him. He ran for nearly a mile, till he rounded the top of the hill.

"Pa can't see me now," he thought. And he

darted into some underbrush at the side of the road and hid.

A minute later Pa passed his hiding place. He stood in the road not ten feet away, puffing and panting and looking about for Davy. Then, shaking his head, he started back for the tavern.

Davy waited until his father was well on his way toward home. At last he stood up.

"Pa will be mad at me now for a week," he thought forlornly. "He has a right to be, too. But I don't dare go home till he gets over it."

Brushing some dry leaves from his clothes, he wondered where he could go and what he had better do next. Suddenly he had an idea.

A man his father knew, named Jesse Cheek, was starting off that very morning to drive a herd of cattle to Virginia.

"I know how to drive cows," Davy said, half aloud. "Maybe Mr. Cheek will hire me to go with him." And he set off at a run for Mr. Cheek's house, several miles away.

CHAPTER EIGHT

Trouble for Davy

Mrs. JOHN GRAY finished the last seam in the coarse blue jacket she was making. Stepping to the kitchen door, she called to the tall, lanky boy who was hoeing the young corn in the field near by.

"Davy," she cried. "Come here a minute."

"I'm a-coming," Davy called back. Dropping his hoe, he ran to the house.

Mrs. Gray held up the jacket so he could see it. "Do you want wooden buttons on this?" she asked. "Or do you want horn buttons?"

Davy looked puzzled. "It don't matter to me, ma'am, just so they button," he replied soberly. "You sure are nice to make that jacket for me. And the shirt and trousers, too."

"I'm charging you a fair price for them," Mrs. Gray said with a smile. "The jacket will be finished tonight. Do those shoes you bought from the peddler yesterday fit all right?"

"Right enough," Davy answered jauntily. "But I don't aim to wear any of my new clothes till I get to Baltimore."

He pulled down the handle of the pump near the kitchen door and stuck his mouth under the stream of water to get a drink.

[*81*]

"You know," he went on, wiping his chin on his arm, "sometimes I can't hardly wait to get to Baltimore. I haven't ever seen a big place like that. It's a breeze of luck for me that Mr. Myer will take me along when he starts tomorrow with his next load of flour."

"Maybe it is," Mrs. Gray said doubtfully. "And maybe it isn't. For some reason, I don't trust that wagoner. I don't know why. Anyway, we'd like to keep you here with us, Davy. You've been a great help to Mr. Gray."

Davy grinned. "Reckon I'd better get back and finish hoeing that corn for him," he said. And he started for the cornfield, feeling very grown up and quite pleased with himself.

More than six months had passed since Davy had run away from Pa and his hickory stick. Busy months! First he had helped Mr. Cheek drive a large herd of cattle to Front Royal, in Virginia. Then he had traveled with the wagoner, Adam Myer, to Gerardstown. When Mr. Myer decided to spend the winter there, Davy had found work on John Gray's farm at twenty-five cents a day.

All winter long he had worked hard for Mr. Gray. He had saved up his money for new clothes which he needed badly. Now they were all paid for and he still had seven dollars left.

"I'll buy Ma and the girls some gimcracks in Baltimore with part of that money," he thought as he hoed the corn. And he wondered how his family was getting along.

He had missed them all sadly, right after he had run away. Indeed, he still missed them. But he wasn't going to try to make his way home just yet. He wanted to see more of the world first. When Mr. Myer stopped his white-topped wagon in front of the Grays' house next morning, Davy was ready to leave.

He said good-by to the Grays and promised to stop to see them if he came back through Gerardstown. Then he handed his bundle of new clothes up to the wagoner and climbed up beside him. Mr. Myer shouted to his horses. Slowly the big wheels began to turn.

All day long the wagon rolled through the beautiful Virginia countryside. Past farms where fruit trees bloomed. Past wide green

[83]

fields. Through little villages where dogs ran out to bark at the horses, and children stopped playing to watch them go by.

In the evening Mr. Myer found a place near a brook to stop for the night. He built a fire and cooked a good meal, while Davy fed and watered the horses.

Not until supper was over did Davy remember the seven dollars which he had put into his pocket. He fished out the money and held it out to Mr. Myer. "I reckon I'd better give this to you for safe keeping," he said. "I might lose it afore we get to Baltimore."

Adam Myer pulled at his stubby red beard and cleared his throat. " 'Deed you might," he replied. "I'll keep it safe for you." And he opened his purse and put the money inside. Then he pulled out his pipe and leaned back against a tree. Soon he was telling Davy a long funny story about one of his trips.

That night he and Davy slept on the ground near the wagon. When the sun rose next morning they set out again. Two days later they rumbled into Baltimore.

Slowly the big wheels began to turn

Davy helped the wagoner unload his barrels of flour and roll them into a store at the edge of town. Then he brushed some flour from his new clothes and set off, whistling gaily, to see the sights. And what a lot of strange new things there were for a backwoods boy to see!

Buildings standing right up against each other. Streets paved with bumpy cobblestones. A market where fine vegetables, fruits, and cakes were on sale. Shops and churches. And more people than trees in a forest.

Up and down the streets Davy wandered until it was nearly dark. Then he asked the way to the tavern where he was to meet the wagoner. There he spent the night.

The next day he started out again, to explore other parts of the little city. At last he came to the wharf which ran out into Chesapeake Bay.

Big sailing ships were coming and going in the harbor. Davy stared at them as though he he could hardly believe his eyes.

"They're like birds a-flying over the water," he thought. "I wonder if I dare step aboard one."

[86]

He sauntered down the wharf, watching sailors load and unload the vessels. Near the end of the wharf lay a ship with her sails furled. There seemed to be no one aboard her.

Davy walked up the gangplank and stepped

on the deck. At that very moment the captain of the ship came out of his cabin.

"Where did you come from?" he asked gruffly. "What do you want here?"

"Just to see what a ship is like," Davy replied, wishing he were back on the wharf.

The captain looked him over slowly from his head to his feet.

"You wouldn't want to take a trip on her, would you?" he asked. "We're sailing for London tomorrow, and I could use a strong boy like you in the crew."

"Where's London?" Davy wanted to know. "Across the ocean?"

The captain smiled and nodded. Davy scratched his head thoughtfully. He hadn't intended to be a sailor. But it would be a wonderful thing to cross the ocean and to see a foreign land.

"Yes," he said eagerly. "I'd like to go. I'll just get my clothes and money, and then I'll be ready to leave."

"Don't you have to ask your parents about it?" the captain asked doubtfully.

"I can't," Davy replied with a quick smile. "They're afar off—in Tennessee. That's a powerful long way off. They won't care."

After a few more words with the captain, Davy ran off, up the wharf. He was nearly bursting with excitement, and eager to tell Adam Myer about his wonderful luck.

First he ran to the tavern where he and Mr.

Myer had spent the night. But Mr. Myer was not there. So Davy hurried to the wagon shop where they had left the big wagon for repairs.

To his surprise, the wagon stood in the street, with the horses hitched and ready to go. Mr. Myer was talking in a loud voice with the owner of the shop. His face was red, as though he had been drinking.

"Where have you been, you young varmint?" he cried gruffly when he saw Davy. "Here I am all set to go with a load for Tennessee, and you keep me standing around half the day. Get up into that wagon."

Davy stared at him in amazement. The wagoner had never yelled at him before. And he knew no reason why he should yell now.

"No," Davy said. "I'm not going with you. Listen, Mr. Myer, I've got a job on a boat sailing to London. Give me my clothes and my money, will you, and I'll—"

"What money?" the wagoner broke in, reaching for his whip.

"My money, that I gave you to keep for me," Davy replied, looking puzzled.

[89]

Adam Myer snorted. "I don't have no money of yours," he declared. "What's more, you ain't going to London on any boat. I'm going to take you home to your folks."

"No," Davy protested. "I've got a job on that boat and I—"

Mr. Myer shook his whip. "Get up into that wagon," he commanded, "or I'll curl this lash right around your legs."

Davy hesitated, but only for a minute. He was in a strange city, without money or friends. If Mr. Myer wanted to make trouble for him he could swear that he was a runaway and have him locked up.

There seemed to be nothing he could do at that moment but to obey. With a heavy heart he climbed up to the high seat. Soon the white-topped wagon had left Baltimore behind and was on its way west.

There were no funny stories told beside a campfire that night. Adam Myer growled whenever Davy spoke to him. He threatened the boy with his whip whenever Davy mentioned his money. He made him sleep in the wagon at his side. And for nearly a week he watched him constantly to see that he did not run away.

Poor Davy did not know what had happened in Baltimore to change the jolly wagoner into a cruel, disagreeable man. But he decided at last that he would not put up with such treatment for another day.

That night Davy did not close his eyes. As soon as it was light enough to see what he was doing, he rose on his elbow and peered closely at Mr. Myer. The wagoner was sleeping soundly.

Slowly and stealthily, Davy crept to the back of the wagon. Dropping lightly to the ground, he ran for all he was worth.

CHAPTER NINE

A Surprise for the Crocketts

I T WAS a blustery March evening nearly two years later. Several wagons stood in the yard of Pa Crockett's tavern. Inside the tavern the wagoners were sitting before the fire, telling jokes, spinning yarns, and waiting for their supper.

Ma Crockett was bustling about, getting the evening meal. Becky and Jane were setting the long table. Wilson was cleaning a rifle. Joey was mending a moccasin. And Pa was talking to one of the men.

He broke off in the middle of a sentence as the door opened. A tall, dark-haired boy in shabby clothing stepped into the dimly lighted room.

"Well, stranger, what can I do for you?" Pa asked.

"I'd like to spend the night here if you've room enough," the boy answered.

"Got any money?" Pa inquired.

The boy nodded.

"Then draw up a stool to the fire and warm yourself," Pa said. And he told Becky to lay another place at the table.

The boy glanced around quickly. Crossing the room, he sat down by the fire with the wagoners. They looked at him curiously, waiting for him to explain who he was and where he had come from. But he stared into the flames without a word, and after a minute or so, they began talking together again.

Soon Ma Crockett said supper was ready. The young stranger followed the wagoners to the table. His plate was piled high with meat, potatoes, cabbage, and beans. But he didn't seem to want to eat a mouthful.

Becky watched him from the other side of the table with a puzzled frown. Suddenly the boy looked up and caught her eye. He winked at her and grinned broadly. In an instant Becky was on her feet.

"Davy!" she cried joyfully. "Ma! Pa! That's our Davy! I knew him the minute he grinned! It's our Davy!"

For an instant Ma Crockett peered at the boy in astonishment. Then she threw her arms around him. Pa set down the dish he was holding, with a thud. Wilson jumped up and began to pound Davy on the back. Joey grabbed him around the neck, while the wagoners looked on wondering what the excitement was about.

[*95*]

Jane pulled on Davy's arm. Little Sally shouted, "Davy's home! Davy's home!" at the top of her voice. And for a moment there was such confusion that no one could hear what anyone else was saying.

Then Pa banged on a plate with his knife.

"Quiet down, now, the whole kit and caboodle of you," he commanded. "We got other folks sitting here besides us Crocketts."

He put his hand on Davy's shoulder and turned to the wagoners.

[96]

"It's my boy, home again, and growed so big I didn't know him," he said proudly. "It's my son, Davy. He's been gone so long we thought he was dead, didn't we, Ma?"

Ma Crockett nodded. She smiled happily and dabbed at her eyes with the corner of her apron. As for Davy—he had been planning this surprise for his family for a long time. Yet now he had such a big lump in his throat that he could hardly speak.

[*97*]

Of course, everyone wanted to hear his story right away. Even the wagoners. So Davy told that story as he ate his supper.

He told about his journey to Virginia with Mr. Cheek. About his work on John Gray's farm. About his trip to Baltimore. And about the wagoner, Adam Myer.

"Soon as I got away from that rascal, Myer, I decided to come home," he said, reaching for a piece of buttered bread. "And I've been on the way ever since."

"It sure took you a long while to get here," Wilson declared, pushing aside his empty plate.

"It sure did," Davy exclaimed. "And I had to do all kinds of jobs afore I could start. I made beaver hats for a hatter, and I worked around in different villages, and I helped on farms and—"

He stopped long enough to eat his last big mouthful of apple pie.

"And sometimes I got paid and sometimes I didn't," he went on, wiping his mouth on his hand. "Anyway, I saved up some money and then I lit out for home as soon as I could.

"Traveling on foot seemed a mite slow, though. So I just grabbed a comet by its tail and sailed across the sky till I saw the Holston River. Then I dropped off to the ground. And here I am!"

The wagoners laughed aloud at this. And even Pa couldn't help smiling, though he had never liked to hear Davy tell tall tales.

"Are you going to stay home now?" Becky asked her brother hopefully.

Davy nodded. He looked down the table at his father.

"I'm all ready to face up to that whipping I ran away from, Pa," he said. "I'll take it any time you want to give it to me."

Pa Crockett shook his head. Hard knocks and working for strangers had already done more for Davy than any hickory stick could ever do.

"You don't need a whipping now," he told his son. "You're 'most a man."

Davy threw back his shoulders proudly. "I aim to work for you now like a man would," he promised. And he meant what he said. Before long he had an excellent chance to prove it.

Pa Crockett was not a good manager. He often borrowed money to keep his tavern going and he found it hard sometimes to pay it back.

"I owe Abe Wilson thirty-six dollars," he told Davy one day, several weeks after the boy had returned. "Abe's growling about that money like a bear with a sore head. Do you reckon you can pay him back for me by working for him?"

"How long would I have to work?" Davy asked.

"Six months," Pa replied.

"All right," Davy said. "I'll do it."

That night he bundled up his clothes. And early the next morning he set off for Abe Wilson's place, not far away.

For six months he worked hard for Mr. Wilson and in this way he paid Pa Crockett's debt. Then Davy learned that Pa owed money to another man—a Quaker named John Kennedy. So off the boy went to Mr. Kennedy's farm. And there he worked for another six months.

One fine Sunday evening Davy returned to the tavern to tell Pa that the debt to Mr. Kennedy had been paid. Ma Crockett watched him proudly as he and his father talked together.

"Land sakes!" she exclaimed, when they had finished. "You've grown so big, Davy, that your clothes don't fit you any better than a rabbit skin would fit a bear. You stay home for a while, now, till I can make you some new ones."

"I can't," Davy said. "Mr. Kennedy wants me to keep on working for him. He'll pay me enough so's I can buy my own clothes pretty soon, Ma. And a rifle, too."

"A brand-new one?" Joey asked admiringly.

Davy nodded. "I aim to practice with it till I can shoot better than anyone in Tennessee," he boasted. "Then maybe I'll even try to get me a wife!"

Ma Crockett's mouth dropped open in surprise at this, and Wilson burst out laughing.

"Just listen to that!" he said to Becky. "He's not seventeen yet, and he's talking about getting a wife!"

[*101*]

Becky giggled. "No girl with any sense will have him till he learns to write his name," she remarked, trying to sound like a young lady.

Davy grinned. "I'll take care of that, too," he declared grandly. And he did.

Davy arranged with Mr. Kennedy to let him go to school four days a week. Before another year had passed he could read and write and figure.

He had bought himself some neat new clothes. He had won several shooting matches with his splendid new rifle. And he had asked pretty, blue-eyed Polly Finley to be his wife.

[102]

CHAPTER TEN

Disturbing News

POLLY CROCKETT stopped the whir-
ring of her spinning wheel. She cocked her
head on one side to listen. Six-year-old Johnny
Crockett was playing on the cabin floor with
his little brother, Will. Johnny looked up
quickly.

"Do you hear him, Ma?" he asked eagerly.

"No," his mother replied. "I reckon that
was just a gabby bird calling. But your pa will
come soon. It's time I started us some supper."

She put aside her spindle. Taking a bucket
from the shelf near the door, she went outside

to get some water from the well. As she started back across the clearing with her bucket brimful, she looked at the cabin and smiled.

What a snug, tight little home Davy had built for his family here in the wilderness of southern Tennessee! How fine it looked, with blue smoke curling from its chimney, and its oiled-paper windows shining in the late afternoon sun.

Pumpkins and yellow gourds were ripening in the corn patch near the log barn. Firewood was piled neatly at the side of the cabin. Raccoon skins were stretched on the outside walls to dry. And Polly knew that many more skins were stacked in the cabin loft.

Some day soon Davy would take those skins to the little settlement of Winchester, ten miles to the north. There he would trade them for flour, sugar, salt, a little coffee, and maybe some gimcracks for herself and the two little boys.

"There couldn't be a better husband in all the world than Davy Crockett," Polly thought proudly. And she hummed a little tune as she pushed open the cabin door.

Johnny scrambled to his feet and ran to shut it for her.

"Pa's never coming," he complained.

But at that very moment a shrill, clear whistle sounded in the woods near by. Johnny was off across the clearing like a shot out of a gun.

"Pa!" he cried. "Pa, did you get a bear?"

Davy Crockett laughed. "Not this time," he

[*105*]

said, popping his coonskin cap on Johnny's head. "But I got us three deer, and a panther near as big as an ox, and a good fat turkey."

He led his two pack horses across the clearing and stopped them in front of the cabin.

Polly had come to the door to meet her husband, with little Willy clinging to her skirts.

Davy handed Polly his rifle and began to unpack his meat and skins.

"Do you reckon you can scare up enough

supper to feed five hungry men?" he asked.

"Five!" Polly gasped in surprise.

Davy grinned. "One of them's me," he said, pushing aside a spotted dog who was nosing at the meat. "The other four are hunters I ran into, up near Buck's Hill. They were aiming to sleep out. But I told them to come along over here when they'd got their deer skinned, and we'd try some candle-snuffing."

"That means I'd better hustle!" Polly exclaimed.

She stepped inside and laid Davy's rifle across the antlers over the fireplace. Then she set about getting supper.

By the time the meal was ready, the hunters had arrived. Stacking their rifles in a corner of the cabin, they sat down at the puncheon table. Everyone was so hungry at first that there was little talking. Finally tall Andy Morgan pushed back his empty plate and stood up, stretching his arms wide.

"You cook as good as your husband can shoot, ma'am," he said to Polly. "Did Davy tell you how he got that big panther today?"

"I know how he got it!" Johnny piped up before his mother could speak. "He got it just the way he got the last one."

"How was that, bub?" drawled old Sol Jones.

"He just grabbed it by the tail," Johnny declared soberly, "and he swung it 'round and 'round over his head, till it lost its breath and died."

The men all laughed at this, and big Mike Bell roughed Johnny's hair up all over his head.

"I reckon there isn't anything your pa can't do," he said. He turned to Sol Jones. "Did you tell Crockett what you heard in Winchester last week about the Creek Indians?" he asked.

Sol shook his head and lighted his pipe with a brand from the fire.

"There ain't much to tell yet," he drawled, puffing out a little cloud of smoke. "Old Chief Tecumseh's been trying to stir them Creeks up against the settlers for a long time. Maybe he'll get them to put on their war paint and—"

"And maybe he won't!" Davy broke in, with

a quick glance toward Polly. "Anyhow, the Creeks live a good piece south from here."

He pushed his chair back from the table and stood up, for he did not want any more talk

about Indians now. Not with Polly beginning to look scared. And the two little boys sitting there, all eyes and ears.

"No use getting *them* all stirred up till there's good reason," he thought. And he reached for the candle which stood on the chimney shelf. "How about this one, Polly?" he asked. "Can we use it for snuffing?"

Polly nodded. She was uneasy about what she had just heard, and she wanted to ask Sol some questions. But Davy didn't give her a chance. Taking down his rifle, he told the men to come along. Then he opened the door and stepped outside.

It was a lovely September evening. Though the light was fading rapidly, it was still possible to see for some distance. So Davy fastened the tip of a fox's tail to a tree at the far side of the clearing.

The men loaded their rifles. Standing near the cabin door, they tried, one after another, to hit the little piece of fur. Johnny sat on the step, hugging his knees and watching them eagerly.

Four times around they tried. Several shots came very close, but none hit the target.

"You'd have to have cat's eyes to see that mark now," Andy Morgan exclaimed at last. "Let's have a try at the candle, Crockett."

"Not yet," Davy said. "I've got one more chance a-coming to shoot at that thing."

Raising his rifle, he took careful aim and fired.

"You hit it!" Mike Bell cried. "You knocked it clean off the tree!"

"It's about time I did," Davy Crockett remarked in disgust. He was put out with himself tonight. Usually he hit any target at which he aimed, with his first shot. And many men were already saying that he was the best marksman in Tennessee.

"I'll do better at snuffing the candle," he told himself. But he didn't.

He had to shoot three times at the lighted candle which he had set up in the crotch of a tree. Three times, before he could shoot off the tip of the wick without putting out the flame. And Mike Bell did the trick with his second bullet.

"What's the matter with you?" Mike asked Davy later in the evening. "You didn't shoot any better tonight than a cross-eyed old man with the tizzick. What's on your mind?"

[*111*]

"Indians," Davy admitted. "If the Creeks do start trouble, Mike, they're likely to push up from the Mississippi Territory right into Tennessee. I'm going to ride to Winchester tomorrow and see if anyone there knows what those Red Sticks are up to."

The next day, as soon as the hunters had left, Davy rode off to Winchester. When he returned after dark, his face was grim. News about the Creeks had reached the settlement that very afternoon. Dreadful news!

"They're on the warpath all right," Davy told Polly as they sat by the fire, after he had stabled his horse. "More than a thousand of them attacked Fort Mims without any warning at all, Poll. They killed all the settlers—even the children."

Polly glanced fearfully at the bed where Johnny and Will were sound asleep.

"How near's Fort Mims?" she asked quickly.

"It's a good way south," Davy assured her. "But those sneaking Red Sticks will come scalping and killing around here next, if we don't stop them.

"Men in Winchester are joining up with the army already, to go and fight them. General Andrew Jackson's going to lead us."

"Us!" Polly repeated in dismay. "You aren't going, are you, Davy? You'd never leave me and the boys! You'll get killed and—"

"I won't get killed any quicker than anyone else," Davy broke in with a little smile. "And I can't stay home, Poll. Not with Red Sticks on the rampage. Do you reckon you can finish that new deerskin shirt with the yellow fringe, that you're making for me, afore I have to go?"

Polly sniffed and blinked back some tears. "I'll get at it right away," she said.

The shirt was finished the next day.

Davy packed his saddlebags with extra clothing and food. He filled his powder horn and bullet pouch, and stuck his sharp knife in his belt.

Then he kissed his wife and children good-by. He set his coonskin cap firmly on his head. And with his rifle slung over his shoulder, he rode away to help General Jackson's army fight the Creeks.

[*113*]

CHAPTER ELEVEN

Redskins on the Rampage

DAVY CROCKETT slid quietly from his saddle. Without a sound he pushed through the bushes until he reached a big oak near the bank of the Tallapoosa River. He stood so close to the oak that he seemed almost part of the trunk, as he peered with keen eyes up and down the river.

There was no living thing in sight. But fresh moccasin tracks in the soft earth of the river bank told Crockett what he wanted to know. Stealthily he slipped back again through the bushes.

In a low tone he spoke to the men who were waiting where he had left his horse.

He peered with keen eyes up and down the river

"The Creeks have passed here," he said, "and headed south. It wasn't long ago, either. What do you want to do now, Major?"

Major Russell glanced at the sky. "Get back to camp before it's too dark to see where we're going," he replied. "All right, men, ride on."

The men turned their horses and rode quietly away. Davy swung himself into his saddle and set off after them.

All day long he and the other scouts had been ranging the woods, in search of Creek Indians. The Creeks had already been defeated in one battle near the Tallapoosa River. And the scouts knew that hundreds of painted warriors were hidden close by, in the forest. Yet they had not seen a single Red Stick.

"They're harder to find than fleas on a black dog," Davy thought. "And some of them are spying on us right this minute, or my name's not Crockett."

He looked about uneasily, as a damp January wind rustled through the trees. Urging his horse on, he caught up with the other men.

Night had fallen by the time the scouts

reached the place where the army of nearly nine hundred men was encamped. And what a strange-looking army it was!

There were officers in soiled white pantaloons and bright red jackets. There were soldiers in dark-blue homespun coats and trousers. There were frontiersmen in leather leggings and deerskin shirts. And there were friendly Indians—each with a white feather or deer's tail in his hair, which showed that they belonged to the white men's forces.

[117]

Some of the men had just come from the settlements to join the army. Others, like Davy Crockett, had already fought in several battles with the Creeks. Most of the men were tired, and they talked in low tones as they gathered around their campfires to eat their evening meal.

There was little food, for it was difficult to get supply wagons to an army deep in the wilderness. And all the game had fled from that part of the country.

One of the newcomers looked in disgust at his small ration of beef.

"It ain't big enough to fill up a field mouse," he complained. "And it would taste a sight better if we had a mite of salt."

Davy Crockett laughed. With his hunting knife he cut his piece of meat in two.

"Here," he said, "have half of mine. We got used to living on next to nothing long afore we licked the Creeks at Taledaga, didn't we, George?"

Young George Russell nodded. "Ate beef hides for three days when we were in Fort

Strother on the Coosa River," he told the new-comer. "And Davy kept us from thinking how hungry we were by telling us jokes and spinning yarns. How about a good tall story now, Davy?"

"You don't need one now," Crockett replied, winking at him. "We just had us a feast!"

He cleaned his knife with a handful of dry grass, and stuck it into his belt. "You better keep your rifles close by, tonight," he said, getting to his feet. "I've got a feeling we're in for trouble. But right this minute I'm too dog-tired to care."

He lay down on the ground and rolled himself up in his blanket. Almost at once he dropped off to sleep, with his head on his knapsack and his rifle beside him.

Before long the rest of the men were sleeping, too, lying like logs beside the dying camp-fires. Even General Jackson's tent was dark. Only the guards were awake, pacing up and down in the starlight.

Hours passed. The men slept peacefully.

The stars marched steadily across the sky. Suddenly there was the sharp crack of a rifle shot.

"Red Sticks! Red Sticks!" shouted one of the guards. Another rifle blazed.

In an instant the camp was aroused. Men sprang to their feet, and grabbed their guns. Bullets from an unseen enemy were flying all around them.

"Mend the fires so that we can see the red devils!" an officer shouted.

"Take to the trees!" called another.

Crockett and some other men leaped to pile brush on the fires. Then they ran for the shelter of the trees. Anxiously they waited for the redskins to rush forward into the firelight. Bullets were still flying, but not an Indian appeared.

"They've got too much sense to show themselves," Crockett muttered, as a soldier near him cried out in pain.

He aimed his rifle quickly at a spot where an Indian gun had just flashed in the darkness, and pulled the trigger. Then he jumped as a bullet whistled past his head.

They ran for the shelter of the trees

The fighting went on for nearly two hours. At daybreak it stopped as suddenly as it had begun. A number of white men lay on the ground, badly wounded. Four had been killed. Not a Creek was in sight.

Immediately General Jackson called his officers together for a meeting. He told them of a plan by which the army might be able to trap the Creeks.

"We must first bury our dead and make litters to carry the wounded," he said. "Then we will start marching north to Fort Strother. In order to reach the fort we must cross the Enotachopco River. I am hoping that the Creeks will track us to the river and attack our rear ranks as they make ready to cross.

"If the Creeks do this, the men in the rear must then stand and fight. The men in the front ranks will quickly recross the river and surround the Red Sticks on three sides. Then we'll have the enemy trapped."

The plan seemed a good one and the officers went at once to give orders to their men. Soon the four dead soldiers were buried. The wounded were placed on litters. And the army set off through the woods.

Davy Crockett and twenty-four other scouts rode midway in the long column of moving men. With keen eyes the scouts scanned the woods on either side, keeping a sharp lookout for spying redskins. But they saw none.

At last the army reached the stream. The men in the front ranks crossed at once and climbed to the steep bank on the opposite side. The scouts on their horses splashed into the cold water. The men in the rear made ready to cross.

Suddenly, behind them, the air was filled with terrific war whoops. Hundreds of painted warriors rushed out from behind rocks and trees. Arrows whizzed through the air. Bullets sang.

Davy Crockett wheeled his horse around in midstream, ready to join in the fight.

"Suffering wildcats!" he yelled. "Look at our men! They're *running!*"

And they were! Throwing their guns aside, they were fleeing for their lives. From the far

bank of the stream, General Jackson shouted
at them to stand and fight. But nothing could
stop the fear-crazed men. Even some of their
officers fled from the screaming Indians.

And the Creeks were everywhere! Shooting
with deadly aim at the men on the opposite
bank. Attacking others who still floundered

helplessly in the water. Chasing those who fled.

Yelling like a wildcat, Crockett dug his heels into his horse's sides. Out of the water he rode, full speed, and up on the bank with the other scouts beside him. Firing, reloading, and firing again, the scouts swept down on the Creeks.

"Give them blazes!" Davy shouted. "Cook them up with lightning! Slam them! Go ahead! Slam them!"

"Slam them!" The other scouts took it up.

Straight into a shower of bullets they rode. Dodging arrows! Driving screaming redskins back from the river! Chasing them off into the forest, and into the neighboring hills!

This gave General Jackson time to rally his troops on the far side of the river. Now they joined in the fight. Other redskins took to their heels, leaving their dead where they fell.

The battle was quickly over. Twenty of Jackson's men had been killed. There were many wounded. The general's plan had not succeeded. But, because of the bravery of Davy Crockett and the other scouts, the Creeks had been defeated again.

"Give them blazes!" Davy shouted.

"Cook them up with lightning! Slam them!"

It was easy to see now that the war against the Creeks would soon be won. Davy Crockett's horse had been badly crippled in the hard ride against the redskins. Crockett, himself, felt that he was no longer needed by the army. He longed to see Polly, Johnny, and little Will.

Soon after the army reached Fort Strother, Davy Crockett asked for a furlough. Then, leading his poor, limping horse, he started his long journey home.

CHAPTER TWELVE

Good Times—and Bad

JOHNNY CROCKETT stuffed one more wad of clay and straw into the chink between the logs of his father's new powder mill. He smoothed it over carefully with his hand. Then he looked across the room at his brother Will.

"I've finished chinking up my half of the mill," he announced. "Jingoes, you're slow, Will! You'll never get through afore Pa comes back. Want some help?"

"Nope," Will replied. "I can do it by myself. Where's Pa gone, anyhow?"

"Over to Jethro Parker's cabin," Johnny said, rubbing his dirty hands down his brown linsey trousers. "They're holding court over there. And Pa's got to decide what to do with that Ed Moon, who was caught stealing hogs."

Will turned around with a puzzled look. "Is that what a justice of the peace does?" he asked. "I thought Pa arrested people."

Johnny shook his head. "Mr. Parker arrests them," he explained. "He's only a constable. But Pa decides how they'll be punished. I'll bet he's the best justice of the peace in Tennessee, too."

He squatted on the floor to wait for Will to finish his chinking. Staring around the empty room, he wondered how it would look when Pa got his powder mill to working. Then his eyes wandered back to his brother. Something about the way Will was standing made Johnny think of his mother.

"I bet you don't remember Ma," he said suddenly.

Will whirled around quickly. "I bet I do," he declared. "I can remember more about her than you can."

Johnny grinned. "Can you remember the day Pa came home from fighting the Indians?"

Will nodded. "And the day Polly was born," he said. "And the day Ma died, and the day Uncle Joey and Aunt Sarah came to take care of us, and—" He stopped to draw a breath.

"And the day Pa brought us home a new ma," Johnny added. "And the time we moved out here from Winchester. I like it better, living here on Shoal Creek, than back east."

"So do I," Will agreed. He turned again to his work.

Johnny watched him for a moment. Then he stood up and went to the open door. His father's powder mill and grist mill were built on a stream some distance from his home. But through the trees Johnny could see the clearing and the cabin.

It was a big cabin, for Davy Crockett now had a big family. He had married a widow with two small children. Since then, three more children had been born. So now there were eight—Johnny, Will, George, Margaret, little Polly, Robert, Rebecca, and tiny Matilda.

This was a lot of people for one man to take care of. But hunting was good in the forests near by. Corn and other crops grew quickly in the rich soil of the clearing.

Davy's wife, Elizabeth, kept the cabin and the children clean and tidy. And the Crocketts did very well after Davy Crockett opened his mills. Settlers came for many miles to get their corn ground and to buy gunpowder.

They admired Davy's neat clearing, his horses, cows, and pigs. They laughed at his jokes and tall stories. They found that not one of them could beat him at target-shooting. And they went home telling each other what a fine man he was.

"Crockett's doing a whopping good job being justice of the peace," Tom Slade remarked to Jethro Parker, as the two men rode away from the mills one day. "I hear he had to practice up some on his writing and his spelling, though, before he could make out law papers."

The constable nodded. "That's right," he

agreed. "But he's doing real well at it now. And he's made up a saying that he writes at the bottom of every one of those law papers."

"What's that?" Slade asked curiously.

"'Be always sure you're right, then go ahead,'" Parker replied.

Tom Slade chuckled. "It's a good saying!" he exclaimed. "Crockett *will* go ahead, too! You just watch him."

And Davy Crockett did go ahead!

The settlers of the Shoal Creek country decided to form a regiment to protect their homes in case of trouble. They remembered how bravely Davy Crockett had fought in the war against the Creek Indians. And they elected him the colonel of the regiment.

When they wanted to send a man to the state capital to help make the laws for Tennessee, they elected Colonel Crockett.

The family had just finished supper one fall evening when Crockett came home with this news. Mrs. Crockett smiled proudly when she heard it. But Crockett himself was not smiling. He settled himself in front of the fire, with little Robert on his knee, and an arm around Polly, who was leaning against his shoulder.

"It beats all why they chose me," Colonel Crockett said to his wife. "I don't know any more about making laws than a coon dog knows about cooking."

"You'll learn," Mrs. Crockett replied quietly, as she warmed up some stew for his supper. "You'll be a good lawmaker, too, Davy, because you're honest and fair, and—"

"And not scared of things, like I am sometimes," Polly added, pushing a long strand of black hair back from her father's ruddy face.

Davy Crockett laughed. "Sure I'm scared sometimes, Polly," he declared. "I'm scared of this lawmaking business right now. But I reckon the only way to lick my scaredness is to grin hard and go ahead."

He gave her a little hug and turned to his wife to talk of other things.

Several months passed before it was time for the lawmakers of Tennessee to meet in Murfreesboro, the capital of the state. Davy Crockett knew that he would be away for some time at this meeting of the legislature. So he had laid in supplies of bear meat and venison for his family. He had also closed and locked his mills.

He spoke to his wife about the mills, as she helped him pack his saddlebags the night before he was to leave.

"I still haven't paid back all the money I had to borrow to build those mills," he told her. "Next year, though, I reckon we'll earn enough to square the debt."

Mrs. Crockett nodded. "I'm sure we will," she said. Then she pushed another clean shirt into one of the saddlebags, and handed the bag to her husband.

The next morning Johnny brought his father's horse around to the cabin door for him. And everyone gathered in the clearing to say good-by. Swinging himself into the saddle, Davy Crockett rode away, waving as he disappeared among the trees.

On a fine day in March he rode through the woods toward home again. Everything had gone well in the capital. He had made many new friends, and learned many things about how the state was governed. As he jogged along, he hummed a jolly tune.

It was dark when he reached the cabin, but light from within gave the oiled-paper windows a cheerful glow. At Davy's clear, shrill whistle the door flew open. Elizabeth and all the children came running out to meet him.

The dogs barked a noisy welcome. Everyone

was overjoyed to see him. But the minute he entered the cabin Davy Crockett knew that something was wrong.

It was Johnny who broke the news, as soon as his father had hung up his coonskin cap.

"The mills are gone, Pa!" Johnny exclaimed. "We had us an awful storm last week, and the stream flooded over—"

"And it washed both the mills clear away," Will broke in excitedly.

Davy Crockett looked at his wife in dismay. "They weren't even paid for yet!" he exclaimed.

"I know it," Mrs. Crockett replied, pulling little Rebecca back from the fire and setting her on her lap. "I've been thinking a lot about what we'd better do, Davy. It looks like we'd better sell everything we have and pay up our debts. Then we can start all over again somewhere else."

Will faced his father eagerly. "Can we do it, Pa?" he asked excitedly. "It would be fun to move. Can we do it, for sure?"

Davy did not reply at once. He sat down by

[*138*]

the fire and glanced slowly around the big comfortable room. At the bearskin rugs, the sturdy furniture, the loom and spinning wheel. Then he smiled at his wife.

"Your ma's a brave woman," he said to Will. "If she don't mind starting again from scratch, I reckon I don't, either. Anyhow, I always do have a hankering to see new places."

"But where'll we go?" Will and Polly both asked at the same moment.

"The Obion River country, about a hundred and fifty miles west of here, might be a good place for poor folks," Davy Crockett replied thoughtfully.

"There's a little village called Jackson a-growing up out near there. But I wouldn't want to go right to Jackson. I'd aim to settle about forty miles north, where there's nothing but deer and bear and a few Indians."

"Friendly Indians?" Mrs. Crockett asked anxiously.

Her husband nodded.

"Then that's where we'll go," declared Mrs. Crockett. And so the matter was settled.

CHAPTER THIRTEEN

Bears

M RS. CROCKETT filled a deerskin pouch with dried meat and fresh cornbread. Then she spoke to Robert, who sat alone at the table, eating an early breakfast.

"Here, Bob," she said, laying the pouch before him. "That's to have in case your pa and Jim McDaniel don't shoot anything afore dinner time. Now watch out for yourself if you go in any canebrakes."

Bob grinned and nodded his head. He was feeling very important that morning. For his father and a neighbor were setting out on a long bear hunt. And he was going with them to tend the pack horses and help cut the meat.

"You talk like I was little Tilda, Ma," he said, as he scraped the last bit of mush from his bowl. "And I'm past ten years old. Haven't I been a good help to you ever since John and Will and George went off to Jackson to work and go to school?"

His mother nodded. "Yes, you have," she said with a smile. "That's why I don't want anything to happen to you."

"Don't you fret," Bob assured her. "I've been hunting with Pa afore. I can take care of myself all right."

Pushing his chair back from the table, he picked up the bag of food. Then he pulled on his coonskin cap and ran out into the frosty morning to find his father.

Within a few minutes, Davy Crockett, his son, and Jim McDaniel were each on horseback, riding into the woods beyond the clearing. Bob and his father each led an extra horse. And eight lively dogs frisked along ahead.

More than four years had passed since the Crocketts had settled in western Tennessee at a place forty miles north of the little village of

Jackson. Other people had come to the Obion country, too. But the settlers' cabins were far apart. And it was still a strange, wild land.

Once an earthquake had made deep long cracks in the ground and split huge trees in two. Then a hurricane had blown over other trees, which were now overgrown with vines and briers. There were miles of deep forests, dense thickets, and canebrakes where the canes sometimes grew thirty feet high.

Panthers, deer, and elk made their homes in these forests and thickets and canebrakes. So did shaggy black bears. Hundreds of them! And Davy Crockett knew where to find them.

Before he and McDaniel and Bob had ridden more than fifteen miles, Crockett spied a huge oak tree, with a hole high up in the trunk. He rode up close to the tree. Dismounting, he examined it carefully while the dogs ran here and there, sniffing and whining.

"This tree's hollow," Crockett said after a moment. "There's a bear in it, too, getting ready to hole up for the winter. A big one! See the scratches his claws made when he climbed up the tree to the hole in the trunk?"

McDaniel looked doubtful. "Maybe old Mr. Bear made those scratches coming *down* the tree," he drawled.

Davy Crockett laughed loudly. "McDaniel, I thought you were a bear hunter!" he exclaimed. "A bear always slips when he's coming *down*, and then he makes longer scratches than these. There's a bear in this tree, and I'm going to prove it."

"How?" asked McDaniel. "That tree's so big around, even you can't climb it. How are you going to get up to that hole so's you can look inside?"

"You'll see," replied Crockett, winking at Bob. "We'll take the horses over there near those bushes. Then we'll chop us down that young pine near the oak. And we'll lay it against the oak so one end of it comes right where that hole is. Then—"

"Then I'll skin up the pine, Pa!" Bob cried. "I can look in the oak and see if there's a bear."

Crockett grinned at the boy and nodded. Soon the two men were hard at work with their

A huge black bear stuck his head out of the hole

tomahawks, cutting down the pine tree. In a short time it was nearly ready to fall. And the dogs were yelping and running about the oak.

"Don't take another lick with your tomahawk till I get those hounds out of the way," Crockett said to McDaniel. "The trunk's liable to fall on one of them."

He ran back a short distance and called the dogs to him. At that instant a huge black bear stuck his head out of the hole in the oak tree.

"Hey, look!" shouted Crockett. "There's the bear, and he's a rip-snorter! Run for it, Bob! He's coming down the tree!"

Davy Crockett sprinted for his rifle. McDaniel ran to get his. Bob raced back to the horses. Barking wildly, the dogs bounded forward to attack the bear. Yapping and snarling, they closed in on him.

By this time McDaniel had his rifle in his hands. He raised it, took aim, and fired. But his shot went wild.

Old Grim howled as the bear's heavy paw raked his back. Over and over rolled the bear and the dogs, down a little hill beyond the oak tree, growling, snarling, fighting. Suddenly Holdfast yelped with pain. Grim howled again.

Bob's heart was in his mouth. "Shoot, Pa! Shoot!" he begged. "He's killing Grim!"

"Can't shoot from here," Crockett cried. "I might hit one of the dogs!"

Running down the hill, he pushed the muzzle of his gun against the bear's body and fired. With a groan, the big animal reared up. Then it sank back on its haunches and fell dead.

Crockett bent down at once to examine old

Grim, who lay panting on the ground. The dog licked his hand and wagged his tail feebly, as Davy gently felt him all over.

"No bad damage," Crockett said to Bob and McDaniel, who had come running down the hill. "He's scratched some and winded. And Holdfast's lost part of his ear. But they'll both be raring to go as soon as we get this monster skinned and cut up."

Pulling his knife from his hunting belt, he began to cut away the skin. McDaniel helped him. Bob went to get one of the pack horses. Before long, the meat and skin were loaded on the horse's back. And the little party set off.

That afternoon Crockett shot three more bears and McDaniel shot one. At dusk they stopped their horses by a stream and made camp for the night.

By the time the stars were out, the horses had been hobbled and fed. The bear meat had been placed on a hastily built scaffold so that no dogs or wolves could get it. And the two men were sitting with Bob, close to a blazing fire, eating hot, juicy bear steaks.

[147]

McDaniel finished eating first. Leaning back against a tree, he looked admiringly at Davy Crockett.

"You can hunt better than any man I ever

knew," he said. "I reckon there ain't a bear in this country that don't hate your name."

"Well," Crockett said slowly, "there's one that don't. I met him up on Whangdoodle Knob last winter when I'd run out of bullets. And he liked me so much he followed me home. Now he's so tame he lives with us.

"He spends his days churning butter and sweeping out the cabin and tending the young 'uns. Night-times he just sits in one corner of the fireplace a-smoking his pipe, while I sit in the other, reading an old newspaper I bought last time I was in Jackson. And we've got to be such good friends we don't hardly need to talk at all. Isn't that right, Bob?"

He turned to Bob and winked. Bob nodded solemnly, trying not to grin. But McDaniel slapped his knee and laughed loudly.

Davy Crockett stood up, stretching out his long arms and yawning. "It's high time we all got to bed," he announced. "I aim to start hunting tomorrow at sunup."

He threw some wood on the fire and strolled over to see that the horses were well hobbled. Soon he, Bob, and McDaniel were all rolled up in their blankets, sleeping soundly.

The next morning they set out early. For five days they hunted. Then, with all the meat and skins the horses could carry, they made their way home.

CHAPTER FOURTEEN

A Bear Hunter Goes to Congress

I T WAS a fine afternoon the following May. The sun shone down on the little town of Jackson, and streamed through the window of the log store.

Davy Crockett looked at the pile of supplies which lay on the counter before him. Then he glanced at the paper in his hand.

"That's all, I reckon, Lem," he said to the storekeeper. "Except a pokeful of sugar-candy for the young 'uns, and two yards of that red ribbon for my wife. I'll load this stuff on the horses while you measure it out."

He swung a big sack of flour to his back. And with another sack full of sugar under one arm, he started to go outside. Lem watched him duck his head as he went through the low door. And he watched him duck it again when he came back fifteen minutes later.

This time Davy Crockett was not alone. He did not go to Jackson often, but he knew many people there. And whenever he was in town, men gathered around him to talk and to listen to his funny stories. Now four men pushed their way into the store behind him.

"We don't aim to buy anything, Lem," announced a big man named Pete Brown. "Davy says he's brought in a few more bearskins, and we just want to get a look at them."

"There they be," Lem said, pointing to the big pile of skins which Davy Crockett had stacked in one corner of the store.

Pete stared at the skins, and his eyes opened wide. Redheaded Jake Tench whistled softly in wonder.

"Where in blue blazes did you get all them?" Jake asked, turning to Davy Crockett.

[151]

"How many bears did you kill this year, any-way?"

Crockett grinned. "I reckon it was about a hundred and five," he replied. "That's counting an old grandpappy bear who tried to hug me to death. I had to kill him with my knife."

He picked up a keg of nails. "Hey, give me a hand with some of these things, will you?" he asked. "My old mother's come a-visiting all the way from Holston River. So I want to get back home tomorrow, if I can. I aim to see my boys afore I leave town, too."

He started out with the nails. The men all turned in to help. And in a short time they were watching Davy Crockett ride down the dusty road, leading his heavily loaded pack horses.

"Too bad we didn't get more time to talk," Pete remarked, sitting down on a bench in front of the store. "That Crockett's got some fine yarns to tell. And I reckon he's the greatest hunter in the whole West."

"He fights as good as he hunts, too," Jake Tench declared. "I knew him in the Creek War. He ain't afeard of anything that breathes. And he'd give you the last bullet in his pouch if you needed it."

Limpy Collins leaned up against a hitching post to rest his bad leg. "I hear Colonel Crockett did right well in the legislature," he drawled. "Stood up like a tiger against laws he didn't think was right, and—"

[*153*]

"Nobody could ever make *Davy* vote for anything wrong," Jake Tench broke in. "He's as honest as the sun. Say, he'd be a good man to send to Congress as a Representative from these parts."

Young Larry Wilson shook his head. "We've two men in this district already who are running for Congress," he said. "Rich men with lots of schooling. Crockett could never get enough votes to lick either one of them."

Jake shrugged his shoulders. Limpy began to talk about hunting. And nothing more was said at that time about Crockett's becoming a Congressman. But many people were thinking about it. And at last, Davy himself decided that he would run for the office of Representative of the Western District of Tennessee.

He was too busy looking after his family to spend much time in trying to get votes, or in speechmaking. But when he did talk, he said sensible things in such a funny way that people laughed and cheered.

Poor settlers liked him because he had been a poor settler himself. Farmers asked him what to do about their crops. Hunters and trappers said he was the best man of them all. He had a host of friends. And on election day there were more votes for Davy Crockett than for either of the other candidates in the Western District.

So it was that on a cold day in December, Congressman Crockett prepared to start for Washington, to help make the laws for the United States. A friend had lent him enough money to buy city clothes when he reached Nashville. And to pay for his long journey by stage from there to the capital.

By eight o'clock in the morning, Crockett's saddlebags were packed and he was ready to leave. He hugged each one of his little girls. He slapped Bob on the shoulder. And he stooped to kiss his wife.

"I'll write to John at Jackson as soon as I can, and send him a letter to bring to you," he promised. "Take good care of yourself, now, while I'm gone."

Mrs. Crockett nodded. Then she stepped back and eyed her husband from head to foot. He looked so strong and handsome in his new

[*155*]

hunting shirt and red-fringed trousers that she smiled at him proudly. Then she handed him his coonskin cap.

"You do as good a job in Congress, now, as you do when you hunt bear," she told him.

"I sure will try," Crockett said, with a grin. And he did. In Washington he went to work at once, learning all that he could about Congress and his duties there.

Some people laughed at his backwoods manners. Others called him "the gamecock of the wildernesss." But everyone liked his tall tales and his breezy talk.

When he made a speech in Congress, people

[*156*]

listened. For he said what he wanted to say, clearly and well. And the voters in Tennessee heard such fine things about him that they elected him for a second term.

It was then that he ran into trouble. And all as a result of the Creek War which had been fought so many years before.

CHAPTER FIFTEEN

"Be Always Sure You're Right—"

FIFTEEN years had passed since General Jackson and his army had won the war against the Creeks. At the end of that war, General Jackson had held a council with the chiefs of the tribe.

"You began this war against us and we've defeated you," the general told the chiefs. "If you want peace now, you must sign a treaty.

"In that treaty you must agree to give half of all your lands to the United States Government. We will promise that your people may keep the rest of their lands forever."

With heavy hearts the chiefs had signed this

treaty and had given up half of their country.
And for fifteen years the Creeks had been living and hunting in the land that was left to
them, just east of the Mississippi River.

Other Indian tribes were also living on land
which the United States Government had
promised they might keep forever. But now
the Indians were in trouble.

The white men had discovered that the
Indian lands were valuable. Andrew Jackson
was now the President of the United States. He
had forgotten the treaty he had made with the

Creeks. And he was urging Congress to pass a bill forcing all Indians to move to the wilderness west of the Mississippi River.

When this matter came up in Congress, Davy Crockett was furious. He told one of his Washington friends about it, as they ate dinner in their boardinghouse near the Capitol.

"A treaty's a promise," he declared, reaching for some butter. "Not even President Jackson has a right to break a promise. And I'll fight against his Indian bill as long as I've a leg to stand on."

"You'd better watch what you say, Davy," his friend warned him. "Andy Jackson's wrong about this bill. But he's right about a lot of other things. And he's well liked everywhere."

"Yes," Crockett agreed, "but—"

"Jackson comes from your state, too," his friend broke in. "The people there are all for him. If you vote against his bill, maybe they won't elect you again."

"Then I'll go home and hunt bear!" Crockett exclaimed. He shook his head. "I'd rather be an old coon dog belonging to a poor man in the forest than do what I know is wrong," he went on. "I've got a saying that I live by. And I'll never go back on it."

"What's that?" his friend asked curiously.

" 'Be always sure you're right, then go ahead,' " Crockett replied with a grin. "And

I'll fight now for what I know is right, no matter what it costs me."

"You'll get in trouble with the people who elected you if you do," his friend warned.

Davy Crockett shrugged his shoulders. And that very afternoon he began his fight against President Jackson's bill. He talked against it

[*161*]

to everyone who would listen to him. In Congress he spoke out against it boldly. He said he knew he was the only Representative from Tennessee who would vote against the bill.

"But if I were the only man in the United States who disapproved of it, I still would vote against it," he declared in ringing tones. "And I would be glad that I did until the day I died.

"I know about these Indians. Many of them live out in my part of the country. They believe in the treaties we've made with them. They've taken up some of the white men's ways. They're farmers now. Peaceful farmers. And I'll never vote to send them across the Mississippi, where they may be attacked by warlike tribes. These Indians have rights, just as we have, and a treaty is the highest law of the land."

Again and again Crockett demanded that the treaties with the Indians be kept. Many people felt as he did, though only a few were bold enough to say so.

The bill was passed at last by Congress. The Indians were forced to move across the Mississippi. And when election time rolled around again, Davy Crockett was defeated. But people all through the country were talking about his courageous stand against President Jackson.

"There's a man who'll fight for what is right and stand up for those who are weaker than he is," they said. And they repeated Crockett's saying: *"Be always sure you're right, then go ahead."*

This saying was printed in newspapers throughout the country. So were many stories about Davy Crockett. Some stories poked fun at him, saying that he could grin a coon out of a tree, and calling him a "coonskin congressman." Other stories told of his fame as a hunter in the backwoods of Tennessee.

Plays were written about him. A piece of music was composed, called "Crockett's March." A book was written about him which told the story of his life. Soon he became so popular that he was elected to serve a third term in Congress.

At the end of this term he decided to take a trip through the East. He wanted to see more of his country. And the people wanted to see Davy Crockett.

Everywhere he went, they flocked around him, eager to get a glimpse of the backwoodsman who had dared to stand up against the President of the United States. Great crowds gathered to meet him. They demanded speeches from him. They pushed forward to shake his hand.

They gave him a beautiful gold seal for his watch, with the words "Go ahead" engraved on it. And a rifle, too—the finest he had ever seen. In cities, in towns, and in villages, people cheered him and shouted his name.

What a trip that was! And what stories Davy Crockett had to tell his family when at last he reached his home in Tennessee.

"I rode on the railroad cars," he told them the first night he was home. "You never saw such a sight! It's like a lot of stagecoaches all strung along behind one machine. We got in, and the engine started to wheeze as though she had the tizzick. Then she began to take little short breaths. And away she went like a blue streak, with sparks flying in all directions."

"Weren't you scared?" Matilda asked, hitching her low stool closer to her father's chair.

Crockett laughed and laid his arm across her shoulders. "Not nearly as scared by that as I was by all the people I saw everywhere," he replied. "Why they all wanted to get a peek at me I just don't know."

"I do," Bob declared, looking proudly at his father. "What are you going to do now, Pa? Are you going back to Congress in the fall?"

"If I'm elected," his father replied, smiling.

But he wasn't! For the western part of Tennessee had changed in the past few years. Many more people had settled there. People who thought Andrew Jackson was the greatest man in the world, and who did not like Crockett because he had stood against Jackson.

So Davy Crockett did not go back to Congress. For more than a year he stayed home, hunting and looking after his crops. Then he made ready to go on a journey—a long journey which was to end with the greatest adventure of his life.

CHAPTER SIXTEEN

"—Then Go Ahead!"

MATILDA was unhappy. She dropped the stocking which she was knitting, into her lap. Then she glanced at her father, who sat near the fire cleaning his rifle. Suddenly tears rushed into her eyes.

"I don't see why you want to go to Texas!" she wailed. "It's thousands of miles away and—"

"Not thousands of miles," Davy Crockett broke in with a chuckle. "Only about eight hundred miles. And I've two good reasons for going.

"One reason is that Texas is a fine rich land. It might be a good place for us to settle, and

[*166*]

I want to find out about it. The other reason is that the Texans are in trouble and need help."

"What's the matter with them?" Matilda asked, wiping her eyes.

Davy Crockett blew down the barrel of his rifle. "Well," he said, laying the rifle across his knees, "it's this way:

"Texas belongs to a country named Mexico. But the Mexicans didn't ever want to live in Texas. So they said that Americans could settle there. Lots of Americans did. They called themselves Texans. And a little while ago they set up their own government.

"Now, the Mexicans have a president who isn't any better than an old rattlesnake. He doesn't like the Texans. And he's sending a big army to chase them out of their homes. Somehow that don't seem just right to me, so—"

"So you're going to help fight the Mexicans," Matilda exclaimed quickly.

"Maybe," Davy Crockett replied with a smile. "And maybe the fuss will be all over by the time I get there."

He stood up and put away his rifle. For he was planning to leave the next day, and he had many things to attend to. Whistling softly, he sat down at the table, and began a letter to his brother Will about Texas.

Davy Crockett was not worried about leaving his family. Bob was nearly a man now, and able to take care of the place. Thirteen-year-old Matilda was a great help to her mother.

And all of the other children were married.

Three good friends were traveling with Crockett to Texas and Davy was looking forward to the journey. Yet, the next day, when Davy Crockett kissed his wife and Matilda good-by, he wished for a moment that he were not going so far away. His eyes were misty when he slapped Bob on the shoulder.

"Take good care of your ma and Tilda while I'm gone," he said, reaching for his coonskin cap.

Bob handed his father's rifle to him. "Take good care of yourself, Pa," he said soberly, "and come back safe."

Crockett nodded. Swinging himself into his saddle, he called good-by, and rode away to meet his friends.

A number of men from Tennessee were going to Texas. Some were going to explore the country. Some, like Davy Crockett, were going chiefly to help the Texans defend themselves against the Mexicans. For the Texans were now determined to fight until they had won their freedom from Mexico.

By the time Crockett reached the town of Nacogdoches, in Texas, he had sixteen men with him. They called themselves "Crockett's Company." All of them had promised to follow Davy Crockett wherever he led them. At Nacogdoches they heard exciting news.

There had already been fighting between the Texans and the Mexicans. Many Texans had been forced to flee from their homes. An army of nearly two thousand soldiers was on its way from Mexico. General Sam Houston was trying to form an army of Texans to stop the Mexicans. And the town of San Antonio de Bexar was in great danger.

"It's the first town the Mexican army will attack," a man in Nacogdoches told Davy Crockett. "There's a fort there called the Alamo. It used to be a Spanish mission.

"Colonel James Bowie is in command there. Young Colonel Travis is with him. But they haven't more than one hundred and forty-five men to defend the fort. They need help badly."

"Then we'll go ahead to San Antonio,"

Davy Crockett declared. And he set off to the southwest with his men.

It was a mild day in February, 1836, when they reached San Antonio de Bexar. They went at once to the Alamo, half a mile from the town. Colonel Bowie and Colonel Travis both gave them a warm welcome, for they had heard of Davy Crockett. Immediately they asked him if he would like to command some of the men.

Crockett shook his head. "I'll fight like a panther and a wildcat rolled up together," he said. "But I'll leave the commanding to you. When do you reckon that Mexican Army's going to arrive?"

"Can't tell," Colonel Bowie replied. "We've sent scouts out to bring us warning of their approach. Now all we can do is to wait."

And wait they did, for several long, uneasy days. Days when Davy Crockett seemed to be everywhere at once. Making friends with the men. Telling them stories so funny that they roared with laughter. And amusing everyone with the tunes he tried to play on an old violin

[*171*]

that he had found somewhere in the town.

At last the waiting was ended. The word came that the Mexican Army was drawing near.

"Let them come," the men shouted. "Let them come!"

These were brave men who shouted so defiantly. For each one was there of his own free will. And each one was determined not to surrender the Alamo to the Mexicans.

From the parapets of the fort they saw the enemy advancing. On they came toward the town, marching steadily. Their swords and rifles gleamed in the sun. Their band played stirring music.

"There are more of them than ants in an anthill!" Crockett exclaimed to the man who stood beside him. "Who's that, leading them?"

"General Santa Anna," the man replied grimly. "He's the President of Mexico and he's one of the most cruel men who ever lived."

Meanwhile the Mexicans were drawing nearer. Into the town they marched. And there they took up quarters for the night. San Antonio was in the hands of the enemy!